Reminisce
HOLIDAY
MEMORIES

Table of **CONTENTS**

EDITORIAL

EDITOR-IN-CHIEF Catherine Cassidy
CREATIVE DIRECTOR Howard Greenberg
EDITORIAL OPERATIONS DIRECTOR Kerri Balliet

MANAGING EDITOR/PRINT & DIGITAL BOOKS Mark Hagen
ASSOCIATE CREATIVE DIRECTOR Edwin Robles Jr.

EDITOR Amy Glander
ASSOCIATE EDITOR Molly Jasinski
ART DIRECTOR Raeann Sundholm
LAYOUT DESIGNER Catherine Fletcher
EDITORIAL PRODUCTION MANAGER Dena Ahlers
COPY CHIEF Deb Warlaumont Mulvey
COPY EDITOR Joanne Weintraub
EDITOR, *REMINISCE* Marija Potkonjak Andric
ASSOCIATE CREATIVE DIRECTOR, *REMINISCE* Sharon K. Nelson

BUSINESS

VICE PRESIDENT, CHIEF SALES OFFICER Mark S. Josephson
VICE PRESIDENT, BUSINESS DEVELOPMENT & MARKETING Alain Begun
VICE PRESIDENT, PUBLISHER Russell S. Ellis
VICE PRESIDENT, DIGITAL EXPERIENCE & E-COMMERCE Jennifer Smith
VICE PRESIDENT, DIRECT TO CONSUMER MARKETING Dave Fiegel

THE READER'S DIGEST ASSOCIATION, INC.

PRESIDENT AND CHIEF EXECUTIVE OFFICER Bonnie Kintzer
VICE PRESIDENT, CHIEF OPERATING OFFICER, NORTH AMERICA Howard Halligan
VICE PRESIDENT, ENTHUSIAST BRANDS, BOOKS & RETAIL Harold Clarke
VICE PRESIDENT, NORTH AMERICAN OPERATIONS Philippe Cloutier
VICE PRESIDENT, CHIEF MARKETING OFFICER Leslie Doty
VICE PRESIDENT, NORTH AMERICAN HUMAN RESOURCES Phyllis E. Gebhardt, SPHR
VICE PRESIDENT, CONSUMER MARKETING PLANNING Jim Woods
EDITOR-IN-CHIEF, READER'S DIGEST Liz Vaccariello

PICTURED ON THE FRONT COVER:
H. Armstrong Roberts/Classicstock.com

THE HAPPIEST HOLIDAY

Precious memories are made during the most glorious time of the year—Christmas. Nothing quite compares to this special holiday brimming with hope and happiness. But it is the Christmases of our childhood that are deeply woven into our memories—the ones we all remember as the most precious and magical.

Reminisce, America's top-selling nostalgia magazine, with more than 1 million readers, invites you to join us in a festive journey through the Christmases of our past. With *Holiday Memories* you can relive the magic and wonder of the most treasured time of the year with poignant, real-life stories from the people who lived them.

Edward Lozon's daughter Debra appears awestruck as she looks up at Santa. She met the jolly old fella in 1960 at an annual Christmas party hosted by Edward's employer, Great Lakes Steel, in Ecorse, Michigan.

Perhaps your fondest yuletide memory is taking an annual trip to a bustling downtown department store to visit Santa, the man with a heart large enough to hold the wishes of every child in the world. Maybe it was unpacking boxes of heirloom ornaments and glittering tinsel as you waited in anticipation for the first unveiling of the Christmas tree. Other cherished memories might be singing carols in the school pageant, baking cookies or helping a neighbor in need.

These colorful pages—graced with more than 400 family stories, photos, vintage ads and more—capture the very best of the past to delight readers young and old. They're filled with our readers' favorite holiday memories of joyful moments, time-honored traditions, unforgettable meals, cherished childhood toys, the spirit of generosity and compassion, and other heartfelt recollections seasoned with love.

So this year, as you make merry with loved ones, rekindling your own special traditions and planting the seeds of holiday memories for younger generations, we invite you to savor the warmth and good cheer of an old-fashioned Christmas with *Holiday Memories*.

Merry Christmas,
The editors of *Reminisce* magazine

CHAPTER 1

FAMILY TRADITIONS

The cherished family customs and time-honored traditions of the Christmas season stir up childlike anticipation in young and old alike. As the big day draws near, our excitement mounts as we delight in baking cookies, hanging mistletoe, singing carols, writing letters to St. Nick, wrapping—and hiding—presents, finding the perfect evergreen and pursuing other joyous forms of merrymaking.

"My favorite time of year was the Christmas season," says Donna Davis of Chattanooga, Tennessee.

"Sometime before Christmas Eve, Dad would go into the woods behind our house and cut down a tree. Then on Christmas Eve, we'd have fun decorating the tree with ornaments and those big Christmas lights. While Daddy was working on the tree, Mama started the Christmas ham. I'll never forget the aroma of that ham cooking and the sight of the windows all fogged up from heat inside our house, where we were all so snug and warm.

"We'd find our stockings for Santa to fill—our cleanest, largest socks—and we'd hang them over the back of the chair in front of the fireplace. We always left a plate of cookies and a glass of milk for Santa. Sometimes Mama and Daddy would recite 'A Visit From St. Nicholas' to help us drift off to sleep.

"When morning arrived, we'd jump out of our warm beds onto the cold floor. Daddy built a roaring fire and we'd check our stockings, which were always filled with an orange, an apple, nuts and sweet hard candy stuffed way down in the toe.

"We were all thankful for this one time of the year—we were all together, enjoying God's goodness."

Turn the page to share in some beloved old-fashioned holiday traditions as these families celebrate the Christmas season.

HOLIDAY MEMORIES
STILL SHINE BRIGHT

A hand-picked tree and lovingly recycled gift tags made every holiday special.
DOROTHY MORRIS • HIGHLAND MILLS, NY

I was born in 1930, during the Great Depression, and while I don't remember going hungry, there were few frills. Still, getting ready for Christmas was memorable. Each September, my father, sister and I hiked into the forest behind our house to choose a Christmas tree. Dad tagged it, and a few days before Christmas, we tramped through the snow, cut the tree and dragged it into our house. Although the tree looked small in the woods, it was always too big to fit through the kitchen door. Mom watched as we emerged from the woods, and her comment was the same year after year: "You're not bringing that into my house."

Dad's response was equally predictable. "Now don't worry, Marge," he would say. "I haven't customized it yet!" Some years his engineering skills failed and even customizing didn't help. But we always thought the tree was perfect.

Next, we retrieved Grandpa Helbing's cast-iron tree stand from the basement, a foot-high triangle with legs and a holder for the trunk but no well for the water. Then came the decorations, some so old they had wax drippings on them from the days of candlelit trees. Each year, Dad told us about the holidays when he was a boy.

After Christmas Day chores and supper, his parents and four brothers adjourned to the unheated parlor, where a tree stood in that cast-iron stand. Dad and his brothers had buckets of water at their feet in case the tree caught on fire. No one was allowed to move. His father lit the candles on the tree one by one, and they provided the only light in the room. Before very long, the candles were extinguished. Each boy was given his one gift from under the tree—an orange! Then it was all over.

After finishing this story, Dad would leave the room and his two daughters took over the decorating. He'd come back when we were done, and our question was always the same: "Do you like it, Daddy?" He always responded: "If it was any better, it would be no good!" We never figured out the logic, and until he passed away at 94, we never questioned it.

Nor did we ever know when or how three

boxes appeared under the tree on Christmas morning. The largest one held jewelry for our mother, while the smaller ones had jewelry for my sister and me. Dad addressed the tags the same way each year.

Mom's said, "To My Sweetheart." I was the older child, so my tag read, "To Daughter #1, Love from your Daddy." The back of the tag said, "Return the tag." After all, there was a Depression on!

As my parents grew older and we left home to raise our own families, their trees were artificial green or silver foil. Dad always complained that they weren't real Christmas trees.

After my mother's untimely death and my father's decision to sell the homestead, he and I decided to revive the old traditions one last time. The less-than-perfect live tree (pictured lower left, opposite page) graced Dad's parlor once again.

The "To My Sweetheart" gift box was missing, but precious memories of our mom loomed large in our thoughts. We were thankful as we reflected on those happy, predictable, secure years.

IN THEIR SUNDAY BEST around 1941 are the author (far left) with her sister Jean and parents, Edgar and Margaret Helbing.

MUSICAL BREAK

A major snowstorm in 1970 created the perfect wintry scene for my family's annual Christmas caroling. We donned a colorful array of sweaters, parkas and gloves, topped off with our matching red plaid scarves. Each of us gathered our musical instruments—tambourine, bells, trumpet, clarinet and triangle—and squeezed into the car.

We went to the neighbors' porch, stood in a semicircle and started playing "I Heard the Bells on Christmas Day." After the first verse, we continued to the second with even more enthusiasm. As the trumpeter dramatically built up to a high note, a loud crash abruptly silenced the music.

We had no idea what the commotion was about until we saw the trumpet player grimacing and rubbing the back of his neck. The vibrations from the instrument's high-pitched note had shattered a large icicle, which fell from the tall roof, hit a porch column and sent a chunk of ice down his back. We were all happy the chunk of ice did nothing more than send a shiver down his spine—literally!

Our neighbors opened their door to a loud blast of laughter. They looked bewildered, but joined in our good humor after we told them the story.

We shared warm wishes for the holidays and handed the family a canister of treats before giggling all the way to the next house to play once more.

CAROLYN JOYNER FREEBAIRN
SALT LAKE CITY, UT

TRADITIONS TO CHERISH

CAPTURING SANTA

One Christmas during the early 1940s, my fun-loving grandfather decided he was going to build a trap to catch Santa.

Papa was always up to some kind of mischief. My brother and I were playing in front of the fireplace when he made a big show of banging open the front door to bring in lumber, chicken wire, nails and a hammer.

"What are you doing, Papa?" we asked.

"Going to catch that jolly ol' fat man, that's what," he replied. "Tired of him messing up my roof with all those animals and making a mess in my fireplace!"

We were absolutely horrified. "Papa! You can't do that!"

"Yes, I can!" he said. "And when I get him, I'm going to invite all the neighbors in to see him. May even charge admission!"

Christmas morning arrived and we ran into the living room—not to see what Santa had brought, but to see if he was in the trap. Of course he wasn't. The cookies Papa had left as bait were gone, though.

"See!" we squealed. "You can't catch Santa!"

"Humph!" grumbled Papa. "Just have to build a better trap next year!"

Santa wasn't in the trap the next year either, nor the year after that. One Christmas we found a note on the door to the trap that just said, "Hah!"

After that we began to realize why Santa never appeared in the trap on Christmas morning. Papa would smile and look at us with those wonderful blue eyes, and we knew that a trap wasn't necessary to capture the Christmas spirit. It had been with us all along.

LYN ARNOLD • CONYERS, GA

CHILDLIKE ANTICIPATION. "When our son Shane saw this tree, he begged, 'Mama, can we get this tree? Little baby tree—my size tree?'" remembers Amber Wohlhoefer, Tacoma, Washington. The curious fawn at right reminded Dawn Kopp, Dryden, Michigan, of a little child on Christmas morning.

BOOTIES HUNG WITH CARE

Living in an apartment house in Queens, New York, in the 1940s left us with two problems at Christmastime: no chimney and a front door that required a key or a buzz-in.

OK, so Santa would use his Christmas magic to get in. (We believed anything that Dad told us in those days.) But we had no fireplace for hanging our stockings, and the landlords didn't like holes in the walls, so we couldn't even tack them up.

Dad told us that if we put our stockings side by side on a chair near the tree, Santa would see them and be sure to fill them with goodies: apples, oranges, nuts, a hankie and the like. Way down in the toe, you might find a dime, or even a quarter!

Booties were also part of our tradition. I was born on Dec. 21, 1941, and Dad bought me a pair of Christmas booties. Every year after that, those booties were the first decoration on our Christmas tree.

When I got married in 1963, my parents gave Bob and me the booties. To this day, they're the first thing we put on our tree.

When our first grandson was born, I got him a pair of booties. Now the tradition continues with his parents each Christmas.

This picture (above) shows my brother George and me, ages 5 and 8, visiting the bearded one at the W.T. Grant five-and-dime on Myrtle Avenue in 1949. My little brother was a bit nervous, so I was told to hold onto his shoulders.

BARBARA SCHMITT PY • SEWELL, NJ

1946

The Season to be Jolly

Christmas again...the wreaths, the tree, the shopping, the presents, the joy.

Pacific Mills wishes you a very merry Christmas and all good things in the new year!

COTTONS
PACIFIC
RAYONS

Pacific

1922

MEETING OLD ST. NICK. Lola Di Giulio De Maci greets Santa Claus (above) during a Christmas celebration with her family (at left).

Fun in Store

BAREFOOT SANTA

Growing up in snowy Canton, Ohio, in the 1940s, I couldn't wait for Christmas and our annual trip downtown, where Santa magically appeared in a department store window, beckoning passers-by on the street to stop inside and shop for awhile.

The closer it got to the big day, the more excited I got. Soon Mom would take my sister, Jackie, and me to see Santa Claus!

The mechanical Santa in the store's window was larger than life, sitting barefoot in his comfy chair, getting ready for the big night. An elf busied himself tickling Santa's big toe with a feather. Santa's booming laugh spilled out over a loudspeaker outside. I felt like Alice in Wonderland gazing through the looking glass.

Santa wore red velvet trousers held up by thick black suspenders, and a white thermal undershirt with long sleeves. No jacket, no boots, no hat. I had convinced myself this was what the real Santa looked like in his workshop at the North Pole, as he relaxed before his big trip around the world.

What I remember most is that jolly barefoot Santa exploding with laughter. The memory of it and the spell it cast on a little girl with a larger-than-life imagination still makes me smile.
LOLA DI GIULIO DE MACI • FONTANA, CA

HOLIDAY EXCURSION

I grew up in the small community of Oldtown, Maryland. Every year, my mother would take us children 20 miles into Cumberland to see the Christmas decorations.

There were nine of us kids, so Mom would take a few at a time. We'd spend the whole day enjoying Cumberland, which was a big bustling city to us back then.

We usually had a little money to spend and would sometimes buy a Santa Claus Surprise Package, a mystery item for kids of different ages. One year, my 25-cent surprise package was a little toy suitcase, which I loved and played with until there was nothing left but bits and pieces of cardboard.

We were always eager to get home and tell the others about everything we had seen and what we had bought. Those jaunts to the big city are memories I'll cherish forever.
BETTY NIXON HUNTER • MELBOURNE, FL

ANNUAL TRIP DOWNTOWN

The Christmas celebrations of my childhood in the early 1960s were all about family and the special things we could do only at that time of year, such as going downtown to see the decorations at all the stores.

That was a big treat for my brother, Ken, my sister, Lucille, and me. We counted the days leading up to the trip. We lived in

Cleveland, Ohio, where the winter weather was usually crisp and cold. Teeming with excitement, we'd climb into our winter coats and boots. I remember putting my hands in Dad's pockets to keep them warm.

My memories of those trips began when I was about 5 years old. I remember there were lots of people, and we eagerly waited our turn to see all the magical window displays. Higbee's on Public Square had the most wonderful animated displays. We went from window to window, making sure not to miss even one!

Inside, kids could shop for Christmas presents with the help of an elf. It was expensive at the time, so we never did it, but I was a bit jealous of the kids who did.

After Higbee's, we headed down Euclid Avenue to Halle's to see Mr. Jingeling, the keeper of the keys to Santa's workshop. Then it was time to visit Santa himself to tell him what we wanted for Christmas. That's me (below) sitting on his lap, ready to tell him my wishes.

The highlight of the trip was the giant Christmas tree at the Sterling-Lindner department store. The tree seemed huge even to the adults, but to us children it was bigger than anything we could have imagined.

Things were much simpler back then. We didn't expect piles of toys under the tree on Christmas morning. Our gifts were a pair of new pajamas, socks and maybe a single toy. Those trips downtown were a special treat, made all the more memorable because we were together as a family. And that's how Christmas should be.

MARY ANN WYNALEK • CLEVELAND, OH

PILES OF PACKAGES. A mother and daughter happily tote their holiday purchases.

RIDING THE UP-AND-DOWN

During the 1930s, it was a tradition for my mother to take us girls with her to help carry packages when she went Christmas shopping at Hudson's in Detroit. We loved to ride the elevators, and Mother sometimes took us on the express elevator for lunch on the 13th floor. The express didn't make any stops until it got to the 10th floor. We got a tickle in our tummies when it went up or down too fast.

My little sister Marion was especially thrilled by these rides—so much so that when she sat on Santa's lap, she asked him to bring her an elevator just like the one at Hudson's.

On Christmas morning, we went into our parents' bedroom to tell them what Santa had brought us. Marion held back until Maxine and I told them what we'd received. When she still didn't say anything, my mother asked, "And what did Santa bring you, Marion?" She hung her head and sadly said, "The old horse's tail didn't bring me no up-and-down."

MERVAL HARVEY • GLENNIE, MI

5889

THE BEST CHRISTMAS GIFT EVER

In a lifetime of happy holidays, the most precious gift was one she didn't know about.

LOIS GUYMER • DOUGLAS, TX

Most people, I think, can quickly name their all-time favorite Christmas gift. It's the one shining brightest amid memories of torn paper and scattered ribbons.

Maybe it was that first real bike or Barbie Dreamhouse or, later, a computer or an iPod. For some it's a kiss under the mistletoe, or a Christmas Eve engagement ring. Sometimes it's the joy on your squealing kids' faces on Christmas morning when they see just what they wanted.

For me, though, a discovery I made just a few years ago about my childhood holidays outshines all other gifts.

When I was a girl, our family had little money. My parents worked night and day at a family business, but times were hard. Our clothes were warm if not fashionable, bought on clearance. There was a roof over our heads, but thanks to a few too many cracks in our old house, we experienced "central air conditioning" each winter. We ate beans and corn bread, soup or whatever the garden was producing, and fried potatoes at every meal.

Sometimes on Sundays, we'd enjoy chicken or meatloaf. Satisfying food—but definitely not fancy. We had few toys, so my brother and I made playhouses and mud pies, had chinaberry wars and waded knee-deep in the ditch when it rained.

It was just the way life was. Everybody we knew was just like us, and we were loved, so we were happy.

Tree Time

Christmas was always exciting. About a week before, Daddy would cut down a cedar tree to bring home. He'd nail a wooden stand to the bottom and place it in front of a window for us to help Mama decorate. We had two strands of lights, a hodgepodge of glass balls large and small (many rolled in glue and glitter to hide peeling paint), paper chains, popcorn strings and some construction paper ornaments made in school. We finished with two strands each of tinsel garland and beads, silver icicles, and a star. Then we admired it, inhaling the heady evergreen aroma.

We could afford to run the lights for only

about an hour each night, so after supper we'd turn off the ceiling light and turn on the tree. From our spots on the floor (Mama and Daddy had the couch), my brother and I would gaze at the shadows dancing as the lights blinked on and off. Mama was a terrific storyteller, so she'd tell tales of Christmas when she was a girl, and we'd sing carols.

Meanwhile, we'd gently shake and poke at the wrapped presents under the tree, all different shapes and sizes, with fascinating rattles. The week crawled by until Christmas Eve. Since there were so few presents during the year, my brother and I could hardly wait for the next morning.

It never failed that on that night, Daddy would have to go somewhere right after supper. A neighbor needed help, or someone was sick. Whatever the reason, he got back well after our bedtime. It seemed so unfair that he missed the last night with our tree. Because it dried out so quickly, we always took the tree down on Christmas afternoon, after a morning exclaiming over a new doll, cowboy boots, pajamas and coloring books.

Christmas Eve Ritual

When Mama and I were reminiscing a few years ago, I recalled how Daddy always had to leave on Christmas Eve.

Mama laughed, throwing her hands up, and said how amazing it was that we never caught on.

"Caught on—to what?" I asked.

Well, she said, back then a few of the stores in town would stay open late on Christmas Eve, marking down toys, candy and other trinkets just to get rid of them. Daddy would take the small amount of Christmas money they had budgeted and go shopping while Mama tucked us into bed at home.

I couldn't believe it. Daddy was never a good shopper, yet he went through picked-over, marked-down toys and brought home magical gifts that always thrilled us.

How astonishing!

But wait—what about all those wrapped boxes we'd spent a week rattling and squeezing?

Those were just decoys, empty boxes she'd filled with various items to give them weight and make them rattle, Mama confessed. When Daddy returned from his shopping excursion, she would unwrap all of those boxes, remove the contents and somehow make our real gifts fit into the boxes before she rewrapped them again.

Knowing how much love went into making those holidays special for us is now my most precious Christmas gift. Especially when I think how easily I might have missed out on learning the secret Mama and Daddy kept for so long.

HEY, NO PEEKING!

We lived in the Pittsburgh suburb of Dormont in the 1950s, when my husband, Pete Lagi, was a salesman at Gimbels department store. We used to follow the old Italian custom of hiding the family's Christmas gifts, and one year Gimbels sent a photographer from the employee magazine, *The Gimbelite*, to our home to take this picture. That's our daughter Linda showing her brother David the presents hidden under the sofa cushions. Chris is next to me on the couch, and I'm holding baby Elizabeth, with Pete looking on.

WILLIE MAE "BEEBE" MARTON • PITTSBURGH, PA

FAMILY MATTERS

GATHER 'ROUND. Dad has his hands full in this photo submitted by Carol Hallgren of Lorain, Ohio. "My parents took us to see our great-aunt in Norwalk on Christmas Day in 1955," says Carol. Her father, Charles Romer, is holding Chuck, the youngest, and Linda. Standing behind them are (from left) Richard, Carol and Barbara.

A QUICK SNAPSHOT of Lawrence and Marjorie Donaldson with their kids was taken on Christmas in 1949. Daughter Pauline Cameron of Merrimack, New Hampshire, says that for her and brother Larry, "the best part was going upstairs, where my grandparents lived, for turkey and more presents."

HOLIDAY EXPRESSIONS ran the gamut for Bob and Ann Leinweber's family in Billings, Montana, in 1960. That's Bob Jr. and Colleen on the floor, with Nancy sitting on Ann's lap and Karen standing at right.

HOLIDAY HOMECOMING. "My grandma (center, holding her daughter, in 1951) has hosted Christmas dinner in her farmhouse for more than 60 years," says Amy Armes from Bright, Ontario. "She's cooked turkeys as large as 49 pounds."

YULE REUNION. For more than half a century, the Weaver family has decked the halls in Arkansas. "We all gather at our parents' homestead," says Mildred McKinney of Camden, standing behind her mom in this 1979 shot.

GRANDPARENTS ARE THE GREATEST. "My cousin and I lived with our grandparents while our mothers worked," writes Elizabeth Hass, Youngtown, Arizona. "We loved them, and I will always remember the feeling of security they gave us."

SEASON STARTED WITH ST. NICK

Her family found joy in the first hint of the Christmas season with their traditional Nicolo Day celebration.

NADINE N. DOUGHTY • EVANSTON, IL

I wasn't quite asleep after all. A tiny sound of crackling cellophane roused me and I opened my eyes. There in the living room, I saw a plump figure—doing what, exactly?

I shut my eyes again quickly. If it was St. Nicholas at work, and he saw me awake, he might vanish!

No, it wasn't Christmas Eve. In our family, we observed St. Nicholas' Day. On December 6, the generous saint of giving celebrated his feast day by filling up children's stockings with goodies.

My parents, who had German and Austrian roots, referred to this as Nicolo Day, and every year they had my three brothers, my sister and me hang our stockings on the old fieldstone fireplace. They had driven special nails into the mortar between the stones just for that purpose.

Ready and Waiting

My red kneesock, my sister's green one and my brothers' white crew socks all made for a cheerful display. But this was nothing compared to the sight we knew would greet us the next morning!

During the night, our parents said, good St. Nick would come to fill those stockings with delightful small surprises, and we'd see them as soon as we woke up. We were so eager that it was almost impossible for us to fall asleep that night.

Sure enough, the next morning, the sight of those bulging stockings had us so excited that we usually didn't wait until our parents were awake to raid them!

What caused us such excitement? Living during the Great Depression was enough to make us see just about anything St. Nick would leave as a genuine treat.

So we'd exclaim over such riches as a pocket comb, or the notebooks we each got, every one with a cover in a different color. The older kids might get a penknife. I still recall fondly the colored pencils that I got, and a blue velvet hair ribbon that I kept for years.

Sweet Treats

We'd all be thrilled to find apple- and banana-shaped marzipan, a delectable almond and sugar candy that was a rare treat for us. And tucked at the very bottom of each stocking were a traditional orange and some nuts we could crack and crunch. We didn't usually eat those oranges right away, but kept them so we could slowly savor the anticipation of the rare and delicious citrus flavor!

After we showed everyone our treasures, the Christmas season was officially under way. There'd be projects to sew, carve, draw or paint as gifts for every family member. Some had already been started, but now we knew we had to hurry to finish them in time for Christmas.

As we grew older, we started to give more elaborate Christmas gifts, often ones that required special shopping trips.

Nicolo, though, remained our family's simple, fun and special way to begin the Christmas season.

A SPECIAL STORY. 'Twas the time for cherubs at Christmas. Jean Parker of Centerville, Utah, says of this 1943 photo, "My two little brothers, Lee (right) and Dennis Lynn Taylor, look like angels, which they were—but not all the time."

Rev. Clement Clarke Moore wrote "A Visit from St. Nicholas," also know as "'Twas the Night Before Christmas," for his family for Christmas in 1822.

RITUAL LIVES ON

In December 2003, my husband had hip replacement surgery, so our two daughters cooked a lovely meal and brought it to the hospital on Christmas Day.

The girls also brought along our gifts and everyone's Christmas stockings. My husband got the usual onion in his, just as he had since our firstborn was not quite 2 years old. That Christmas, he had asked her what Santa was going to put in his stocking, and she told him, "An onion." Why, I don't know.

My husband has since passed away. On Christmas Eve, we took his stocking, with an onion in it, to the cemetery. We just couldn't let Christmas go by without him getting his onion.

JEAN LYNCH • BONHAM, TX

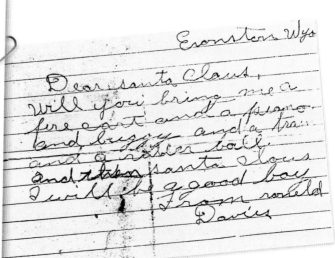

catching the flue bug

My grandparents' house was small, but to my cousins and me, it was a welcoming home where we could always expect a lot of love.

The house in Evanston, Wyoming, had belonged to Great-Grandpa Davies and was passed on to my grandparents, who raised their four children there. The 2$\frac{1}{2}$-bedroom cottage saw many changes over the years.

A bathroom was added on, as was an enclosed porch. An electric stove eventually replaced the coal-burning one. Paint colors and wallpaper patterns came and went.

But one thing never altered—a small crack in the side of the chimney, which made its way up to the ceiling in the kitchen and eventually sent billows of smoke into the cold, dark blue skies of winter.

As a little girl in the 1930s, I learned about the crack—but I didn't know about the importance of that opening until one especially memorable Christmas.

Grandma told us to write our letters to Santa Claus at her kitchen table. My generation wasn't the first to follow this ritual. My father, his brothers and his sister wrote Christmas lists in this kitchen, too.

We then had to mail our letters, but not

at the post office. The notes were folded and pushed through that crack in the side of the chimney.

Grandma said the wind would catch our letters and lift them up the chimney and on to Santa at the North Pole. You had to believe her. After all, she was Grandma!

Later, it was my children and my cousins' children writing their letters and mailing them through the little crack in the chimney.

Time went by, and here I was, a grandma myself, in 1996. The years had taken their toll on my grandparents' home. When I heard my uncle was going to tear it down, I asked him to look around the chimney rubble once it was down to see if any letters remained. He laughed but said he would look.

A few days later, I got a call from my aunt. One of those many letters had been found. My father had written this one (pictured on opposite page, top right) to Santa around 1919, when he was 6 or 7 years old .

The letter read exactly like this:

"Dear santa Claus,

"Will you bring me a fire cart and a piano and buggy and a train and a rubber ball. and then santa claus I will be a good boy

"From roneld Davies"

Santa may not have received his letter, but it was waiting in the chimney to become one of my great treasures—a testament to our ancestral connection through generations of family tradition.

DEANNA HOYT • MURRAY, UT

I found a letter I'd written to Santa Claus (right) when I was 7 years old, asking for a sled and a pair of skis. This was in my mother's personal effects after she passed away. Note the letter's date.

Elmer Stringham • Spring Hill, FL

Dec. 7, 1941
Covert, Mich.
Dear Santa Claus.

I will TRy to be a good boy from now on! My mother said I am a good boy. I would like a pair of skis, and a big sled, and any Thing you would like to bring me. Please bring grandmother and grandfather a present, and my father and mother something and take care of all The Poor Children. Thank you very much.

Elmer Stringham
Route 1. Box 104
Covert Michigan

Mr. Santa Claus
ToyLand
north Pole

Outsmarting the
SUPER SNOOP

I was all of 9 years old when I finally acknowledged there was no Santa Claus. That was the year I found my much-desired bicycle in the cotton gin office. (My daddy was the manager of the two cotton gins in Tynan, Texas.)

My mother and father also owned a small drugstore, and our living quarters were attached to the rear of the store. In the summer, our store was the gathering place for older ladies to come and enjoy cool refreshments. The post office was located next door, and the postmistress often had lunch with us.

The year I turned 13, I began my usual snooping for Christmas presents as soon as December arrived. I carefully checked out our living quarters—no luck. I also volunteered more than usual to help in the drugstore and used the time between customers to search the store. Again, no luck. Remembering the "bicycle Christmas," I went to search the cotton gin. Still, no luck.

Mother had threatened me for years, saying my behavior was so bad that "Santa Claus" wouldn't come to see me anymore. I was fast reaching the conclusion this was the year it would happen. On Christmas Eve, I went to bed feeling completely dejected.

The next morning I checked under the little Christmas tree, just in case. Imagine my surprise when I found a pearl necklace, a silver bracelet featuring a gold initialed heart, and other small presents.

Mother waited several years—after we moved away from Tynan, in fact—before she revealed the secret hiding place. She'd been conspiring with the postmistress to hide my gifts in the post office safe!

ELAINE HOLT • BEEVILLE, TX

SAVVY SLEUTH. Elaine Holt was pretty good at finding her Christmas gifts—until her clever mom found a way to outsmart her.

ORDER AND CHAOS. Seen here is the calm before the storm of flying bows, shredded wrappings and laughter (right) at the Rindt home in 1971.

'IS THE BUICK FOR ME...
OR WILL I GET THE POST TOASTIES?'

My grandparents Anne and Leo Rindt came up with a creative way to ward off snooping children during the holidays. Each year, at the beginning of December, they would put all the presents out around their tree (above). Displaying the gifts that early usually led to the big question: "Who's going to get the big present this year?"

To prevent any of us from knowing which person was getting which gifts, they replaced our names on the gift tags with categories. One year we'd find street names on our tags; the next year, it might be TV shows. They used everything from brands of cereal and song titles to car models.

The tradition lasted more than 30 years, until gifts finally gave way to gift certificates. But it was always fun to guess what would be on our gift tags.

KIMBERLY KENDGIA • OAKMONT, PA

MAKING OUR CHRISTMAS SWEET

The Sears wish book meant chocolates and the most important decision of the season. **LYN MINK** • BEAVERTON, OR

It was the most exciting day of the year, more anxiously awaited than the first day of school and more anticipated than any holiday during my childhood in the 1950s: the day the Sears Christmas Book arrived in our northern Illinois mailbox.

As soon as I saw the mail truck, I would bundle up in my red wool coat and matching mittens, gray furry hat and sturdy black boots, and walk down our long, snow-packed driveway, hoping that today was The Day.

Fred, our mailman, never hinted when it was The Day, but I think he knew what I was waiting for, because he was so careful with the package—it was never torn or creased. When I opened the mailbox and saw the

brown paper and the thickness of the parcel, I knew the treasured Christmas wish book had finally arrived.

I would run back to the house clutching the book tight, taking great care not to drop it in the snow. Mother let me have the honor of opening it. First, I tried to gently slide the book out of the wrapper. Then impatience would take hold and I would tear off the paper, eager for a thrilling glimpse of the cover. Some years it was Santa Claus or a nutcracker, but my favorite was a colorful, brightly lit Christmas tree.

I would sit on the living room floor and turn the wish book over, so I could start at the back with the toys. I'd linger over the

LIFE IS LIKE A BOX OF CHOCOLATES. Finding the perfect piece of chocolate was a highly anticipated event for Lyn Mink (opposite). She pored over the wish book (left) every December, studying each colorful page.

dolls, but they were only the second most important things within the book's pages. I skipped past the fur coats and the frilly dresses to the front of the book and there they were—chocolates!

Every year, my mother ordered the 5-pound box of chocolates. It arrived in December, and that was the only time we ever had an entire box. We would go to the little Sears store in town and pick it up at the desk (along with other packages I wasn't permitted to see). I got to hold the heavy box in my lap during the drive home. Later my mother put it safely in a high cabinet in the kitchen, where I couldn't sneak a piece.

After dinner on Christmas Eve, she would bring out the chocolate box. It was wrapped in holiday paper, usually white with red and green holly or ornaments. I ripped off the paper and lifted the lid.

The distinctive sweet scent of chocolate filled the air and made me hungry all over again. Glorious multishaped candies lay before me, divided into four sections and two layers.

Choosing the right chocolate was a big decision, since I was allowed only two pieces on Christmas Eve. Usually I could tell what was inside each one, but once in a while I was fooled—like the time I bit into what I thought was chocolate cream and got a piece of pineapple instead.

By the time I was 7, I learned to study the chocolates carefully before choosing. It was serious business—and it still is!

Christmas Day in our upstate New York home brought a treat that was allowed only once a year in the war years of the 1940s.

On that special day, Dad carried on a tradition his father started. He drilled a hole in one side of a lemon, then showed us how to slide a peppermint stick in the hole and gently suck up the lemon's juice.

But surprise! The sugar from the candy combined with the sour lemon juice to create a wonderful sweet-tart taste.

This simple, inexpensive treat was a highlight of our Christmases. Years later, my brother, sister and I realized the importance of this tradition, as it made up for the gifts my parents couldn't afford to buy. I'll always feel lucky that despite the hardship of these years, we had this sweet ritual to savor.

David Hudson • Canandaigua, NY

OUR BACKYARD TREE FARM

In 1968, when I was 5 years old, my family moved to South Plainfield, New Jersey. Compared to our small yard on Staten Island, the new property felt like "the country." Little did I know that our more spacious yard would bring a family tradition that I cherish to this day.

The first November at the new house, Dad decided that our family of eight should pile into our old station wagon and go to a tree farm to select a live Christmas tree. After we came to a consensus on the tree, we tagged it for later pickup. The day we picked out our prized tree began the holiday season for us.

My dad and older brother dug a hole in the yard and covered it with plywood. This spot would be the future home of our Christmas tree! I remember how methodical my dad was, even making my brother box up dirt from the hole and move it into the garage so it wouldn't freeze.

We picked up our tree the first week of December and kept it in the garage for a few days so the warmth of our home didn't "shock" it. In the meantime, we rearranged furniture so the tree and its washtub would fit just right. Once the tree was in place, we decorated it. Mom had the honor of placing the white sheet above the roots, while Dad was in charge of the watering.

I enjoyed every minute of sitting under that tree with my family, opening presents and sharing stories and laughter. After Christmas each year, the tree would be planted in its new home—the hole my dad and brother had dug weeks earlier. They would plant it the week after New Year's.

Over the years, I lost track of how many trees were planted on the property, but I still remember the location of the very first tree. Eventually we ran out of room in our yard and Dad began donating our trees to the local parish our family attended. Once my brother married, I was given the honor of helping my dad with the tree preparation. I was overjoyed to have an important role in such a memorable family tradition.

PHILIP ECKEL • LAKE ARIEL, PA

O CHRISTMAS TREE. Philip Eckel is pictured at right with sister Sally Eckel Gillis in 1970. They are also seen above with siblings Peter Eckel (in red coat), Pat Eckel Meleo (in brown coat) and Cindy Eckel (behind Philip).

Storybook Tradition

This is my favorite picture. That's me at age 3, just before Christmas in 1947.

My family lived with my grandparents Joseph and Alfretta Wheller in Paxtang, Pennsylvania. Whenever I asked, "Grandpa, please hold me," he would pull me onto his lap and read to me.

Here he is reading from my favorite illustrated storybook, *Night Before Christmas*.

A few years later it would be the first book I learned to read.

My father, John Eslinger, took the photo and developed it. My talented mother, Jo, did the tinting.

This is such a sweet moment. I treasure this picture and the memories of my grandfather.

BONNIE BAIR • MANCHESTER, MD

CHAPTER 2

DECK THE HALLS

There's no place like home for the holidays, especially when it's trimmed from top to bottom, front door to back, with flickering candles, bright bows, sprigs of holly, colorful cards, miniature villages and, of course, the centerpiece of yuletide decor—the stunning Christmas tree aglow with shiny ornaments and sparkling tinsel.

For Clancy Strock of Gainesville, Florida, the decoration that most evoked the spirit of Christmas was the string of gleaming lights wrapped around the tree.

"My mother remembered Christmas trees illuminated with candles," he says. "That's hard to imagine in these safety-conscious times, but during the days of kerosene lamps, candles were the only way to make Christmas trees come alive with light. Trouble was, candles were also capable of torching the tree!

"Except for lights, most people made their own tree decorations during the Depression. We strung popcorn and cranberries on strong thread. One year, we tried marshmallows for ornaments. Somehow those tasty white blobs slowly disappeared through the holidays.

"No matter how small or grand the room, Christmas lights and their accompanying decorations instantly transformed it into a new, magical place, and the wonderment never ends, no matter how old we become."

Enjoy more stories and photographs depicting the creative ways readers decked the halls to create delightfully nostalgic memories.

UNCLE BOB'S CHRISTMAS

Magic radiated through a Chicago bungalow filled with holiday spirit.

DONNA PIEHL · ALGONQUIN, IL

My sister and I were raised in Chicago in the 1940s and '50s. We lived in a small apartment on the city's north side, although it didn't seem small when we were little ourselves.

Our Christmas Eves were pure magic, helped in a big way by my uncle Bob Carlsen, a tall, strapping Dane with a smile and laugh to match. He would gather family and friends at his home on Christmas Eve. This man knew how to deck the halls, and he did everything in his power to make the holiday wonderful.

Uncle Bob lived in a typical Chicago brick bungalow, built by his father, on Harding Avenue. Compared to our city apartment, it was huge. The entrance was on the side of

the house, and when we arrived and walked up the stairs, we were greeted by wonderful aromas that emanated from the kitchen.

As we reached the top of the side stairs, there was a hallway to the left. On the right was a swinging door made of heavy, shiny dark wood with small panes of beveled glass and lace curtains. We were not allowed to enter that room until after dinner, but all of us children tried, in vain, to peek through that lace curtain to see what treasures and decorations lay on the other side.

Dinner seemed a long time away, but while the adults gathered, we went to play in the basement. This was also a special place.

We could reach it the normal way, by going down the stairs. But if you were lucky enough to be small, you could get there by sliding down the short, angled clothes chute located in the main-floor bathroom, dropping into a big canvas hamper.

Once downstairs, we found a player piano, toys, books and so many things to investigate. The floor was raised, slatted wood, so your feet wouldn't get cold, although you could lose a crayon or pencil through the gaps.

Soon we were called for dinner and ran up the stairs to the dining room. There was a large table set with a beautiful tablecloth, china dishes, silver, crystal glasses and, the best part, a Christmas candle at every plate. They were small colorful candles depicting snowmen, Santa Clauses, Christmas trees, angels, deer, choir singers and tin soldiers.

As the candles were lit, the room was filled with the warm glow of peace and love, family and friends together, all orchestrated by a warm, caring, loving man who wanted to make all of it special.

After supper, we children were not allowed to leave the table until we were excused. Then we could play downstairs again, eagerly waiting for the adults to finish their meal and conversation.

Finally, it was time. Uncle Bob would call us up. When we were all lined up in the hallway, he would open the swinging door and the magic would begin—the beautiful tree, candles, lights, decorations, music— and then, just as we entered, a noise by the fireplace.

We turned...and there stood Santa Claus, brushing the soot from the chimney off his red suit! What child would not have been enchanted?

This is the memory my Uncle Bob gave to all of us, a wonderful kind of Christmas magic. That magic remains in my heart, and every year I relive the memories of those special nights.

A SPECIAL MAN. The author and her sister Judy posed with Uncle Bob in 1950 (above). Opposite: Donna's mom, Verna, with Uncle Bob (bottom) and the house where the magic happened (top).

A CHRISTMAS WONDER

Christmas is a time for surprises, but our family got a special one in the late 1940s, when my father revealed a side of himself we'd never seen.

Our rural area didn't experience the wonder of electricity until years later. To me, electricity meant wealth. I looked forward to our December rides to the county seat for shopping, because the houses with warm lamplight inside and colored lights outside seemed wondrous to me.

My father was a quiet man and he didn't get involved in the frivolity of the season. That's why everyone in the family recalls the year we set up the tree in the living room and Dad told us not to put any decorations on it.

He had been working for days with wire and automobile taillight bulbs. Now I saw why he had asked to use my watercolors, a request that had puzzled me. Dad had painted the clear glass bulbs and fashioned a string of lights. Behind the tree, he placed a wooden box that held a battery and attached the contacts at the end of the wires. We had lights on our Christmas tree for the very first time!

Dad was as delighted as we were, and I wondered why he'd ever wanted to hide his enjoyment of the season.
RUTH MARTIN • WEST ALEXANDER, PA

TREE LIT UP NEIGHBORHOOD

Christmas was an exciting time for me and my sister, Sylvia. We had come with our family from Germany to Teaneck, New Jersey, in 1929.

Our Christmas tree had candles on it instead of electric lights. They were lit on Christmas Eve when our family sang "Silent Night" in German. Then Mom would extinguish the candles while we opened our gifts. The candles were lit again the next night and allowed to burn down to about 1 inch. Mom would then replace them and light them again a few days later.

The neighborhood kids, who all had electric lights on their trees, were fascinated by the candles. Mom would often let them come in for a closer look.
RALPH GERRICK • WILMINGTON, DE

BRANCHES OF LOVE

On Dec. 23, 1943, I stood in line for more than an hour with a nickel clutched in my palm and waited to buy a piece of Dubble Bubble gum. When my turn came, I parted with my coin reluctantly, but it was well worth the price. I carefully unwrapped the waxed-paper square and waited for the gum's sweetness to perfume the air.

Long after the bubble gum lost its flavor, I preserved the pink wad in a glass of water on the kitchen table. The next morning after breakfast, I chewed it again—even in school, until Miss Miller caught me.

Dummy! Should've left it in the glass, I thought as I maneuvered my gum to form one last bubble. It popped prematurely and was gone as I spit it into the wastebasket.

I had collected discarded lead weights from double-hung sash windows at 10 cents a pound to earn that nickel for the gum, and now both the money and the treat were gone. I didn't know when the scrap man would return to buy more metal. I panicked. Days or weeks without Dubble Bubble gum! Even at 7 years old, I understood the war's

demands for rationing. I planned my gum and candy purchases as carefully as Mom planned the weekly amount of sugar, fat and meat she bought with her coupon book.

When I got home, Mom was taking the eyebrow pencil out of her makeup case. As I watched, she squatted behind her sister and drew one perfectly straight dark-brown line down the back of each of Aunt Frances' legs. When Mom finished, Frances surveyed her elder sister's handiwork and commented, "Pretty good, Mary. The lines match. Thanks."

The line extending from mid-thigh down to Aunt Frances' heel was meant to simulate the seam of a stocking. It made her feel like she had nylon hose, a luxury the stylish 20-year-old couldn't afford.

Mom and her five sisters moved in with widowed Nana while their husbands were overseas fighting the war. We shared a two-bedroom railroad flat on Manhattan's Lower East Side. It was cramped, but we didn't mind. I loved all my aunts but felt a special kinship with Aunt Frances. Maybe it was her soft voice, her patience, her artistic ability or just the fact that she was always there for me.

"Let's go," Aunt Frances said after she bundled me up. There was snow in the air, and it was Christmas Eve afternoon. Down the five flights we raced. Our mission: to buy a Christmas tree. We traipsed from one stand to another, down Attorney Street to Madison Street, past Grand and St. Mary's Roman Catholic Church, where we'd later attend midnight Mass.

But with each block we became more and more disillusioned.

"Skeletons," Aunt Frances muttered under her breath as she surveyed the trees stacked against the schoolyard fence. "What nerve to call them Christmas trees! Outrageous prices! You can count the number of branches on each tree!"

I nodded in agreement. We pushed on while the temperature dropped. We warmed our hands over the trash-can fires the sellers lit to keep warm.

As we walked, Aunt Frances picked up discarded branches of pine and fir. I figured she would put them on our windowsills and dressers to give the house a seasonal air.

By 8 p.m., we were tired, hungry, cold—and treeless. I was disappointed as we trudged home. My thoughts drifted to my father, who was off on a Pacific island whose name I couldn't even pronounce. He probably didn't have a tree, either. I expected a Christmas morning with a bare spot where the fir should have been.

But I was wrong. I woke to discover Aunt Frances had bored holes in an old broomstick and inserted the branches she'd collected into the holes. Then she had decorated our broomstick tree with Popeye lights she had bought just for me!

As I reminisce about Christmas of 1943, I remember how Aunt Frances taught me the meaning of the holiday with branches of love.

ROBERT KOVNER, AS TOLD TO HIS WIFE, BONNIE YARRY • MAITLAND, FL

PLENTY UNDER THE TREE. "Our sad little tree, sort of like Charlie Brown's, had no store-bought decorations, yet it still added to the wonder of Christmas for us in 1952," writes Collene Burgess of Hesperia, California. The Stouvenel kids—from left, Collene, Collette, Mike and Betty—were excited that Santa had come to their home in Clinton, Iowa.

SEASON'S GREETINGS

Getting holiday greetings in the mail is like a surprise visit from friends and family. The cards on these pages used a variety of messages and festive images to send warm yuletide wishes. In many households, these cards not only warmed the hearts of loved ones, but became part of the holiday decor. See pages 40-41 for a glimpse of the unique and interesting ways many families displayed these cards so all their visitors could enjoy them.

A Happy Christmas

St. NIKLAS

MERRY CHRISTMAS

Here's to tell U t 🎩 I hope U will 🐝 happy Christmas Day. 🎵 wish U 🚶 y gifts, a 🛷 some 📚, perhaps a 🔫 I'd like to 🐝 a 💡 bright, a 🕯 shining on your Christmas To give a 🪶 of cheer to 🎈 and ⏲ your Christmas fun.

Merry Christmas, DAD

Here's to Dad with loads of love
And lots of loud applause --
The grandest guy who ever played

Hearty Christmas
I'm sending Kris Kringle
With laughter and mirth
To deliver this jingle
And best wishe on earth

WHITE CHRISTMAS. Sherri Owens and brother Don, ages 3 and 6, sit next to their dad's spray-painted tree at their home on First Street in Henderson, Kentucky, in 1948.

DAD'S TREE ARTISTRY

Before the Christmas tree went up, her father took several days to improve on what Mother Nature had started. **SHERRI OWENS** • CINCINNATI, OH

Christmas in our family was always an exciting time for my brother Don and me. There were always lots of presents, but almost as exciting was the perfect white Christmas tree.

When we were kids in the 1940s and early '50s, white Christmas trees were unusual. But we always had a white tree, and a perfect one at that. Dad would meticulously choose the most perfectly shaped tree he could find and make it even more perfect at home. It took several days and a lot of effort before that tree could meet Dad's standards.

After attaching the trunk to the base, he would stand back, take a long look at the tree and reach for his saw. First he would remove all of the lower branches—creating plenty of room for presents underneath—and

carefully put the branches aside for later. He'd step back and walk around the tree several times, contemplating his next move.

It was then the real artistry began. Dad would get his brace and bit, choose a bit size slightly smaller than the base of a specific tree branch he had cut off earlier, then push his way through the branches to drill a hole. A chosen branch was pushed in the hole and voila! A once-bare spot was no longer bare.

When Dad was done shaping, he brought out the paint sprayer and sprayed until every single inch of that tree was white as snow.

Every year it seemed our tree was more breathtaking than the last, as if it had been in a beautiful snowstorm. My brother and I will never forget those perfect white trees Dad created in the garage.

TRIMMING THE TREE. "As was custom, I cut the top off a large tree on my parents' 'back forty' in Aitkin, Minnesota, for this Christmas tree in 1957," says Ben Reem (left) of Detroit Lakes. Above: Sandy Flood of Morris, Illinois, shared this photo from the 1940s or '50s from a collection inherited from Charolette Bihlmeier, who lived in Chicago.

THE YEAR WE (ALMOST) HAD NO CHRISTMAS TREE

In December of 1947, my mother told my sister and me that we wouldn't be getting a Christmas tree because the three of us were going to spend Christmas with Mom's family in Des Moines, Iowa. My father would stay behind on our Missouri farm to milk the cows and tend to the other livestock. Since we weren't going to be home for Christmas, she saw no reason to get a tree.

One Saturday a couple of weeks before Christmas, after listening to us girls bemoan the situation one more time, my father said, "I know where we can get a Christmas tree, and it won't cost us anything." Within a few minutes, he had the tractor hitched up to a wagon, which held a ladder, rope and saw.

We traveled down the road about half a mile to an abandoned farmhouse that had a tall cedar tree in the front yard. My father got out his ladder, tied the rope around his waist and, with the saw in one hand, went up the tree. When he got as high as he could, he threw one end of the rope over a tall branch and proceeded to inch his way up to the very top. He'd been a telephone lineman, so he knew how to use a rope to make his way up a pole or tree.

When he gotten as far as he thought he needed to go, he started sawing. Soon he shouted, "Get back, girls, it's coming down." He cut off the top 5 feet of that tree, which was the perfect size.

When we got back home, my sister and I got our family's two boxes of Christmas ornaments. We decorated the tree with our usual pride and gusto, and even my mother had to admit that it was a fine-looking tree!

PAT DALBEY JORGENSON • MEAD, CO

Holiday Whistle Stop Tour

THE DAY HIS TRAIN CAME IN

That cold December morning in 1932 started like any other, but it was one our family will never forget.

I was 11 and my little brother, Billy, was 6. Our family lived in Indianapolis, Indiana. The Depression days were still affecting us, so Christmas would again mean a small tree and inexpensive gifts beneath—not much for two little kids to look forward to.

My little brother, however, was filled with expectation. He flew around the dining room gathering his coat, scarf, helmet hat and gloves, urging me to hurry up so we could get to the Rivoli theater.

He really believed he might win the Lionel train set to be given away that afternoon. He wanted an electric train so much. Mother had explained many times that it was out of the question. They were too expensive, and only necessities could be purchased on our dad's meager salary.

We walked the three blocks to the theater. I listened the whole way to Billy's constant chatter about the "'lectric train" he was going to win.

We took our place in the long line that had formed in front of the ticket window. All our school friends were there, talking about the train *they* were going to win, as Billy told them *he* was going to win it.

We finally got to the window, bought our 10-cent tickets and went inside. The usher tore them and put half in a special box, giving me the other stubs. We found some seats near the front and sat through the main feature, a cowboy serial and the Pathé News.

By this time, everyone was talking and getting more excited, especially Billy. I managed to keep him quiet and in his seat. At last, the lights came on. The curtains were drawn together, covering the huge screen, and everyone grew quiet.

The theater manager came out and walked to the center of the stage. He was carrying a box under one arm and the larger train box in his other arm. He put both boxes down.

"I think this is what you've all been waiting for," he said, smiling and looking out over the many little upturned faces. He picked up the smaller box, shook it briskly, reached in and pullet out a ticket stub.

In a loud voice, the manager called out four numbers, "4-5-7-2."

Billy grabbed my arm and exclaimed, "Sister, sister!"

I looked at our tickets and couldn't believe what I saw! Then I laughed and said, "Here's the ticket, honey. Go get your train."

He had *won*! Billy flew up to the stage to collect his prize.

We were eager to show our parents that Billy had indeed won the train set. He carried the long box all the way home, although I offered to help. How his little arms managed, I'll never know.

That Christmas, the Lionel track circled our tree with the train happily going round and round. An equally happy little boy sat for hours, watching. It became a tradition to place that beloved train around our tree.

Many years later, the train charmed Bill's four children. Today, Bill lives in Mattoon, Illinois, and the train will again be part of Christmas for his family.

E. GERALDINE ALFORD • GREENFIELD, IN

ENCIRCLED WITH LOVE. Lyndall Maxwell, pictured at home in 1938 with her father, Walter Earl Maxwell, is fascinated with the toy train going around her. The photo was taken in Houston, where she still lives.

DAD'S CHRISTMAS VILLAGE

At a time when most families were talking about how many people could fit around their dining room table for dinner on Thanksgiving, my dad, G. Wylie Overly, was moving our dining table and chairs to the basement.

He was making room for the Christmas village that he spent so much time designing and building. It had a farm, a church, an armory, an airport, a lumber mill, an Indian tepee, a person fishing, a circus, a house and a road under construction, horseback riders, a zoo and, of course, Santa and his reindeer. Santa can be seen coming down a street located to the center right of the picture. Dad was a perfectionist, so the buildings, vehicles and figures were close to scale and lit by Christmas tree lights. (Wiring ran beneath the sturdy platform.)

Dad made the tunnel at the base of the tree from papier-mâché painted to look like a real mountain. He dyed sponges green for the bushes and trees. The tree trunks, made from sticks, were anchored with small pieces of wood for stability. The pretend lake in the

DAD'S GIRLS got in on the fun of running the Christmas village, too. Ann (right) ran the train while Louise turned the fountain on and off, to the delight of their guests.

center was made of metal and fit tightly in the wooden base. It was a treat to watch the train go over the bridge.

My sister, Ann, ran the train and worked the switches while I turned the fountain on and off.

Dad welcomed people into our home to see the village on weeknights during the first three weeks of December. At that time of year there was always snow on the ground in our part of Pennsylvania. Many people arrived wearing snow-covered boots or shoes, but this didn't seem to bother my family a bit.

Dad worked many evenings and weekends in November to get the display ready. This was indeed a labor of love that brought holiday delight to those who visited our home. I cherish these childhood memories.
LOUISE OVERLY CULP • COOKEVILLE, TN

BY GOLLY, IT'S JOLLY!

THE ABUNDANCE of cards, greetings and gifts surrounding this couple and their humble tree shows how much love and generosity came their way. This image comes from Nettie Whitney of Dorchester, Massachusetts.

SEASON'S GREETINGS decorated the banister at the home of Leslie and Frances Brudvig in 1956. "This is one of many slides that my 80-year-old father recently put on CDs for each of his three kids," says Scott Brudvig of Richmond, Virginia. "Many, like this one of my siblings, Linda and Allan, with my mother, capture the feel of the 1950s."

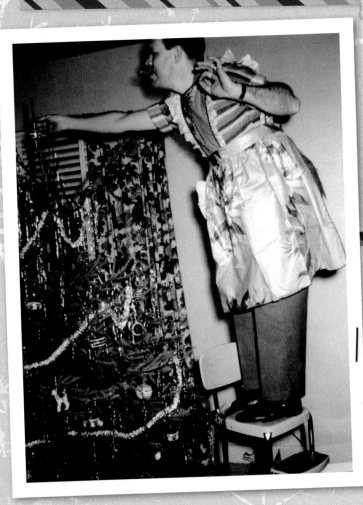

SURPRISE! "On our first Christmas together, in 1957, my husband, Doug, surprised me by preparing dinner, hence the apron," writes Dorothy Kelshaw of Lansing, Michigan. "His hobby was gourmet cooking. He also surprised me with this Christmas tree. I just had to capture the moment of this macho man, with cigar and apron, putting the final touches on the tree."

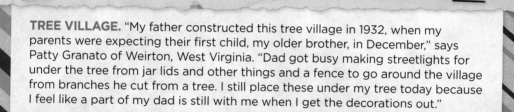

TREE VILLAGE. "My father constructed this tree village in 1932, when my parents were expecting their first child, my older brother, in December," says Patty Granato of Weirton, West Virginia. "Dad got busy making streetlights for under the tree from jar lids and other things and a fence to go around the village from branches he cut from a tree. I still place these under my tree today because I feel like a part of my dad is still with me when I get the decorations out."

IS IT TIME YET?
The anticipation of toys left by Santa Claus is evident on the faces of brothers Dennis (left) and John Houseman in 1960 at the family home in Philadelphia. Their mother, Joan Houseman, shares the photo.

FINISHING TOUCHES

CHRISTMAS ANGELS

This 1946 photo (above) is especially meaningful to me because it was the first Christmas my sister and I spent with our new father and mother, who had adopted us the summer before (above right).

Joyce was 7 and I was 5 that year, yet this was the first time we had ever experienced Christmas—up until then, we had no idea how most people celebrated Christ's birth.

My sister and I had been abandoned in Appalachia and spent two weeks in a Christian orphanage. The news was put in area church bulletins to find a home for us, and Robert and Helen Willis of Hopkinsville, Kentucky, answered the call. They were in their 40s and had never had children.

Joyce and I barely made it through the anticipation leading up to Christmas, and both of us woke up very early on a cold but sunny 25th. For the longest time, all we could do was sit on the warm floor and stare at the gifts, the shimmering tree and the large, bright angel perched on top.

Mother took this picture of us sitting there in awe and joy at the scene before us—it was a wonderful day for all of us. When I saw the printed photograph, I noticed several bright lights that were hovering in back of me and asked Mother what they were. "Those are your guardian angels!" she told me. "The Lord must have sent them to watch over you and your sister."

Through the years, Mother and Father set the example for me to follow Christ, and I eventually came to realize that my parents were my real guardian angels.

KEN WILLIS • OWENSBORO, KY

WAXING ARTISTIC

My favorite memory of Christmas 1955, when I was 5 years old, is decorating with Glass Wax. It was a cleaning paste you applied to windows and mirrors, allowed to dry, and then wiped off with a damp cloth to remove any smudges.

Around the holidays, the company that made it provided Christmas stencils for decorating windows. I don't remember if we used the official ones or made our own, but we created wonderful window designs in our New Jersey home.

You taped the stencils to the window and then dabbed on Glass Wax with a sponge. When the wax dried, you removed the stencil and ended up with snowy stars, Christmas trees, snowmen, and Santa and his sleigh.

When the holidays were over, you just wiped off the wax and the windows would be clean. Maybe that was how Mom got us to do some cleaning!

LOIS HENDERSON • MORRISTOWN, TN

FIRE PLACING. "It wasn't Christmas till our dad, James, set up our cardboard fireplace," says Jeff Lewis of Scranton, Pennsylvania. "Jack (left) and I surprised Mom (Jean Ann) in 1970 with the mini wheelbarrows, made in Cub Scouts."

STOCKINGS HUNG WITH CARE. "I made the stockings tacked onto the mantel of our Philadelphia house, which was more than 100 years old when this photo was taken on Christmas Eve in 1964," says Betty Johnson Backes of Spring Hill, Florida. "My daughters, Donna, 8, and Kim, 6, are with their cousins Greg, 1, and Steve Ridge, 7 months."

Hanging Christmas stockings on the mantel, staircase or other area—with the expectation they will be filled with small gifts from good old St. Nick— is a festive tradition enjoyed by children around the world.

LADDER OF SUCCESS?

This small bit of family drama took place rather frequently in my house in Alton, Illinois, in the late '20s:

"If only I had a ladder that reached to the ceiling, I could hang my pongee curtains myself." Yes, my mother said this over and over, year after year, until I had the complaint etched in my ears like a name on a gravestone.

When he hung the silk curtains, Daddy always got the pinch pleats crooked, and one panel sagged dejectedly. My parents then yelled and fought about it.

When I was 10, however, Daddy had the brilliant idea of giving my mother a 12-foot ladder for Christmas. This would allow her to hang her pongee curtains, not to mention making holiday decorating a breeze. He took my sister Jean and me into his confidence, and we all giggled and whispered together like conspirators.

The metal ladder was big, heavy and expensive, about $10. Now Daddy had the problem of where to hide it so Mother wouldn't find it before Christmas.

He decided to ask a neighbor to keep it. Mother's best friend, Patsy Hulsenburg, lived two doors down. Daddy asked her husband, Gus, to hide the ladder. Being a friendly guy, Gus said he'd find room in his shed. He also thought the present would be a success and would help preserve domestic harmony when it was time to hang those curtains or trim the Christmas tree.

Patsy, who was a big talker and gossip around the neighborhood, told the Kramers and the Gills about the Christmas surprise coming for Irma Lampert. Everyone was delighted and knew all the details.

Christmas Day arrived at last, and Daddy had a twinkle in his eye. After we girls got our presents, he put Mother's favorite record, "Hearts and Flowers," on the Victrola. Then he disappeared.

Soon, Daddy reappeared with Gus, carrying the enormous ladder with a huge red ribbon tied to its peak.

Mother was aghast. She sank to the couch and began to cry. She had been hoping for something romantic and glamorous, like a diamond ring or perhaps a sparkling rhinestone necklace.

But as she looked at Daddy, she knew the ladder was absolutely the most perfect gift he could offer. Daddy took her hand, and they kissed long and lovingly. "I hope we never fight about the curtains again," he said. "I love you so much, and I hate it when we bicker and shout."

There was a knock on the door, and all the neighbors piled in—the Hulsenburgs, the Kramers, the Gills and all their kids. Everyone hugged Mother and told her that she had a wonderful, thoughtful husband.

Mother just kept crying big, splashy, happy tears. The neighbors brought punch and cookies, and Patsy took pictures of each family on the steps of the ladder. Mother brought in her big jar of cookies, and we ate and danced and played carols on the Victrola.

After that, I don't think Daddy and Mother ever argued over the small stuff. When feathers began to fly, they just brought out that big old monster ladder to remind them of their love and laughed their troubles away.

LOUISE LARSEN
ST. LOUIS, MO

LITTLE LOUISE is pictured at 2 months with her father, Anson Lampert, in April 1918 and at age 10 with her mother, Irma.

it wouldn't be Christmas without *Jewels by* TRIFARI

From left to right: "Duchess" Necklace $20, Earrings $15, matching Bracelet (not shown) $20, "Queen of Diamonds" (on large green ball) Necklace $15, Pin $5, Earrings $5, Bracelet (not shown) $10, "Gem of India" Bracelet (hanging) $15, Necklace (on red ball) $10, Pin (on silver ball) $7.50, Earrings (on green ball) $7.50, "Stardust" (on blue ball) Pin $10, Earrings $7.50, "Golden Fleece" Necklace $7.50, Bracelet $5, Earrings $3. All prices plus tax.

THEIR FIRST NOEL. "Back in 1923, my mother- and father-in-law (top) were real Christmas romantics," says Sally Eshelman of Swannanoa, North Carolina. "It was their first holiday as a married couple." Above, Cita (Droemer) and Bill Jacobs celebrate their first Christmas in 1953 in Gardenville, Pennsylvania. Daughter Carol Jacobs Norwood of nearby Myerstown says, "As you can see, they were expecting a baby—me!"

Here's for happier holidays in your home!

Easy ways to make your home gayer and brighter with G-E Christmas Tree Lights

Brighten doorways with gay holiday decorations. It's easy. Simply string colorful General Electric lights over grocery.

A lighted wreath above your fireplace lends a festive touch. Lighted wreaths available—or light your own with G-E bulbs.

For a gay decoration put G-E lights in a deep bowl and cover with the ornaments. Edge with sprigs of holly.

Sparkling tree in the dining room too, adds Christmas cheer. You can get lighted artificial tree, or trim a small tree.

For a brighter Christmas, be sure your bulbs are marked G-E

Greet friends through cheery windows. G-E bulbs in candle outfits or wreaths will send your holiday welcome out.

Get free booklet "Bright Ideas". Shows many ways to decorate indoors and out. Write General Electric, Dept. 166-L, Nela Park, Cleveland 12, Ohio.

C-6 G-E lamps in bright colors for series strings. Available in red, blue, green, orange and white. Look for the G-E on bulbs you buy.

C-7½ for use indoors in multiple strings. If one goes out, rest stay lit. Also new inside-color bulbs for OUTDOORS in approved strings.

C-9 outdoor multiple lights. Inside color so they're weather and scratch-proof. Use in approved strings to say "Merry Christmas" outdoors.

You can put your confidence in—

GENERAL ELECTRIC

Very Merry

FESTIVE FLIVVER. "In the 1940s, my husband's aunt and uncle decked out their old car and delivered gifts to their nieces and nephews," says Bernie Hauser of Menomonee Falls, Wisconsin.

CRUISING ON DREAM STREET

Back in the 1940s, the holiday decorations in our part of Detroit's east side were pretty scant.

So a bunch of us would pile in a car and ride out to Lake Shore Drive. On one side was huge Lake St. Clair, frozen over and shimmering like diamonds. On the other side, always back off the road, stood the enormous mansions with thousand of lights in every holiday shape and form. Even the towering evergreens were aglow.

We were awestruck and wondered what it could possibly be like to live in that fashion.

Today, I live not far from that dream street, and still take my grandchildren on a drive to see the wondrous display.

But I don't wonder what it's like to live there anymore. I just drive back to our little house, make eggnog and watch the kids open their presents. Nothing can top that.

SHIRLEY PASKE • HARPER WOODS, MI

A COTTON CHRISTMAS. As missionaries in Brazil, Florine Hawkins' family celebrated the holidays in summer. "In 1963, our twins and neighbors made a tree out of cotton," she says from Odessa, Missouri.

HIT THE LIGHTS!

In December 1948, when I was 7, we lived on a farm near Precept, Nebraska. My dad and we three kids had installed a wind charger that summer, so it was the first winter that we had electricity. We cut a tree from the pasture and decorated it with strings of popcorn and ornaments. My older brother made lights for it with old wire and bulbs we'd painted.

We couldn't leave the lights on too long because the paint would burn off, plus we would be wasting precious electricity, so I watched out the north window and my sister watched out the south window as my brother stayed near the plug. When we saw car lights coming we would holler, "Car!" and he would plug the lights in. That way, whoever drove by would know we had a lit Christmas tree!

BEULAH VAHLE • LONG ISLAND, KS

First Christmas

My daughter, Janet Lou, was completely enchanted by our small pink Christmas tree adorned with bright, shiny ornaments and glittering tinsel. It was her first Christmas in 1958. I was enchanted with it, too, but even more so with our new baby!
SHARON KOEHNE • SPRINGFIELD, IL

CHAPTER 3

SPIRIT OF THE SEASON

Christmas is the most wonderful time of the year. It's also one of the best times to make someone else's day a little brighter. Despite the hardships of the Depression years and rationing during World War II, the contagious spirit of generosity was alive in bighearted folks who knew it was far better to give than to receive.

"In 1933, our family could not afford a Christmas tree," says Phyllis Upright of Independence, Oregon. "To an 8-year-old like me, that was devastating.

"My older brothers found a juniper bush in a neighbor's yard, cut off a good-sized limb and dragged it home for our Christmas tree. We carefully decorated it, but it didn't look much like a Christmas tree.

"My older sister Maxine had a boyfriend named Howard who owned a yellow roadster. One day he came over to visit Maxine, and the first thing he saw was our makeshift tree. Without saying a word, he turned and drove away.

"When he returned about an hour later, there in his car's rumble seat was an honest-to-goodness Christmas tree with decorations already in place. He had gone home and taken the tree right out of his parents' living room and brought it to us. He thought we kids needed a tree more than his parents, and they agreed."

From chance encounters to unexpected blessings to random acts of kindness, these stories will remind you of the goodness that prevails during this special time of year.

PUTTING THE 'SHARE' IN SHARECROPPING

Texas twins made do at Christmas and split their gift. **ALTA CONDRAN** • KAUFMAN, TX

During my 1950s childhood in Hedley, Texas—population 600, including cats and dogs—our family, the Butlers, were sharecroppers, working the cotton fields in the area.

We were a large but close-knit family. Eight of us lived in a one-bedroom house, with three girls in one bed and three boys in the other. We were allowed one game in the house, dominoes, since we didn't have a television. We were allowed to play on Monday until bedtime and on Saturdays if we had our Sunday school shoes polished. This left us lots of time to get creative with finding ways to entertain ourselves, which usually involved some kind of outdoor play.

We never had much money for presents or a tree, but this didn't stop us from enjoying the holiday season. Christmas at school was particularly exciting. We'd be sitting at our desks when all of a sudden we would hear a loud siren and bells ringing. Looking out the window, we'd see Santa Claus riding on top of a fire truck, carrying wrapped presents. What a sight!

We would all gather around the school Christmas tree, waiting for Santa to hand us a present that would be our very own. We weren't interested in sitting on Santa's lap because we were too busy admiring our gifts. Each of us was so thankful for that one gift that none of us asked for anything else from this magical man.

The school Christmas tree was especially important to us, because it often determined whether we would have a tree at home to decorate. Every year after the holiday party at school, the janitor would take down the tree and carry it to the burning area, which was surrounded by a wire fence. Since there were many poor families in town, lots of children—including my twin brother, Alvie, and me—would rush to save the tree and carry it home.

One year, we were the first to arrive and were excited about getting a tree, but in Alvie's efforts to save the tree from burning, his pant leg caught on fire. As the other children looked on, one boy began to throw dirt and smother the fire on Alvie's pant leg. Alvie gave him the tree to thank him for saving his clothes.

Without a tree, we went tumbleweed

GOOD CROP OF KIDS. The author's mother (above) holds her young twins at a Texas cotton field. At right, three of the Butler children (from left), Alta May, Alvie Ray and R.E., with their dad.

hunting. Whether we had a tumbleweed or a tree, we still decorated it with the same things. We took icicles from the school tree, made garland out of paper, and used buttons to decorate the tree and canning lids to top it. We were so proud of our efforts.

Every year, we looked forward to seeing the "Christmas fruit man," as Alvie and I called him. This man would load his truck with bushels of fresh fruits, mainly apples and oranges, and sell them door to door. If the cotton crop was good that year, Dad would buy one of each as a special Christmas treat.

Also, if we had a good year, we knew we would get to order a crate of baby chickens, which would arrive in the spring, and two pairs of new shoes—one for working in the fields and everyday wear, and the other for school and church on Sundays.

The crop also determined our Christmas presents. If it had not been good, we got gifts at the electric company, where people brought their children's used toys. If the crop had been good, we would get a brand-new gift. However, Dad couldn't afford a gift for each of us six kids, so we drew sticks to see if it would be a boy gift or girl gift. In 1954, I pulled the short stick. But being a tomboy, I was pretty excited when our gift turned out to be a BB gun.

On the Sunday after Christmas, Alvie and I raced home after church to see who'd get to use the gun to hunt rabbits and squirrels for meat for the family. Both of us grabbed the gun, with the barrel resting on Alvie's shoe. I told him to turn the barrel loose or I would shoot his toe. He didn't turn it loose, and I pulled the trigger. I then looked down to see a hole in his Sunday school shoe. Fortunately, we always bought larger shoes than we needed so we could grow into them, so the BB missed his toe.

Alvie shrieked! I knew I was in trouble, so I ran outside. We had a fun game of cat and mouse, chasing each other around the barn. As I peeked around the corner to catch a glimpse of him, he saw my nose and shot. To this day, I still have a dimple on the tip of my nose from the BB.

Mom spanked both of us that day, Alvie for forgetting to change his shoes after church and me for putting a hole in one of them.

I'll always have fond memories of that Christmas and all the fun times I had with my twin brother. That year was also special because we received a cherished Bible storybook that we shared and read to each other for many years after. We never minded sharing because even though we may not have had much, we always had each other.

A REASON TO SMILE. Helen Carey Blair, the girl with the big smile and gingham dress half-sitting on a desk in front, was thrilled after receiving the book at right.

The Golden Rule

SOMEWHERE OUT OF NOWHERE

During the Christmas season of 1939, I was in the sixth grade at Parker Elementary School in Chicago. We held a small gift exchange, each of us buying a present for 25 cents to give someone in the class. I did a lot of baby-sitting to earn my 25 cents and bought a nice flower pin for a girl.

Everyone opened their gifts—hair ribbons, pins, yo-yos, tops, model cars and other toys and trinkets. But when I opened up my gift, I was disappointed to find a pad of rough arithmetic paper.

Then the teacher, Miss Williams, called me up to the front of the room and handed me a package with a pretty ribbon around it. I opened it up and found a book titled *Helen Carey: Somewhere in America*, a story about a young girl brought up on a ranch.

I was surprised. My name was Helen Carey, too! I felt like the most important person in that room; I think I floated back to my seat. Everyone came to look at the book and said how lucky I was.

I lost the book when my family moved to Arizona, but I was lucky to get my hands on another copy years later from a kind stranger I connected with on the Internet—another nice thing someone did for me. Today I'm proud to show the book to my grandchildren and great-grandchildren.

HELEN CAREY BLAIR • PHOENIX, AZ

SANTA CLAUS IN A BLACK SEDAN

Christmas 1953 started out looking like a rather scaled-down affair. The tree wasn't as big as usual, and we five kids were informed, "Santa Claus is kind of poor this year." Evidently, it had been a bad year for farming all through the Midwest, including our farm in Guinea Bend, Illinois.

It was with great expectation, then, that I looked forward to the school gift exchange. On the last day before winter vacation, we brought our 25-cent gifts and placed them under the classroom tree.

When my present was handed out, I felt through the wrapping and determined it was a book—my favorite gift, for I loved to read.

"Why aren't you opening your present?" asked my fifth-grade teacher, Miss Tarrant. Students all around me were eagerly tearing off wrappings.

"My mom said I was to get just one present this year," I explained shyly, "and I wanted to take this home and put it under the tree." Miss Tarrant didn't say anything more.

On Christmas morning, a big black '40s sedan pulled up right in front of our house. Then out stepped Miss Tarrant, carrying a cardboard box.

"Santa Claus dropped these off at the wrong house," she said, "and I thought you might be able to take them off my hands."

Inside the box were several small presents, carefully wrapped in pretty paper, some for girls and some for boys.

There was one package, larger than all the others, that Miss Tarrant said she was pretty sure Santa would want me to have myself. It contained two books and an assortment of items not unlike some that I had seen on Miss Tarrant's school desk on the afternoon of the gift exchange.

That Christmas turned out to be one of the most memorable I ever had.
DIANA SCHUTZ • CATLIN, IL

HOLIDAY SPIRIT REMAINS

Back in the mid-1950s, when I was in grade school in Rockwell, Iowa, a holiday gift exchange was popular. At 50 cents, the price limit wasn't that steep for most of us.

It was the last year before we became too old for the exchange, and I was excited. The only problem was, one boy in our class was from a family that was very poor.

Of course, he drew my name. I resigned myself to no gift, knowing money was tight with them. I also had begun to learn that it was better to give than to receive.

Imagine my surprise when I got a large gift on the day of the exchange. I opened it and found a model airplane valued at $1.

I thanked the boy and walked on air for months, until we left for summer vacation.

Looking back, I realized that the teacher probably bought that plane and put my name on it. Regardless, I still treasure that time and try to believe Santa Claus worked his magic.

It was the kindest thing if the teacher did it, but if the boy did it, it was even better.
MIKE FATLAND • MASON CITY, IA

ANGELS ON EARTH

SANTA WORE BOBBY SOCKS

Christmas 1940 makes me misty-eyed every time I think about it. I was attending high school in California's San Joaquin Valley. In the hard times of the era, people depended on one another. We collected food, clothing, bedding and household items and gave them to the needy.

We saved the toys we collected for Christmas. The home economics classes made new dresses for the dolls, while the shop classes turned lumber into trucks, games and other toys.

As Christmas approached, we students wrapped the toys and loaded the packages for delivery. As we presented the gifts, we saw joy in many faces, especially those of the children.

We had a few more visits to make on Christmas morning. The air was heavy and chilled us to the bone. A rancher offered us his truck for deliveries, and we gratefully accepted. For several hours, we knocked on doors. But as the cold hours passed, our enthusiasm gradually waned.

When we finally headed home, someone pointed to a small house down a canal bank. Although there were no electric or telephone lines running to the structure, smoke curled from the chimney. The house stood bleakly in the forlorn terrain that surrounded it.

None of us knew who lived there, and we wondered if there were children. We still had a doll, two trucks, some small toys, chocolate Santas and a box of groceries. We decided to make one last visit. We climbed down from the truck and gathered the gifts.

Mud sucked at our boots, slowing our progress. When we knocked on the door, a young woman whose dark hair was tied back with a red ribbon answered it. Three small children peeked from behind her skirt—a girl of about 2, and boys perhaps 4 and 5 years old. The mother put an arm around the toddler and looked at us questioningly.

"Merry Christmas," we chorused as we bent down and handed the gift-wrapped packages to the children and the box of

RANDOM ACTS OF KINDNESS. In the 1940s, the author, seen working on her family's ranch in California, learned it is more blessed to give than to receive.

groceries to the mother, whose eyes widened with amazement. She slowly smiled, then quickly said, "Come in."

The catch in her voice was sufficient for us to accept her invitation. We removed our boots and stepped inside.

I knelt to reach the little girl, and it was then that I looked around the room. The linoleum floor was worn but spotless. Bleached flour-sack curtains hung at the windows. Neatly made beds occupied one corner of the room, and the kitchen another. A small stove furnished heat.

As I turned back to the children, dressed in clean, neatly patched clothes, I noticed several green tree branches standing upright in a dirt-filled pot. A red cloth circled the base. Can lids and paper angels hung on strings, and a paper star graced the top. Streamers of popcorn completed the tree.

The room was silent as the children looked at their mother, wondering if the gifts were really for them. The little girl hugged her doll, and the boys grasped the trucks as they sought an answer. She put her arms around them and said in a choked voice, "I told you Santa Claus would come."

BEVERLY ROBERTS JOSTAD • SALEM, OR

SISTERLY LOVE

In 1946, my mother was a widow caring for seven children, all under age 16, and times were hard for us. My two older brothers had gone to work a few hours a day for the Sisters of Loretto, so things were looking a little better.

There was much talk around our house about being good and Santa watching, but my younger brothers and I knew this year was different.

Imagine our surprise when we came home from midnight Mass to find treasures under the tree. Mine included a doll that cried and a red reversible raincoat. I was thrilled to see my brothers had received toy cars and warm shirts and boots, and my sister had gotten a vanity set and some new clothes. It was years before I learned the good Sisters of Loretto had sent most of our Christmas presents home with my two older brothers.

On Christmas morning, we went skating on our pond. A hole had been chopped in the ice so the cows and horses could get water. Of course, I fell through it and, after I was pulled to safety, spent the rest of the day inside, warming up.

How loved I felt that day, wrapped in a blanket, holding my doll and watching my new coat steam by the fireplace. I remember rocking away, listening to my mother sing in the kitchen and thinking that I was very wealthy indeed.

MARY CECIL • NEW HAVEN, KY

FRIENDS DID NOT FORGET THEM

My father was sent overseas in July 1944, and it wasn't long afterward that we received a telegram saying he was missing in action.

A few days later, there was a knock on the door, and we learned he had died at Normandy. My mother became a widow with three young children to raise—my brother, age 8; my sister, 3; and me, at 6.

It looked like Christmas would be a dark time for our family. Mom didn't have money to buy presents and a tree. Then we received an invitation from Jake and Ruth Wise, some friends who farmed near Fernald, Iowa, to spend our Christmas holiday with them.

You can imagine how excited we were when we got the news we were going to ride the train from Des Moines to Nevada, Iowa.

Christmas morning was an exciting time. There were presents under the tree for us, and candy and fruit in our stockings. There was a sumptuous dinner and then an even bigger treat: Snow was plentiful, and Jake had a sleigh and horses to take us on our first sleigh ride.

It was great until the horses got loose and ran away. The sleigh tipped over, and I got snow up my coat sleeves.

Each Christmas season, I look back at that time and realize how much it now means to me that they would remember a sad widow and her children.

BEVERLY GRAEBER • JONESBOROUGH, TN

THE SMITHSON FAMILY in early '40s included the author (right), with siblings Terry and Myrna, and their parents, Bob and Helen, in Odessa, Missouri.

PRINCE OF PEACE

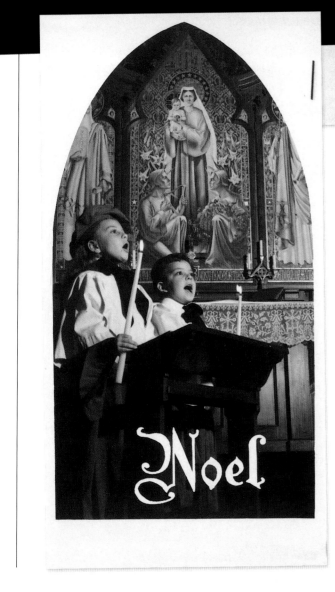

SPIRIT SHINES BRIGHTLY. Year after year during the 1950s, outdoor displays that depicted the true meaning of Christmas cast a welcoming light at the Harold Gerbers family home in Fort Wayne, Indiana.

REASONS TO REJOICE

POWER OF PRAYER

After the Christmas program at our little rural schoolhouse, everyone went downstairs to the basement for refreshments. I was serving punch while our 6-year-old daughter, Katrina, was playing with the other children.

All of a sudden, I heard the cry of a child. Someone grabbed my arm and said it was my daughter. I ran to her—she had fallen and hit her head on the basement's cement floor. Seconds later, she stopped crying. To my horror, I saw she was unconscious.

My husband scooped her up, and we ran to the car. The hospital was nearly 35 miles away. Katrina's breathing was very shallow, and her tiny body felt lifeless. It was the longest 40 minutes of our lives.

At the hospital, Katrina still wasn't

responding. I stood next to her as she lay in bed, now hooked up to IVs and wearing a neck brace. Suddenly, she looked up at me and said, "Mommy?" I burst into tears.

The doctors told us that she had a severe concussion but would be OK. Later, we found out that, after we left the school, everyone had gathered to pray for Katrina. We know she was in the Lord's hands, and He gave her back to us.

BRENDA NISSLEY • BLOOMFIELD, MT

GOOD NEIGHBORS

In December 1963, my father told my two sisters and me that he couldn't afford presents that year, not even our traditional treats of chocolates, nuts and fruit. My mother suffered a stroke the year before and was constantly going to the hospital, so there was no money for Christmas.

On Christmas Eve, we heard a knock on the door. Two ladies came in and gave us new coats, along with some holiday treats. Our neighbor across the street had told her church about our situation, and the people of the congregation wanted to help.

I will never forget our kind neighbor and the members of her generous church.

SHEILA DEANE • CHATTANOOGA, TN

COLLECTED KINDNESS

We were in the 18th month of my husband's layoff, and money was very tight. Christmas was right around the corner, and we had three daughters under the age of 7.

I did my best to come up with inexpensive gifts, buying clearance items and making what I could by hand. But it broke my heart to know that the sparkle would not be in the girls' eyes on Christmas morning.

We attended church together as a family on Christmas Eve, as usual. After the service, we walked back to our car in the parking lot... and everything changed.

As we opened the car doors, bags and boxes of gifts began spilling out. The back seat was packed with presents, trinkets, candy—everything a little girl could hope for.

And that wasn't all. Back at home, we found an envelope of money taped to the door. Shortly afterward, visitors arrived carrying bags and a handful of more cash.

We didn't know it at the time, but the offering that had just been collected at church had been destined for us.

Though it was years ago and our girls were very young, they still talk about the miracle of that Christmas.

VICKIE ALLISON • BESSEMER, PA

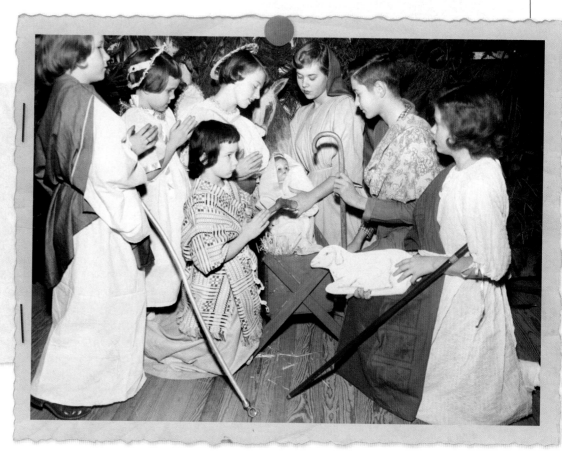

AWAY IN A MANGER. "This photo of children kneeling before the Baby Jesus reminds me of the December of 1938 when my family was invited to attend a second-grade Christmas pageant," says Beatrice Demmel of Escondido, California.

SECRET GIFTS

A doctor's patients received a gift they never knew about—
and one his family would never forget.

JOHN McCLENDON • BRANDON, MS

The Depression was sapping the life from my dad. You could see the toll in his lined and haggard face, his hollow eyes, the slump of his shoulders. His devotion to the medical needs of our rural county, which was beset with unemployment and hopelessness, gave him little rest.

"You need to eat and get some rest, William," Mom pleaded. "What if you get sick? What will your patients do then? And what about me and the kids?"

"You should see them, Ellen. They have given up hope. Their health is going, along with everything else."

After meals, Dad pulled a large, worn ledger from his desk and added the names of the patients he'd seen that day.

Once my sister, Jane, asked, "Why do you waste time on the ledger, Dad? Those people won't pay, and you won't ever ask them."

"They can't pay," Dad replied patiently. "Times will get better. Then my patients will come around. They have so little now, and pride and honor are what they value most."

Despite Mom's fretting, she couldn't imagine her rock of strength could ever crumble. She was as shocked as the rest of us when Dad died of a coronary after helping a young mother through a difficult delivery.

His funeral was the largest our community had ever seen. Mom reached deep for inner strength, calmly accepting the condolences offered by Dad's patients.

After the funeral, we sat at the kitchen table. "What will we do?" Jane asked.

"We'll make it," Mom answered firmly. "William left a little money, and I have three strong children to help."

"Be realistic, Mom," Jane said. "What can two boys and I do when half the men in the county can't find work?"

Gestures of gratitude

My sister looked at the ledger on Dad's desk. "There's our answer. Ask people who are working to pay something on their bills."

Mom frowned. "I can't do that. Those who are working can't make ends meet. William wouldn't ask, and neither will I."

Unmoved, Jane said, "There are collection agencies that will do it for us."

Mom flushed. "I know you're trying to help, but we'll not discuss this any further."

A few weeks later, a letter came from an agency offering to collect the unpaid bills for a fee. Jane confessed that she'd contacted the agency. Mom tore up the letter.

"Those agencies are run by cold-hearted people," she said. "I don't want them making life miserable for the people Bill loved."

FUN WAS IN THE BAG for children her brother and a few whiskered volunteers visited with gifts in 1958. Charlene Heryla of Seattle, Washington, sent the photo.

She dropped the shreds into the fire, turned to me, and said, "Come on, John. We need to find a spot for the garden."

As it turned out, we needn't have even worried about a garden. The first ripening of vegetables brought a stream of produce to our door. Dad's patients came with beans, tomatoes, corn, eggs and butter. When Mom thanked them, they looked down humbly.

"He helped us when we needed help," a woman said. "I wish we could do more."

A precious secret gift

Summer gave way to fall. The produce changed, but there was no change in quantity. Apples, pears, canned fruit and late vegetables continued to arrive.

Letters from the collection agency kept coming and went to the firebox. The ledger was put away. As Christmas neared, Mom tried to prepare us for a meager holiday.

Again we failed to gauge the depth of Dad's patients' gratitude. The last cold days of Christmas week, we received gifts of pies, cured hams, fresh beef, cakes, knitted mittens and scarves, even a hand-sewn quilt.

Our spirits lifted as we opened boxes of ornaments to decorate a pine tree a neighbor had brought us.

On Christmas Eve, we gathered around the fireplace. Mom looked at the presents under the tree and said, "We're having a wonderful Christmas, thanks to the good people who have shared with us. They're gifts from your father, too. He gave himself to the people, and they have returned it to us.

"There's something we can give, too." She paused and glanced at Jane. "Get the ledger."

Mom leafed through the book, reading names in Dad's handwriting. "This will be a secret gift," she said. "You must promise you will never tell anyone."

Mom tore the first page from the ledger and threw it into the fire. We watched as the paper burst into flame. Then she nodded to me, and I did the same with the next page. Bob had his turn, then Jane. Page after page, we threw the debts into the fire.

Mom was serene as she looked at the charred remains. Her smile radiated enough love to encompass each of us around the fire—and all our friends who would never know about their secret Christmas gift.

THE GOOD DOCTOR

The harsh winters in New York City were too much for me in the 1950s, and at the age of 6, I suffered from asthma, followed by bouts of pneumonia.

It was then that we met a wonderful "country doctor" right in the heart of Queens. When I close my eyes, I can still recall Dr. Goldman's kind face, warm eyes and gentle smile.

One day, during a blizzard around Christmas, my mother called Dr. Goldman to our home. He appeared in his sturdy old Chevy station wagon with big, cumbersome snow chains on the tires.

I peeked out the window just in time to see him trudge through the snowdrifts up to our front door.

He examined me and gave me a shot of penicillin, which helped immediately. I thought him an angel.

I watched as he checked on each of my six siblings, and I thought him patient.

Dr. Goldman later complimented my mom on what a good and caring mother she was, and I thought him kind. He charged only $10 for the lengthy house call, and I thought him my hero.

In 2008, 50 years after my first asthma attack, I graduated from medical school, inspired by Dr. Goldman's example.

My hero's bedside manner had influenced me all through the years I practiced as a registered nurse, and I was determined to follow in his footsteps and become a doctor. During the ceremonies, as I recited the Hippocratic Oath and crossed the stage to receive my diploma, Dr. Goldman's spirit was certainly with me.

ELEANOR LOPEZ • HUDSON, FL

GOING HOME FOR CHRISTMAS

Stranded in a blizzard, they were blessed by good Samaritans.

PAMELA BRESSLER WILLIAMS • JAMESVILLE, VA

Holidays without family would be unimaginable, so two days before Christmas, my husband and I stuffed the Buick with gifts and began the nine-hour trek from Cincinnati, Ohio, to York, Pennsylvania. Full of Christmas spirit, we donned the handmade Mr. and Mrs. Claus hats my mother had made, and set out.

As night approached, we were crossing the western mountains of Pennsylvania and singing along with Nat King Cole's "The Christmas Song" when we saw smoke rising from under the hood! We quickly pulled over, shut off the engine and looked under

JOINT VENTURE. The author and her husband open a gift together.

the hood, then decided it would be best to leave the motor off until we could get help. It was around then that the first snowflake floated down—and as we hadn't bothered to check the forecast before leaving, we had no blanket, no candles, no flashlight and, since this was 30 years ago, no cellphone.

In what seemed like minutes, there were 3 inches of snow on the ground. The wind began howling and we saw almost no cars on the road. As darkness descended, we shivered and huddled together in silence.

Soon the snowfall was 6 inches deep, the car was covered, and we feared that even if cars did pass, they would think ours was abandoned, since the emergency flashers were buried. As fast as we pushed the snow off, we were covered up again. Getting out of the car seemed even more dangerous than freezing inside.

I was delighted to see flashing lights as a state police car rolled up next to us and the trooper said, "Jump in and warm up!" But after only five glorious minutes of heat, he apologetically sent us back out into the snow, explaining that the cold was stopping diesel-powered vehicles in the passing lanes, and those were his first priority. The good news was that a tow truck was on its way.

After those toasty moments, the Buick seemed even colder. But finally, the tow truck appeared. The driver attached our car and we scrambled into the warm cab. Now the question became where to go. It was late, we were in the mountains, and the few motels we passed were filled or closed.

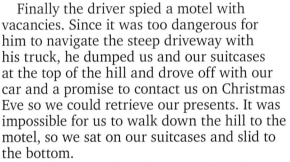

JOLLY FAMILY. The author's sister and brother-in-law, Kathy and Richard Kern, in Mom's hats (right) and with the author's parents, J.F. and Gloria Bressler (above, foreground); husband, Lance (in hat); daughter Donna.

Finally the driver spied a motel with vacancies. Since it was too dangerous for him to navigate the steep driveway with his truck, he dumped us and our suitcases at the top of the hill and drove off with our car and a promise to contact us on Christmas Eve so we could retrieve our presents. It was impossible for us to walk down the hill to the motel, so we sat on our suitcases and slid to the bottom.

Luckily for us, the folks at the Laurel Highlands Motel in Donegal absolutely exemplified the Christmas spirit. Normally they closed up a large portion of their place in winter, but that night they opened every room. We settled into one of the remaining rooms and called the family to tell them we were OK.

Soon the lobby was crowded with more stranded people, and the owners reopened their restaurant. We all crowded around the lobby television to watch the local news and discovered the wind chill was 40 degrees below zero. I was living proof of that: In a few days, my face peeled as if I had suffered a bad sunburn.

The next day the tow truck driver took us back to our car, which couldn't be fixed. In the bitter cold, we started to load the gifts into the tow truck to begin the 20-mile drive to the nearest car rental agency. When the driver removed his gloves to help shift the gifts around, I demanded in my best teacher's voice that he put them back on. He quietly replied, "I just didn't want to mess up the pretty presents."

We had another lucky break on Christmas Eve. Despite the brutal weather, we were able to rent the agency's last car, a gorgeous navy blue Cougar, and drive on to be with our family. We were almost speechless with joy. Since we already had our Christmas miracle, no further gifts were required.

HARD AT WORK

CHRISTMAS SUDDENLY ON HOLD

It was Christmas morning 1956 on our dairy farm outside of Menomonie, Wisconsin, and I was 7 years old, the youngest of three kids.

We already had a foot of snow on the ground, and the temperature plummeted below zero overnight. As my dad and my brother bundled up to head to the barn for the morning milking, Mother went down to the basement to add some more wood to the furnace.

I was inquisitively inspecting the brightly wrapped gifts under the tree when our Christmas plans hit a roadblock. Dad came inside to announce that the electric pump that brought water from our well was out. He'd try to fix it, and we would still be able to draw some water, but we would have to conserve as much as possible. Leaving my

brother to the milking chores, Dad headed back out with his tools.

The pump stood about 20 feet from the back of the house, fully exposed to the icy wind. Soon Dad came back inside, red-faced from the cold, to say he couldn't repair the pump. Now my parents wondered if they would even find a repairman on Christmas willing to brave the cold. And would the needed part be available?

We'd have enough water for coffee and to boil potatoes, but we would have to keep dish-washing to a minimum. There was water for washing hands but not for bathing. That meant no church for us that Christmas Day. No self-respecting farmer who handled barn animals would head for town without a thorough scrubbing! We wouldn't be able to use the toilet, either, but there was still the old outhouse in the yard. Although unused for many years, it was functional.

So, yes—we could survive for a day. But caring for the animals and milking were another matter entirely.

Each milking required two huge tubs of water to clean the milkers and milk pails. Every morning, the milkman would come and pump out our milk tank, followed by a thorough cleaning of the tank, using more water. Not to mention that 40 head of cattle would require many gallons of drinking water in 24 hours.

Dad had to find someone to fix our pump. He tried a few numbers but got no answer. Finally, he reached one and happily reported that a repairman was on his way.

As the repairman headed out to the pump, I pressed my nose to the window to track his progress. When I saw him remove his gloves, I rushed to Mother to let her know of this strange development. She explained that he had no choice but to take off his gloves to handle the small parts that were needed to fix the pump, but that he'd have to work fast before his fingers stiffened in the cold.

After fixing the pump, the repairman returned to the house. I remember my dad asking him how much he owed him, and the man replying, "Five dollars and 60 cents."

Not believing his ears, Dad asked him again, "*How* much?"

Apparently the repairman thought that Dad was challenging the price and explained, "It's 60 cents for the part, and I'd like $5 for my work."

Dad said, "Well, you'll have to take more than that for coming out on Christmas."

I recall Dad opening his billfold and hesitating. I think he was wondering how much he should give the man to compensate him for his work without making him feel foolish for asking for so little. I believe it was a $20 bill that changed hands that morning.

Then Dad asked if he had a hot dinner waiting. The man was a bachelor and said he'd fix himself something once he got home. Dad invited him to stay for dinner, and he gratefully accepted. Mother set a festive holiday table for us, and we were grateful for our many blessings—including the pump man who joined us that day.

MARY DRAKE • FREEPORT, IL

IN THE ST. NICK OF TIME

My dad was a rural mail carrier in Smethport, Pennsylvania, for more than 40 years.

One Christmas Eve in the late 1940s, he returned to the post office after finishing his route and noticed that a pile of packages had arrived on the afternoon truck. The boxes were addressed to a large family that that lived out in Irish Hollow.

Dad brought the packages home and called the father of the family, telling him that he could pick them up at our house. With gratitude in his voice, the man told my dad that he had to tell his kids there would be no gifts that Christmas because the parcels hadn't arrived.

That is one Christmas Eve I will never forget, because it made me so happy to see my father make another family's Christmas merry.

JERRY KLEISATH • PREBLE, NY

1954
▼

WISE MEN STILL SEEK HIM

★ ★ ★ Moses sought Him on a mountain; St. Augustine in his books; Washington at Valley Forge; Albert Schweitzer in the heat of the African jungle; President Eisenhower in his own heart and the hearts of his people; Konrad Adenauer in the Cathedral of Cologne. ★ And one cold night long ago the Wise Men found Him . . . and Angels singing, "Glory to God in the highest, and on earth peace to men of good will."

EXECUTIVE OFFICES • THE CONRAD HILTON • CHICAGO 5, ILLINOIS

AROUND THE WORLD

Hilton Hotels

CONRAD N. HILTON, president

The Joy of Giving

BEST PRESENT OF ALL

In the 1940s, I lived with my mother, Edna Mae Metz (above), in a small duplex on the east side of Huntington, Indiana.

My mother worked hard, holding down two jobs, one as a winder at a Fort Wayne factory, which meant driving 25 miles back and forth five days a week. Her second job was as a waitress at the La Fontaine Hotel, where she occasionally filled in as desk clerk.

Christmas was just around the corner, and the wonder and excitement of the holiday filled my 10-year-old heart with excitement.

It was my mother's habit to shop for groceries on Saturday evening. On one occasion, we didn't go to her store of choice, which had the best meat products. Instead, we went to Riorden's grocery store, which had the best oranges. It must be Christmas, I thought—oranges!

The few people in the store included a boy my age and a little girl about 6. In those days, kids often ran to the store for their mothers.

We selected our groceries, spending lots of time choosing our turkey and carefully examining the oranges for the very best. With our baskets full, we moved to the cash register counter and waited our turn in line. A man who worked for Mr. Riorden was clerking that night. I remember him as very thin, grim and unsmiling.

Now it was the children's turn in line at the register. The boy had a quart of milk and a loaf of day-old bread. He said to the clerk, "My mother said I was to have you put this on our bill."

The clerk stared down at the boy and girl and said, "Your mother has not paid her bill for three weeks. Now you put those things back, go home and tell her no more groceries until she pays her bill!"

Suddenly, I felt ill and my heart sank. The children were crushed, staring down at the floor, not knowing what to do. I looked up at my mother, and I remember her beautiful face to this day. Her mouth quivered as her eyes changed from gleaming to glaring. There was anger in those eyes.

My mother turned to me and told me, "Barbara, we will take our turn now." Then she turned to the boy and girl and said, "Please wait a few minutes, children."

She walked over to a counter and chose two caps and two pairs of mittens. The clerk added up our purchases, and my mother paid the bill in question. She then turned to the grim man and said, "We will never shop here again."

Once outside the store, my mother handed over our grocery bags, along with the caps and mittens, to the two children. "Merry Christmas," she said to them. Then she took my hand, and we headed for home.

My mother kept my hand in hers as we walked silently for a block or so. It was a cold evening, but I was snug in my early Christmas gifts—a beautiful matching blue wool cap and mittens, knit by my mother. Now I knew they would be my only presents. No oranges, turkey or doll, and no watercolors or sled. But what a special gift I received that night.

Soon we stopped near a curb under a streetlight, and my mother looked down at me and asked, "Do you mind, dear?" My heart was full, and I loved her more, at that moment, than I ever had before.

BARBARA BEEMER • HUNTINGTON, IN

SPUR-OF-THE-MOMENT CHARITY

Our family had just finished dinner on Christmas Eve 1942 when my friend Sylvia knocked on our door. Both 14 and looking for something to do, we decided to walk to the five-and-ten and buy a jigsaw puzzle to put together.

It was a cold night, but we enjoyed the walk with the brightly lit decorations and Christmas trees on display in windows.

A block from Woolworth's, we passed the Catholic orphanage, where a nun was sweeping snow from the steps.

"Merry Christmas, Sister Ana Marie," I said.

"Merry Christmas, girls," she replied.

"Is the tree decorated?" I asked.

"The children will decorate it after dinner. There aren't many gifts this year," she added a little sadly as she went indoors.

"How much money do you have?" Sylvia asked me.

I looked in my wallet and found $4. "How much do you have?" I asked her.

"I have $3 from baby-sitting."

A big sign on the five-and-ten—"Clearance Sale"—suddenly gave me an idea.

"Why don't we buy things for the children instead of ourselves?" I asked Sylvia, who quickly agreed.

It felt good to get out of the cold into the warm store. And so many items were on sale! Jigsaw puzzles were 25 cents, so we picked out four. Children's hardcover books also cost a quarter, so we chose four of those, too. Knitted caps were 50 cents, so we bought two in blue and two in red.

On a nearby table were sheets of holiday wrapping paper for just 2 cents each; we bought 12. Then we chose 14 candy canes for a penny each. The two extra were for us, because why shouldn't we have a treat, too?

"How are we going to wrap the gifts and

give them to the nuns?" Sylvia asked.

"The library hallway is always open for people to return books," I remembered. "Let's go there."

We walked the two blocks. "This is a great idea," Sylvia said. "It's nice and warm inside."

As we savored our candy canes, we wrapped the gifts in the pretty paper. Then we started to walk to the orphanage, but changed our minds, returned to the store and bought some big 5-cent cookies. What a treat they would be!

When we reached the orphanage, the children were already in bed. Sylvia and I put the presents under the decorated tree and stood there looking at it. Now the kids would have extra gifts. What a good feeling!

Then the nuns invited us into the kitchen for homemade fudge. "In the Bible, it says, 'Do a good deed,'" Sister Ana Marie said. "Girls, you have done a good deed."

"Thank you for having charity in your hearts," added Sister Grace.

We thanked them for the delicious fudge and walked to my house. It was 9 o'clock and time for Sylvia to go home.

When I went upstairs, I discovered that my older brother had bought a jigsaw puzzle, and all six of us children gathered eagerly around the dining room table to start it.

DORA SILVERS • NORWALK, CA

Gifts From the Heart

JUST LOVE

At Christmastime in 1957, Dad gave each of us $10 to buy presents.

I needed to buy gifts for two sisters, two brothers, Mom, Dad, Grandpa and Grandma. I could make that happen if I went up to the Kresge five-and-dime on Warren, or maybe Cunningham Drugs on the corner of Warren and Outer Drive. Both were on the east side of Detroit, where we lived.

I knew the key to getting the best gifts was having my shopping done way before my sister Judy, 15, and my brother Ken, 12.

I started with Grandpa's gift. I adored my grandfather and wanted so much to give him something he would love. I remembered that he liked chocolate-covered cherries, R.G. Dun miniature cigars and handkerchiefs (either white with an embroidered "F" for Fred, or the red bandanna kind that he always had in his pocket while gardening).

I decided on the cigars. Maybe Grandpa would teach me how to blow smoke rings, just as he had taught Ken (things were different back then, although Grandma might have given Grandpa a good talking-to if she learned of it). I thought if I could get Grandpa to actually say he wanted those cigars, it would make my gift even more spectacular!

"Grandpa, what would you like for Christmas?" I asked.

"Just love, little Mary," said Grandpa.

"I already love you, Grandpa, so what do you want for Christmas?" I continued.

Again he came back with the same answer: "Just love."

"Yes, I know that, Grandpa, but if you had to choose one thing that you really, really wanted for Christmas, what would that be?" I persisted.

"Just love. Love is all I need," he said.

Then Grandpa gave me a big hug and left for home in his two-toned turquoise Buick.

Well, no time to waste. I made my way up to Cunningham's and quickly found the holiday two-pack of R.G. Dun miniature cigars. There were five to a package, and they cost just under a dollar. The alluring, red-lipped Edie Adams stood there as a life-sized cutout for Muriel cigars, but I would not be swayed from my choice!

I plunked my money down, and the lady behind the counter quickly put the cigars in a bag. "These are for my grandpa for Christmas!" I told her.

I guess I felt as though I needed to explain that I would never smoke cigars—well, at least not without Grandpa. She didn't seem to care, though, and out the door I went. I ran home, eager to tell Judy and Ken that they had been "snuffed out" by a 10-year-old. Victory was mine!

Christmas morning came and it was wonderful! I heard jingle bells ringing downstairs and then, "Ho, ho, ho! Merry Christmas!" followed by the slamming of the front door. I remember running down the stairs, only to hear Dad say (as he would each Christmas), "Too bad, you just missed Santa Claus!"

I always wanted to ask why Santa left by the front door rather than the chimney, but the presents under the tree took priority.

When Grandma and Grandpa arrived, I was eager to have Grandpa open my gift.

"Thank you, little Mary, for the cigars!" said Grandpa.

"You're welcome, Grandpa. Remember, you said that you wanted 'just love,' but you can't wrap that!" I said.

"Oh, but you can," said Grandpa. Then he put his arms around me and said, "This is how you wrap love."

To this day, whenever I hear anyone ask, "What would you like for Christmas?" I can hear my grandfather saying, "Just love."

Wrap it up by hugging someone close to you. It's the best gift of all. It always fits, and the best part is you can always regift it—and feel really good in doing so!

MARILYN J. VAN TIEM • BRIGHTON, MI

TWELVE DAYS OF FUN

My son lives in Alaska, and one Christmas season, my daughter was also away. A very special family lived to the south of me, and their children decided to surprise me.

Each night, they gave me a gift from the song, "The 12 Days of Christmas." On the first night, I found on my back step a small Christmas tree with a bird, representing the partridge in a pear tree. The three French hens were tiny chicken replicas. The funniest gift was the one representing five gold rings: five glazed doughnuts in a paper sack.

At first, I had no idea who was behind all this. One night, I opened the back door and almost caught the two little girls, who were hiding behind my car.

The same family invited me to enjoy a lovely Christmas Eve dinner with them. It is all a beautiful memory of a wonderful family.

BETTY SCHNEIDER • IDAHO FALLS, ID

A PENNY SAVED...

Many years ago, when I was making 75 cents an hour, my three children asked for bicycles for Christmas, but I couldn't afford them.

So that January, I put three bikes on layaway. I paid all through the year, but a week before Christmas, I still owed $14.50 on the bikes.

The Saturday before Christmas, my son Ricky (above) asked how much I still owed. When I told him, he asked if he could pour the pennies out of the penny jug we kept. I said, "Son, I don't care, but I know there's not $14.50 worth of pennies in there."

Ricky poured them out, counted them and said, "Mom, there's $15.50 worth of pennies." Ecstatic, I told him to count out $1 for gas so I could go get the bikes.

I've always thought of this as our little miracle. It was as blessed a Christmas as anyone could ever have.

DOT WILLIAMS • CANTON, GA

Benevolent Bosses

HUNDRED-DOLLAR HANDSHAKE

In 1946, after coming home from World War II, I had a job in a lithographic company, but my pay as an apprentice was low.

Christmas was near, and my wife had put a doll on layaway for our 3-year-old girl, but we didn't know how we'd pay for it in time.

I happened to work on Christmas Eve. Imagine my surprise when the owner of the plant drove up, parked his car, walked over to me and extended his hand. He wished my family and me a very merry Christmas and walked away. In my hand he had placed five $20 bills!

Our daughter got her doll on Christmas morning, and I have never forgotten my employer for his kindness.

CARL SHERFIELD • PORTAGE, MI

IT'S ABOUT TIME TO SKATE

In the heart of the Great Depression, when I was 10 years old, Mother and I lived in La Crosse, Wisconsin, where she was working at Auto-Lite.

Mother came to me in September 1938 and said she would be getting laid off about a week before Christmas. She asked me what I wanted for Christmas, and I told her I'd like a pair of ice skates. I picked out a pair at Tietze's Hardware for around $5. Mother could pay 25 cents a week and I could pay 10 cents a week, since I had a paper route. At that rate, we would have them paid for by Christmas.

It turned out that Mother was laid off early, in the middle of November. I told Mr. Tietze what had happened, saying that I could keep paying my 10 cents, but it would take me until around March to get the skates paid for. He agreed to hold onto them for me until then.

On Christmas Eve, we heard a knock at the door, and there stood Mr. Tietze with the skates. I reminded him that I could not pay yet, but he just said, "You need them now,

not in March. They are paid in full, and merry Christmas!"

I still get tears in my eyes when I think of Mr. Tietze's kindness.

BRIAN ROBACH • RICE LAKE, WI

GIFT WAS HEAVEN SCENT

Snow had fallen on our little town of Lonsdale, Rhode Island, and I was standing outside Glancy's Drugstore with my dad's snow shovel.

In Glancy's window was an exotic Evening in Paris set. It was just the Christmas gift for my mom in 1945.

I'd already shoveled the sidewalks of three neighbors but was far from my goal. Mr. Glancy would never pay to have a path cleared for his customers, but good-natured Mr. Miller next door might. He owned the town's only grocery store and put a lot of people's groceries "on the tab."

I shoveled his door to the street, then from left to right of his storefront. This meant that I stopped just before Glancy's unshoveled sidewalk, a fact that Mr. Miller seemed to relish.

"What are you going to do with all your money?" Mr. Miller joked. I told him I was going to get my mom the Evening in Paris perfume set in Glancy's window. Mr. Miller just grunted.

While he and Mr. Glancy weren't fighting for the same customers, they still had a competitive relationship.

After shoveling his walk, I went inside to collect my money. Then Mr. Miller asked if I was interested in taking some groceries to one of his better customers. I put the box on a Miller's sled and trudged through the heavy snow as cold winds blew.

The warmth of Miller's store after trudging across town in the cold felt good. He handed me the money and asked if I'd like to deliver groceries after school.

Sometimes, I filled the orders I delivered. But after Mr. Miller checked my math a few times, I was relieved of that duty. I placed boxes and cans of food on the shelves. Some fragrant oranges arrived, and I placed them on display.

As the days wore on and Christmas

ILLUSTRATION: CHERYL MICHALEK

neared, my funds were still not enough for my mom's gift. Then things began to unravel.

Occasionally, when filling orders, I'd forget and leave an item off the list. Or I'd struggle so hard trying to get groceries up to second-story apartments that the customers would have to help. Or sometimes I'd arrive late because I'd stopped to watch my buddies shooting basketballs in the school yard.

One afternoon, Mr. Miller told me there were too many complaints. He handed me a dollar bill and patted my shoulder.

Christmas was only a few days away. With the money I had, I took the bus to Pawtucket and bought my mother some toilet water from Woolworth's. I placed the package under the tree along with the small hand viewer I'd bought Dad for his slides.

On Christmas morning, we all opened our gifts and Mom and Dad thanked me for theirs.

Soon, there was a knock at the door. We all wondered who would be calling this early in the morning. Mom opened the door, picked up a corrugated box and brought it into the living room. Inside was a gift-wrapped item and a note that said, "To Mom. From you son, Lewis."

When she opened the gift, there was the Evening in Paris set I had wanted so much for her. She came over to hug me. And I'll tell you, the scent of oranges on the wrapping paper was overwhelming.

LOU BRIERLEY • COLUMBIA, SC

WAVES ON A FENDER. Author Idabelle Swarts (on right) with fellow Waves Isabel Hanley (left) and Erma Hunter, in San Francisco in 1945. Below: Idabelle (left) with her sister, Mickey. They worked at the railroad shack in Montana (above) before joining the service.

ALMOST LIKE HOME
FOR CHRISTMAS

On a troop train going across the country, a homesick Wave found the Christmas spirit was alive in Indiana. **IDABELLE SWARTS** • SEASIDE, OR

My sister, Mickey, and I went to work as telegraphers for the Northern Pacific Railroad in 1943. We ended up in West End, Montana, between Bozeman and Livingston, where we lived in an old converted railroad coach.

On Thanksgiving, we cooked dinner for two friends who were leaving for military service. About 6 p.m., a blizzard moved in.

With the snow came freezing cold. It was so frigid, the thermometer broke. We moved into the bedroom, which had a coal stove, and ate our meals at work.

The cold weather lasted until spring. In fact, it wasn't until Easter Sunday that it was warm enough to clear away the dishes from the Thanksgiving dinner!

We vowed to never again live like that. So when September came around, Mickey and I joined the WAVES and departed for boot camp at Hunter College, New York.

My sister and I had been inseparable all our lives. But after boot camp, Mickey was assigned to the medical corps in Bethesda, Maryland, and I was sent to the 13th Naval

District in San Francisco. It turned out that I was the only one from my company going west. But when the bus came to take us to the train, I met Mary Thomas from Missouri, who suffered the same fate.

We became friends on the train and called each other "Missouri" and "Montana" after our home states. From then on, few knew me by any other name.

On Christmas Day, we pulled into Marion, Indiana. It was my first Christmas away from family and I was very homesick.

I wasn't the only one. The coach was very quiet when we pulled into Marion, and soon a lot of the Waves were reminiscing about holidays gone by.

Then I looked out the window and saw a group of women carrying baskets. They came on the train and gave each of us a present and something to eat. Most of the women were the age of my mother, which brought memories of her in Montana. Then she did not seem so far away.

I've never forgotten those women on that Christmas 58 years ago. I only wish I had told them how much it meant to me.

ON-THE-ROAD CHRISTMAS GIFT

In 1958, I was a first-year high school teacher in Beatty, Nevada. On Dec. 22, I headed home to Idaho in my 1951 Hudson to spend Christmas with my parents.

Just south of Fillmore, Utah, a radiator hose broke and the car started to overheat. I hitchhiked into Fillmore and got a ride to a Chevron station. I explained my plight to the owner, Dan Brinkerhoff, who sent a tow truck to bring in my car.

Dan discovered the engine had become so hot it had warped the head, so he called a nearby wrecking yard and found the needed part. I boarded a Greyhound bus, bought the part and then caught a return bus to Fillmore.

By that time it was dark, and Dan had closed the station. He immediately went to work on my car, laboring for several hours while I slept curled up in the backseat.

Finally, he woke me and announced that I was ready to go. When I went to settle up, he would not take a dime for anything he had done.

I was able to spend the holidays with my parents, and I shall forever remember Dan for the wonderful thing he did for me.

GLEN GILLETTE • LAS VEGAS, NV

A HOLIDAY FARE

Just before Christmas around 1919, my foster mother took me and four other girls in her charge on a bus ride from East Rutherford, New Jersey, to Passaic to see the beautiful Christmas lights and Santa's many helpers.

We were the last passengers on the bus ride home and began singing "Stille Nacht" (Silent Night) and "O Tannenbaum" in German.

When we were ready to disembark, the driver placed his hand atop the coin box and said, "No fare, ma'am. Those kids made my night. I really enjoyed them."

"Mama," who knew only broken English, swelled with pride over us girls, ages about 5 to 13, and I imagine our little chests swelled as well. After all, we had saved Mama 35 cents, quite a bit of money in those days.

HELEN HALKER DECKER • WANAQUE, NJ

YULETIDE VOYAGE LAUNCHED SWEET MEMORIES

A holiday homecoming is vivid in my memory as my best-ever Christmas present.

It was a snowy December in 1963, and we seven teens were eager to leave our mainland school and enjoy Christmas break with our families. We came from an island in the Northumberland Strait, and our only way to get home in winter was on a mail plane with seating for the pilot and one passenger.

There were just two of us left to transport when a blizzard bulletin was issued. My eyes welled up with tears as I watched the plane being covered with a tarp. We would not be going home after all.

Somehow, the word of our plight reaeded the island, and arrangements were made to drive us to Caribou Wharf. It was nearly dark when we saw a small boat approach, manned by my dad and one of his friends, dressed in oilskins and hip boots.

As our two "rescuers" maneuvered the boat through the gale, we passengers huddled in the bow. After 7 miles and two hours on the water, we were spotted by an islander with binoculars. The call went out, "They made it home safe!"

That night, the entire community turned out for the annual Christmas concert. Listening to the sweet carols, I was grateful for the love and courage of my island family and for the gift of being home for the holidays.

ROSE DEWOLFE • DARTMOUTH, NS

Humor & Hardship

She has fond memories of the difficult Depression years.
HARRIET BEULAH SMITH GUARDINO • SPRINGFIELD, OR

In the early 1930s, my parents owned a small dairy farm in Grants Pass, Oregon. As the Depression engulfed the nation, the long hours of hard work and constant worry over a dwindling income took their toll on my family. My mother, Catherine Dobbie Smith, collapsed from nervous exhaustion.

My father, John Reynolds Smith, was forced to sell the farm. With the money from the sale, he decided to make his last stand on the Croxton Ranch, a 200-acre dryland spread on Louse Creek, about 5 miles north of Grants Pass. I remember the day that, on foot, we drove our small herd of cattle down the back roads of town and across the highway onto a dirt trail that meandered through the wooded hills to our destination. I felt like a pioneer.

Although we always had enough to eat, times were tough for our small family. But we were grateful for everything we did have. Food was scarce in a lot of homes, and there were stories of men who took potato peelings to work in their lunch pails.

The second year we lived at Louse Creek—in 1932, when I was 11—was especially hard. The dry ground didn't yield enough for us to make a living. Near Christmas, my beloved horse, Dollie, who was used for both plowing and riding, got sick. My parents tried to treat what they suspected was a severe case of colic, but Dollie bolted and ran until she collapsed and died. Her death dampened the holiday spirit considerably.

On top of that, there was little under the Christmas tree except a couple of packages from a kind stranger. The tag was bluntly marked: "To some poor little girls."

But my attention was drawn to a brightly wrapped gift for me from my older sister, Virginia, whom I called Ginna. What could be inside? I felt it and shook it, trying to guess. My mother and Ginna sat nearby, not saying a word, but their sly smiles portended mischief.

Eagerly, I tore open the wrapping and found, to my dismay, a dried-out "horse biscuit"—manure chunk—with a note that read: "Sorry. I got you another horse for Christmas but it ran away." I laugh about it now, but at the time, I failed to see the humor and furiously threw the package at my giggling sister.

Somehow, my parents never lost faith, not even when the brutal winter temperatures plummeted below zero and one of their most valuable heifers died while giving birth.

It was so cold that winter that the creek froze over 2 inches thick. But my father, in his usual fashion, turned tragedy to triumph. He went down to the creek with an ax, a pick and a wheelbarrow, which he loaded with ice to bring back to the house.

Meanwhile, my mother hunted out the ice cream freezer and filled it with enough ingredients to make 2 quarts of fresh ice cream. Ginna and I took turns churning, and when the treat was finally frozen, the four of us gathered around a blazing fire, wrapped in our heavy winter coats, and savored every luscious bite.

It was a tough time, but with humor and faith we made it through. And what amazes me to this day is that some of my fondest memories come from those very grim years.

For you!

IT'S ALL GOOD. Harriet Guardino is seen on her horse, Dollie (below, at right), in 1932 and in her high school graduation photo in 1938.

CRAFTY CHRISTMAS

Back in the early '70s, when our kids were young, we didn't have a lot of money, but we managed to buy Christmas gifts for each child.

Still, every year someone complained that a sibling had received something that was bigger or better. Finally, I had had enough and announced that next year was going to be a homemade holiday.

Each of the kids came up with something special to make for their dad and me, and for each of their brothers and sisters.

Bob Jr. took all the school photos for that year and laminated them onto a block of wood. Teri baked loaves of lemon nut bread and decorated them with plastic holly. Rick painted pictures on pieces of wood and made plaques. And Anne made Christmas ornaments out of scrap fabric.

I sewed matching pajamas for the whole family, and my husband laminated sets of coins minted that year onto pieces of wood.

The next Christmas we went back to buying gifts for everyone, but to this day we all remember how much fun that Christmas was.

ARLENE SHOVALD • SALIDA, CO

A WEST TEXAS **CHRISTMAS**

The winter wind whistled across the West Texas plains. Tumbleweeds drifted into our barbed-wire fence, and laundry froze stiff on the line. Christmas 1944 was just days away, and I hoped a deep snow would come with it.

One morning, my brother, Bobby, and I stepped outside and watched a battered truck pull up beside the rundown house down the road. Kids piled out and scattered across the yard, moving too fast to count.

After lunch, I heard someone in the backyard. It was one of the new kids, and he was on my red scooter. I tried to be nice, because I knew Mother was watching me, but I didn't want him on that scooter.

The boy's name was Herbert, and he wanted to know if we had anything else to play with. Bobby picked up a baseball and asked if he wanted to play catch. Herbert

threw down my scooter, and I escaped down the road with it, where I had a not-so-nice discussion about the new kids with our neighbors Patsy and Jane Palmer.

On top of that, we didn't have a Christmas tree yet and Mother told us we weren't going to my grandparents' this year. My father had only one day off, and we didn't have enough time or money for the trip.

No family at Christmas! No Grandmother to hug me and fix my favorite food. No Granddaddy to dance his jig and make us laugh. No aunts, uncles or cousins. It would be the first Christmas I could remember without family. I wanted to cry. The howling wind made it worse.

The next day, Herbert and two of his brothers were playing in our yard again. Mother made sugar cookies and handed them out the kitchen door to us. Those boys gobbled them down as if they'd never eaten cookies before.

While we sat on the doorstep, I mentioned that Santa was coming on Saturday. Herbert munched his cookie and matter-of-factly told us Santa had never been to his house. I felt so terrible I didn't know what to say.

At supper, I told Mother what Herbert had said. She looked at my dad, and I saw the sadness in her eyes. My father told us Santa might have had trouble finding Herbert's family because they probably moved a lot.

The next morning, Mother rushed off to see Mrs. Phillips and Mrs. Palmer. They were planning something.

When Daddy got home, Mother told us we were going to help Herbert's family. It had to be a secret; we couldn't talk about it all, not even with our friends.

We had no money to buy gifts, so Mother asked us to make or find something to give the children. The Phillips and Palmer families would do the same.

We didn't have many store-bought toys. Bobby had a slingshot, but the rubber band was broken. I had an old rubber Betsy Wetsy. I hated that doll, and I didn't think the new neighbors would like her any better than I did. I wanted to give them something special that they'd really love.

That night, my mind churned as I tried to think of the perfect gift. When I came up with an idea, I really wished I hadn't.

I liked my scooter better than anything I had. It wasn't new when I got it, but I thought it was the best scooter in the world because Aunt Winnie had given it to me. I tossed and turned, trying to make up my mind.

The next morning, I told my parents that I wanted to give Herbert my scooter. They looked surprised. "Are you sure?" my father asked. I was. Daddy suggested I paint it a new color so Herbert wouldn't recognize it.

That night, Daddy brought home a paper sack with a small can of pretty blue paint and a little bell for the handlebars. Mother put newspapers on the kitchen floor, and Bobby and I painted the scooter.

Then Bobby got his baseball from his bedroom and wrote "Babe Ruth" on it in black crayon so Herbert wouldn't know it had been his.

It must have been as hard for him to give up that beat-up ball as it was for me to give away my scooter. He and J.C. Phillips played

a lot of catch.

The lump in my throat was so big that I could hardly swallow. I wanted to hug Bobby, which is what Mother did, but I figured he'd kick me in the shin.

On Christmas Eve, Daddy brought home our tree, a blue spruce from the nursery where he worked. After supper, we walked down to the Palmers' with our gifts for Herbert's family. The Phillips family was already there. It was like a grand, happy party. Mrs. Palmer made punch, and Mother and Mrs. Phillips brought fudge and cookies.

As we walked home, a million stars twinkled in the clear black sky. The Christmas star seemed to shine right down upon us.

We walked quietly, holding hands. I felt like my heart would explode with love and happiness. I started singing "O Holy Night," and the family joined in. We sang the rest of the way home.

Daddy was reading the Christmas story from the Bible when we heard a car pull up. Who could be visiting us this late on Christmas Eve?

We couldn't believe our eyes: Aunt Frances, Uncle Raney and their children, Judy and Little Raney, had driven from California to surprise us. Mother fried the hen she'd planned for Christmas dinner. We decorated the tree, sang carols and hung up our socks.

Overnight, we got about a foot of snow. Big flakes were still fluttering down when I went out to help Daddy feed the dogs. I could hear kids talking.

Daddy and I sneaked over to where we could see Herbert's porch without him seeing us. Herbert was yelling, "He came! He came!" I blinked back tears. Daddy took my hand, and we walked back to our full little house.

I've often wondered if Herbert and his family weren't really angels sent down to help us understand the joy of giving and the spirit of Christmas. Our gifts were small, but the Lord poured out His blessings in a way I will never forget.

CLAUDIA GRISHAM • SPRING, TX

HOLIDAY GENEROSITY

SMILING GIRLS with gifts remind Viola Zumault of Kansas City, Missouri, how much she enjoyed taking freshly baked cookies to friends, neighbors and shut-ins. "That was such a lovely custom," she says.

A NEW FRIEND. "I was finishing a year overseas when I received a care package from my home containing one of my niece's dolls," writes Don Grudt from Port Charlotte, Florida. "My sister asked me to give the doll to a Korean orphan. I got a pass to Seoul and found a new friend among a group of about 50 orphans. This little girl made my Christmas in 1953."

HOUSE CALLS. "Like the family at left, we loved going from house to house on Christmas, visiting aunts, uncles and cousins. The feeling of giving was never so strong as then," says Eleanor Behman from North Royalton, Ohio.

SANTA CLAUS, M.D. A 1959 visit from St. Nick looks like good medicine for these kids at Gillette Hospital in Minneapolis. "My brother Clayton Cacas took this when he and the Minneapolis Gopher Post Band were involved with the hospital," says Charlene Heryla of Des Moines, Washington.

CHRISTMAS IS GIVING, the old saying goes, and it was the reason for this 1936 gathering. The Depression was in full swing, so the *Journal-Courier* in Lafayette, Indiana, invited needy families to a Christmas party. Newspaper representatives felt the true spirit of Christmas as they passed out toys to eager boys and girls.

ROOTED IN LOVE

PINING FOR THE PERFECT TREE

Because of my father's poor health during World War II, our family (pictured below) moved from a tenant farm in the Virginia hills to the city of Harrisonburg so my mother could work in a silk mill, making parachutes for the soldiers overseas.

On Christmas Eve, I felt lonely and misplaced as I listened to the strange city noises, so different from the familiar sounds of the countryside. To my dismay, the family had been so busy moving that we didn't have a tree to decorate.

As a 5-year-old, I yearned for a real tree; my older brothers had always enjoyed selecting a cedar or pine from the nearby woods when we lived on the farm. My brother Gary sensed that something was bothering me and asked, "What's the matter, Janie? Why are you so sad?"

"We don't have a tree, and it's Christmas Eve," I told him. "Where will Santa leave our presents?"

To soothe my nostalgic tears, my older brother found a large paper sack, upon which he drew a beautiful green Christmas tree with big red and blue bulbs and bright yellow tinsel.

"This will have to do this year," Gary told me. "I'm sure Santa will understand."

The next morning, I received a tiny toy phone from Santa and homemade popcorn balls from Mother and Daddy, but my special gift was my brother's work of love: the paper tree hanging on the wall.
JANE ALLEN • ARAB, AL

BRANCHING OUT

In 1956, I heard my father say that he couldn't afford a Christmas tree. He offered the man at the lot $10 for a tree, but the man said he would throw a tree into the river before he would sell it for that little. Taking this in, my mother promised, "The kids will have a tree."

The next day, I saw her go out into the yard with a steak knife in the stinging cold, wind whipping in her hair as she cut the branches off a peach tree. When she came in she placed the branches in a vase, tucked a small towel in the vase to steady the branches, and then put an old cotton tree skirt with glitter on it around the vase.

She placed this on an end table and wrapped chimney paper around the legs of the table. Next she draped Red Cross cotton on the branches to make it look like snow. Then she strung blue lights on the tree along and added ornaments and mounds of tinsel. When she finished and turned on the lights, the branch tree was beautiful in a magical way.

That Christmas my father got a huge industrial drum of all kinds of used toys—in good condition—from the Salvation Army and poured them out under the blue lights of the branch tree. It was truly a Christmas to remember.
BARBARA MARCH • CHEYENNE, WY

GRATEFUL FAMILY. Money was tight for Jane Allen's family in '45, but the Shulls felt blessed to have each other. In front, from left, are Gary, Jane, Yvonne and mom Stella; in back are Jimmy, dad Ernest and Garland.

A Tree for the Holidays

I took my first teaching job in 1959 in a working-class neighborhood in Ludlow, Massachusetts. As the holidays approached, our principal announced that the Lions Club would donate a Christmas tree to each classroom. One morning, a man brought a scrawny little tree to our room. It was already dropping needles, but like the students in this photo, my kids looked at in awe, as many of them did not have a Christmas tree at home. We decided to decorate our shabby little sapling with handmade ornaments, cotton balls and lights. There were shouts of glee when it was finished—our little tree glowed and shimmered as if transformed by magic.

PATRICIA CARLEY • MOUNT DORA, FL

CHAPTER 4

MAGICAL HOLIDAY MOMENTS

One of the great joys of Christmas is being filled with the magic of childlike wonder as we make merry with loved ones and soak up everything the season has to offer.

"My brother, Buck, and I always enjoyed the fruits of believing in Santa Claus," recalls Joretta Hayes from Mebane, North Carolina. "Every Christmas morning, we'd awake to find gifts left by this benevolent gift-giver whom we had never seen.

"But Christmas Eve back in 1954 was different. That evening, Mother announced that Santa was coming to our house, and we'd get to meet jolly old St. Nick. We were filled with excitement and a little fear at the prospect of meeting someone so larger than life.

"Suddenly, a giant figure dressed in red appeared at the window and, in a loud voice, shouted, 'Ho! Ho! Ho!'

"Then there was a knock at the door—Santa! The excitement was almost more than Buck and I could stand. Mother opened the door, and there he was—the biggest thing I'd ever seen, with his red suit, hat and white beard. He reached into his bag and pulled out an orange for Buck and an apple for me. Then he was gone out the door.

"Years later, my mother told me that one of our neighbors had rented a Santa suit for a party and was happy to stop at our house on Christmas Eve to surprise us with a visit. This was just one of many things Mother and Father did to make that Christmas extraordinary."

Enjoy more magical memories from yesteryear with these enchanting stories.

TRULY SPECIAL DELIVERY

Christmas was running very late for this fifth-grade girl. **SUSAN J. SIMONS** • WAUKESHA, WI

My favorite Christmas story is the one my mother, Charmian Beaty Buhrandt, has long told about her fifth-grade class in 1945.

My mother grew up in Hackettstown, New Jersey. It was a small town filled with post-Civil War Victorian homes with wraparound porches—a town where everyone knew each other and all the kids played together. My mother had particularly fond memories of skating, sledding and playing in the snow in winter.

This is how her story goes:

"As Christmas drew close, plans were made for the party and gift exchange at school. How difficult it was not to reveal whose name we had drawn from a hat and what sort of gift we had made or purchased for the recipient.

"The gifts were brought in during the last week before Christmas vacation. Excitement was in the air. We were allowed to look under the tree, which we all took part in decorating, and find out which of the brightly wrapped presents was for whom.

"On Tuesday, I looked under the tree and spied the present I bought. I searched for the one with my name on it, but it wasn't there.

"I checked the tree again on Wednesday and Thursday. More and more presents piled up, but nothing had my name on it.

"Finally, Friday came. It was the day of the party. *There must be something there now*, I thought. I looked under the tree casually, and then frantically, but there was nothing for me.

"I returned to my desk and sat in despair. Out of 25 children, I was the only one without a present. I tried my best not to cry as the day lingered on.

"When our class' teacher, Mrs. Wheeler, announced it was time for the party, the other kids cheered. I only hoped that someone had hidden my present.

"Mrs. Wheeler called out the children's names one by one and handed out the presents, but my name was not called. I sat at my desk in quiet tears while the other kids played with their new trinkets or ate their penny candy.

"With the party winding down, a knock came at the door. My classmate David's mother was standing in the doorway and holding an enormous box. The other children were captivated. She apologized for being late and said she had a special gift for Charmian Beaty. I stood up in shock. *This enormous gift was for me?*

"The children all gathered around me as I stood on tiptoes to open the top of the box. Inside, to my surprise, was a fuzzy brown puppy—so cute, with one ear up and one ear down. I was the hit of the class!

"I happily walked home in the falling snow with my coat over the box to keep my new puppy warm. Only then did I begin worrying if my folks would let me keep the puppy. I did not know the gift had been prearranged with my parents.

"I named the puppy Fritzy and loved and played with that dog endlessly. Even after all this time, I remember Fritzy as the best Christmas present ever."

CHRISTMAS MEMORY UNLEASHED. "One Christmas I received a blond cocker spaniel puppy named Taffy," says Toni Fulco of East Stroudsburg, Pennsylvania. "After all our relatives left our house Christmas night, we discovered Taffy was missing. We feared she'd slipped out the door, until we found her under the Christmas tree—fast asleep in the manger!"

FELINE FANCY. "To stretch the Christmas season as long as possible, we would always decorate on the day after Thanksgiving and then leave our decorations up until after New Year's," says Elaine Graham of Rangely, Colorado. Her cat, like this one, loved sitting beneath the tree. "When it finally came down, he'd lie on the floor and meow where the tree had been," she says.

PUPPY LOVE. Balynda and Brad Thornton, great-niece and great-nephew of Ruth Jo Eppley from Nappanee, Indiana, were more than a little excited about a new puppy for Christmas in 1967.

Unforgettable Fashions

DADDY'S SHIRT

Hand-me-downs were just a fact of country life. Clothes were passed on from brother to brother, sister to sister and father to son. Shirts, pants, dresses and even coats were handmade from flour sacks, cornmeal bags and cloth from a traveling salesman's truck. If someone gave you an article of store-bought clothing apart from shoes, it was a treasured possession.

Just before Christmas 1954, when I was 12, my brothers, sisters and I decided to pool our money to buy our parents something special. The blackberries had been plentiful that year, and I made $7.

After buying school supplies, I had $1.25 to give for the gifts. For Mama, we decided on a two-pocket apron made from material with images of cakes and pies. For Daddy, we chose a fancy short-sleeve shirt with a buttoned collar. As my sister Anna Ruth and my brother Harold left for town, each of us gave our advice.

"Make sure it has all the same color buttons," I warned, glancing at my shirt, which did not.

"And be sure the sleeves are the same length," Buddy Earl said, holding his arms out. Sure enough, the left sleeve was an inch shorter than the right.

When they returned, all of us flocked to see the gifts. The girls oohed and aahed when they saw the apron. Then came Daddy's shirt.

The buttons at the collar matched perfectly and the sleeves were the same length—but best of all, it was multicolored. I had never seen such a beautiful shirt, and I wanted one just like it.

When Christmas came, Mama received her apron with lots of hugs and tears. Daddy was not given to emotion, but tears shone in his eyes, too, when he saw the new shirt.

Daddy worked most of the time and rarely had an opportunity to wear his store-bought shirt. He did put it on for Sunday dinner, but mostly it hung in his bedroom. I often asked if I could put it on just to see if it fit me. Each time Daddy said, "Someday when you grow up and fill out a little bit."

On my 16th birthday, Daddy sat down next to me at the breakfast table and handed me

DAPPER DUDE. Douglas, at age 16, models the store-bought shirt he and his siblings gave their dad for Christmas.

a paper package tied with string. Thinking it was the usual pair of socks or undershirt, I pushed it off to the side.

"Well, ain't you going to open it?" Daddy asked, handing me his pocketknife.

I cut the string and tore open the package. There lay Daddy's store-bought shirt, all starched and ironed. After four years, it still looked brand-new.

"How does it look?" I asked, holding the shirt in front of me.

"Like it was made just for you," Daddy replied.

I wore the shirt for five years. It's now part of a quilt my sister owns. For $1.25, that shirt was one of the best things I ever invested in.
DOUGLAS SCOTT CLARK • MARYVILLE, TN

BEAUTIFUL BROWN BOOTS

Christmas Eve 1942 stands out in my memory as one of the best. I was in first grade and thrilled about Santa Claus' expected visit.

Our white farmhouse in the hills of middle Tennessee had been scrubbed from bottom to top and the cedar tree Daddy brought down off the hillside stood by the front window, decorated with popcorn strings and various other homemade decorations.

A country ham had been boiled the day before, and the cakes were baked and stored in lard cans.

My mother and sister were busy cooking the rest of the meal on the old wood stove in the kitchen. They occasionally called me away from my paper dolls, carefully cut from the Sears Roebuck catalog, to bring in sticks of wood for the stove or to chase the cat out of the kitchen.

My older brother left the farm after high school and went to work at Vultee Air Craft in Nashville, 60 miles away from home. I missed him terribly, and looking forward to having him home for Christmas added to my excitement.

He arrived just before suppertime. I immediately jumped up and down, shrieking with joy when I saw that he was loaded with packages. I wanted to open my gift right then and there. He must have been as eager as I was, because he handed me a rumpled brown bag.

I couldn't believe my eyes when I pulled out a pair of brown leather boots! I knew then why, during an earlier visit home, he had played a game with me that involved tracing my feet on a sheet of paper.

He went out with friends after we ate, and when he came home Mother told him to check on me before he went upstairs to bed. I was sound asleep in my bed with my feet sticking out from under the quilts. I just couldn't bear to take off my beautiful boots before going to bed. He knew then he had selected the perfect present.

I don't even remember anything else Santa brought that year.

SARAH OLDHAM
NASHVILLE, TN

PRETTY IN PINK

I was 8 years old in December 1951. My parents and I had just left war-torn Germany for Detroit, where we were living in a small room in the dilapidated Earl Hotel. It had two creaky beds and smelled of dust and stale cigarette smoke. Not even winter sunlight streaming through the streaked windows could brighten this sad, cramped room.

Adding to the gloom, I feared we would have no visit from the Christkind. German children believed the Christkind, or Christ Child, and His little angels brought presents on Christmas Eve. How, I wondered, could the Christkind find me so far from home?

On Christmas Eve, we went downtown to see the department store windows. The lights, decorations and gifts behind all that sparkling glass were mesmerizing.

For the evening's dinner, we got butter and salami from the window ledge that served as our refrigerator and made thick rye bread sandwiches. Then my parents told me it was time to go to bed because the Christkind might soon arrive. I sincerely doubted that, but I eventually fell asleep.

Next thing I knew, the delicate ringing of a tiny bell woke me. In Germany, a ringing bell meant the Christkind had come and I could go see what surprises He had brought.

I rubbed my eyes, barely able to believe what I saw. I found a brown box tied with red ribbon. As I hugged my parents, they had tears in their eyes. "You see, Anita," Mother said, "I knew the Christkind would find you."

I carefully untied the ribbon and opened the box to discover a beautiful pink dress with a white lace collar and three pearl buttons. It was my very first new dress. In Germany, Mother had sewn my dresses out of hand-me-down clothes. And now here I was in America with a brand-new dress!

In that tired old room at the Earl Hotel, we sang "Silent Night" and "O Christmas Tree" in German. Even though it was so long ago, I clearly remember thinking I'd never known such happiness.

ANITA HAMMERLE • PERRY, MI

ALL SMILES. Above, from left, are Debbie Berger and sisters Melanie and Suzie in 1957. Debbie's future husband, David, had his photo taken on Santa's lap (left) in 1958—at the same Sears store she writes about visiting that year.

Sweet Visit to Sears

The tires of our station wagon crunched in the icy ruts of the parking lot of the Sears, Roebuck and Co. store in downtown Louisville, Kentucky. It was about two weeks before Christmas 1958, and my family and I had arrived to do our holiday shopping. We lived in the suburbs, so it was a special treat to go downtown for gifts.

Santa Claus, the rotund bearded man in the fire-engine-red suit, waved and boomed a jolly "Merry Christmas!" and "Ho-ho-ho!" to all who came to do their shopping.

A Salvation Army greeter rang his bell for donations. As he held the store door open for us, the heat from inside carried the aroma of roasted cashews and peanuts, two of our favorite treats.

Just 5 years old, I was overwhelmed by the enticing smells of caramel corn, buttered popcorn, air-spun cotton candy and candied fruitcakes.

My mouth watered when I saw row after row of candy and nut displays, and I joined the people lined up at the counter, holding two shiny quarters in my mittened hands.

I ordered a 15-cent bag of hot, salty cashews, a bag of popcorn and three coconut bonbons. My two sisters and I shared this delicious bounty, digging in all at once, taking a little from each bag and squabbling over who got which bonbon.

Savoring the sweet round candy, I bit into the hard, waxy shell until it yielded to the moist shredded coconut. Then I followed the sweet taste with a handful of salty popcorn.

Melodic sounds of Christmas carols, piped through the speakers, filled the air. The elevator bell rang, and shoe heels clicked the tile floors.

Glittering jewelry, racks of fluffy chenille robes and piles of shining Christmas tree ornaments competed for my attention. I was fascinated by the aluminum tree illuminated by a color wheel that rotated beneath it. I watched this scene, mesmerized, until my parents reminded me I had shopping to do. So I joined the crowded aisles of rushing shoppers searching for gifts.

I picked out a lace-edged handkerchief embroidered with flowers for my mother, a shiny key chain for my father and a tube of multicolored Pick-Up Sticks for my sisters to share.

I proudly carried my purchases in their crisp white paper bag to the car. Waving a silent goodbye to Sears for another year, I sat back in the car seat, listening to "Silent Night" on the radio. I stared out at the bells and garlands hanging from the lampposts. I watched Christmas lights flashing in the store windows as we left downtown and headed home to the suburbs, sweet visions of our shopping trip dancing in my head.

DEBBIE BERGER
CLARKSVILLE, IN

During the heyday of department stores, three of the most popular and prestigious were Macy's, Hudson's and Marshall Field & Company.

SUNDAY SCHOOL at the Bethel Mission was run by Grace Jepson, who's pictured in back on the far right.

THE RICHNESS OF YOUTH

A pageant on the poor side of town held a wealth of Christmas spirit.
RICHARD STEELE • FREEPORT, IL

The nighttime Christmas program at the Bethel Mission was the most anticipated winter event in the poor area of Freeport, Illinois, known as the Organ Factory. It was especially so in the 1940s for the kids who didn't expect any gifts on Christmas Day.

On the night of one such program at Bethel, I cut through the empty lots behind my home, guided by the soft yellow light streaming through the windows of the one-room clapboard chapel.

Each year, we children had a presentation of the first Christmas, putting on a pageant. The chapel's few decorations included a wreath on the door, a lit fir tree in a corner and red paper bells on the window shades.

As the cast members, we wore simple costumes, mostly old army blankets draped around our shoulders and heads to look like the sort of clothing worn by the men in ancient Bethlehem.

A backdrop of folding screens, old sheets and a few blankets created a stable setting. The Nativity scene and our production, however simple and disjointed, were always well received.

After our Bible skit, an older boy, Harold Sager, played the old upright piano as we sang Christmas carols. The program came to a close when we softly sang "Silent Night" and said the parting prayer. As we left the chapel, someone gave each of us a brown paper bag and told us, almost in a whisper, "Merry Christmas."

The bags were gifts from the Baptist church members downtown. For many of the poorest kids in the Organ Factory, the bags were the only gifts they would get. Each sack contained a couple of apples and oranges, some nuts and hard candy, usually a small tree ornament and, in some years, a miniature doll or toy.

I thanked the lady who handed me my bag, stepped out into the cold moonlit night and started for home.

Before heading into our kitchen, I glanced back across the snowy fields and saw the lights go out at Bethel Mission for another year.

Lying in my bed that night, I smiled as I recalled the evening's events and softly hummed Christmas carols before drifting off to sleep.

I often think back to those childhood days, when we were blissfully ignorant about the state of our lives, and when even the smallest kindness was deeply appreciated by the poor but cheerful kids who attended the little Bethel Mission.

SHEPHERD: DON CONDON; ANGELS: ANEAL VOHRA/UNICORN STOCK PHOTOS

CALLING ALL ANGELS

In December 1938, my parents, two brothers, 2-year-old sister and I were invited to attend a second-grade Christmas pageant.

The stage was set with the stable and manger. The angels were hiding behind the stable, waiting to make their appearance and sing.

When the music started, the performers entered in solemn procession. When the hidden angels stood up, my little sister burst out, "Ha, ha! I see you!" Everyone started laughing. The teacher was not happy and the performance had to begin again. Mother was mortified and quickly took my sister out.

BEATRICE DEMMEL • ESCONDIDO, CA

RELATIVELY ANGELIC

Our son, Seth, was 7 when he was cast as an angel in our Sunday school Christmas play. Tinsel was woven into halos, and old junior choir robes became flowing angel gowns.

Helping Seth into his costume, I noticed something inked in black inside its collar. To my surprise, it read "Carol Sherman," my maiden name. I had worn that robe over 30 years before!

As the children marched in, one of the angels winked at me. I still recall that Christmas coincidence and smile.

CAROL S. CARPENTER
MOUNT VERNON, OH

HOLIDAY THRILLS

UP, UP AND AWAY!

My hometown of Calimesa, California, had its own brand of Americana, especially at Christmas. I remember one holiday season in the late 1960s when Santa Claus jumped out of a helicopter with a bag of candy.

I hadn't believed in Santa for quite some time, but I thought the stunt was a marvelous idea! The very thought of someone as crazy as I was—and totally willing to prove it—had enormous appeal for me.

So I dove headfirst into the front seat of my dad's faded Plymouth and we headed out to the landing zone. When we arrived, kids were already forming a line around an empty field.

All those small faces looked up, searching the chilly December sky for the arrival of our hero. When the helicopter finally appeared, we could see Santa's beard flapping furiously in the turbulent air through the side of the craft. When the helicopter reached the necessary altitude, a brave young man in a red suit stepped out onto its landing skids.

A hush fell over the crowd. An imaginary drum roll started in my head. When Santa leaped, the parachute blossomed and started its descent. But before long, it became apparent that St. Nick and his sweet cargo were drifting dangerously off course, well away from the drop zone in the center of the empty field.

We started guessing where he was going to land. My father told me to look away as Santa helplessly floundered toward the power lines, but I peeked anyway—and he blew past! Then he disappeared from view nearly a block away. Parents gave hot pursuit, hopping over fences and running through backyards. According to some accounts, our wayward Santa was found distracted and entangled in some rose bushes, wrestling with the plants' long, thorny arms.

Santa and his candy were retrieved, and in the end we all had a good time. I would like to thank Mr. Claus for a priceless childhood memory.

GORDON FORBES • CALIMESA, CA

◄ 1950

Kodak produced the first cameras simple enough for amateur use. The earliest models had the film sealed inside; the user had to mail the entire camera back to the company to process the photos.

DAREDEVIL SANTAS like this one free-falling from an airplane in 1967 took holiday celebrations to new heights.

ANOTHER WAY TO ADD SPARKLE TO THE HOLIDAYS

In 1939, when I was 12 years old, my good friends John and Vernon and I ran around so much together, people called us the Three Musketeers. John had a paper route and was the only one with an income of any kind.

We lived in Kitts, a town owned by a coal company in Harlan County, Kentucky. The company store faced the railroad tracks. A row of company houses sat between the tracks and the river, with another row of houses across the river.

On the evening of Dec. 22, the three of us were together as usual. John said he'd buy us some fireworks. He went to the company store and bought five skyrockets. We just needed a place to shoot them. One of us suggested the riverbank as a safe spot.

A widow who lived across the river was a mean one—she hated seeing anyone on God's green earth getting any pleasure out of life. When we played games, fished or went for a swim, she often screamed at us, threatening to call the police.

John set up a forked stick so we could point the skyrockets up for vertical shots. He had shot two of them and was in the process of lighting the third when the widow flung open her back door and yelled, "I'll call the police if you light one more of those things!"

John jumped up, tripped, and knocked the stick down. The skyrocket took off straight

across the river, through the widow's backyard, across her porch, between her feet and right into her house. In about one second, that was the best-lit-up house in all of Kentucky.

The lady turned in her doorway at about the same time her big hound dog came flying through it in the other direction. Down they went, along with two big old cats that must have thought it was time to abandon ship. With all the screams from the woman, the dog and the cats, the Three Musketeers decided to hit the trail, hoping no one had seen us in the dark. Thankfully, no one was hurt and the house didn't burn.

The coal mines closed years ago, people moved away, and most of the houses washed away in a flood. The river and the memories of the good old days are about all that are left. And every Dec. 22, I remember the night of the wild skyrocket.

WASH ESTILL KETRON • KEMP, TX

Is He Real?

THE MAN WITH ALL THE TOYS

I was 8 and my sister Martha was less than two years younger, and we loved Christmas and Santa Claus. Our parents went to great lengths to keep the magic of the Christmas season alive. Our home was always completely decorated from top to bottom even though our family was on a limited budget.

Each year we would have an early visit from Santa Claus. About a month before Christmas, our nicest dolls, doll beds, and table and chair set would disappear. Santa would always leave a note explaining that they were being taken to the North Pole so the elves could repair them for us for Christmas.

Sure enough, each Christmas Eve the furniture would be under the tree with a new coat of paint, new clothes for the dolls, and even new mattresses for the doll beds. We never doubted for even a moment where they had been. This practice was repeated every year.

In 1942 Mama began renting out some of the rooms in our house in Baltimore, and they had to be kept neat and ready for guests. We were never allowed to go into the spare rooms to play. About a week before Christmas we were fooling around upstairs and ran into one of those rooms without thinking. What a surprise it was to find newspapers all over the floor and our furniture and dolls being painted and fixed up. At first we were afraid to admit we'd gone inside the forbidden rooms, but we just couldn't keep this kind of news to ourselves. We excitedly told Mama what we had found.

Without a moment's hesitation, she replied, "Oh my gosh, Daddy and I have been hearing some strange noises and thought that it was just this old house creaking!"

She went on, "Santa probably didn't have time to take them with him and has been sneaking back in here with his elves and fixing them!" Our eyes were as big as saucers. We believed her. Then she added, "But you can't let anyone know that you found out or you will spoil his surprise!"

We never told a soul, and early on Christmas morning she shook us awake and whispered, "Get up, Santa just took your stuff downstairs. If you hurry, you can get to see him!"

We rushed down the stairs just in time to hear the front door shut, the sound of bells jingling and a loud "Ho! Ho! Ho!" We ran outside and saw large footprints, sleigh marks and deer tracks in the snow, but he was gone. Back in the house, under the tree, as promised, were our refurbished toys and a note from Santa Claus thanking us for keeping his secret. We told this story to all our friends and were the envy of the whole neighborhood.

The wonderful story of Santa was real to us until we were much older. Mama finally told us, and the next Christmas we went to Evansville, Indiana, to be with Mama and Daddy's families. We felt a little low because Santa was not going to be a part of our Christmas anymore.

Suddenly we spied a sleigh with Santa, toys, and horses with antlers attached. Someone was planning a big surprise for their family. Once again we thought we had been lied to, because here was Santa in the flesh. It was even harder to lose him again!

CARMEN WILLIAMS HAMILTON
NEW SMYRNA BEACH, FL

THE SANTA SCHEME

Christmas was just around the corner, and there was a problem brewing. I was 9, and the way I saw it by then, the notion of Santa Claus had as many holes as the fenders on the neighbors' 1935 Ford.

It was just after Thanksgiving when my mom turned up the heat by asking me, "Have you written your letter to Santa yet?" I did all I could to wiggle around the subject, but the fates were against me.

I was back in school only a couple of days when I got sick—not a little bit sick, but the-nun-had-to-send-me-home kind of sick. Mom worked for Ma Bell, so it was up to Grandma to nurse me back to health. We had moved in with her after my mother divorced.

During a game of go fish, Grandma asked me if I felt well enough to write my Santa letter. I replied: "Do you have any fours?"

Grandma folded her cards and adjusted her glasses, and I finally admitted I didn't believe in Santa. My grandmother had raised nine kids, so this was old hat to her. "And why do you feel that way, may I ask?"

I began to fidget. "Well, geez, Grandma, there are a gazillion people in the world, and that means there must be a gazillion-times-two kids! How can one person deliver toys to all those kids in one night?"

After a moment or two she explained, "Remember, Santa is an elf, like a fairy, and fairies can use magic."

The elf part I could buy, but a fairy? Fairies were really tiny—with wings. My mother had taken me to the A&S department store every year to see Santa, and he was as big as a linebacker, with no wings in sight.

Ah, but magic! Now there was something I'd never considered. To lower the heat, I said, "You're right, Grandma. Maybe I should write that letter." I had to hedge my bets; what if I were wrong?

So I came up with a plan that would either prove the existence of Santa or ruin my entire Christmas. I hadn't yet said a word to anyone about the one toy I really wanted, the Ideal Jet Fighter. It looked like the cockpit of a jet and projected enemy fighter images on a wall, which you could shoot at with rubber darts. Quickly and silently, I wrote a letter to Santa asking for the jet fighter. I put it in an envelope, addressed it to Santa and even stuck a stamp on it. The next day I watched through the window as Grandma handed my letter to the mailman.

Soon it was Christmas Eve. I don't know how long I slept that night before my mother yanked me out of my nice warm bed, saying, "Hurry, Tommy, Santa is downstairs, and he's waiting for you!"

Who was downstairs? Did she say Santa? Now I was wide awake. Mom dragged me down the 14 steps to the main floor. I hesitated, but she placed a hand on my back and propelled me into the living room.

"Well, hello, Tommy!" a deep voice boomed. "What a pleasure it is to meet you!"

There, bathed in the glow of the Christmas lights, was a man with his hands on his hips. I did a quick survey. Red suit, white beard, big round belly: check, check, check! Holy smokes, it was Santa!

I wasn't even sure I was breathing when he said, "I have something for you, Tommy!" Out of his bag came the jet fighter!

It wasn't long after that holiday season that I realized Santa was in our hearts and not in our living rooms. But what about that night? It turns out Santa was a friend of my mom's who'd been playing the part down at the firehouse and agreed to stop at our place, too. And my letter? My grandmother set it all up with our mailman, who gave the letter back to her the next day.

Still, my mother and grandmother had kept the Christmas magic going for one more year. They left me with a memory—no, a gift—that has lasted all these years.

TOM SHAW • WEST ISLIP, NY

UNKIE BOBBER'S CHRISTMAS

It looked like a bomb had gone off under the tree—and that was
before the family opened their presents!

GERI DAVIS • PRESCOTT, AZ

DURING Christmastime in 1943, Mother and I were living with my Grandpa and Grandma Miner in Coventry, Connecticut. The whole family was praying that Uncle Tom and Uncle Ed (both stationed at the naval base in New London, Connecticut) would be able to make it home for the holidays.

Everything was ready. A beautiful fir tree stood in all its decorated glory in the wide front window of our family's 200-year-old farmhouse. Underneath, a pile of lovingly wrapped gifts was growing daily, and our stockings were hung on the fireplace mantel.

That year, my Uncle Bobby and I were both only 3 years old. The grown-ups in the family got a big kick out of using my name for him, "Unkie Bobber."

Neither of us could yet understand why each morning when we woke, our stockings were still empty, or why we weren't allowed to touch the Christmas tree, or anything on or underneath it.

SNOW BUNNIES. The author and her "Unkie Bobber" enjoyed a snowy day in Coventry, Connecticut, in 1945, two Christmases after "Bobber," also known as Robert Miner, got into some mischief and made for a memorable holiday.

The Wait Was Unbearable

That ever-growing heap of presents was a constant enticement to Bobby and me. Each day we'd beg to open gifts, only to be told we had to wait for Christmas…had to wait for Santa…had to wait for Uncle Tom and Uncle Ed.

We were shooed away from the tree so often that the exasperated grown-ups finally closed the living room door and warned us not to enter until Christmas.

By bedtime on Christmas Eve, neither uncle had yet come home. We kids both put up a fuss to open presents. "Wanna unwap!" Bobby pouted. But the answer was still the same: We'd have to wait for Christmas morning, Santa, Uncle Tom and Uncle Ed.

Sometime after we'd been put to bed, my grown uncles finally arrived. I overheard the joyful welcome downstairs and fell asleep happy, knowing we'd be able to open our presents in the morning.

A Chaotic Surprise

Bobby must have overheard as well, but for him, the temptation proved to be too great. The next morning, when all the grown-ups trooped into the living room in anticipation, there sat Bobby in the midst of chaos! All around him lay a jumble of bright wrapping paper, ribbons, tags, toys, various items of clothing and other gifts. Nearly every package had been torn open and its contents strewn about.

There were shocked gasps. "Oh, no! Bobby! What did you do?"

"Unkie Bobber unwapped kissmus," he laughed gleefully. That explained it all.

It took the rest of the morning to sort out the confusion Bobby's eagerness had created. Everyone was trying to figure out who had given what to whom. There were even a few items that no one claimed as giver or intended recipient!

Every holiday since, when those precious "remember when" stories are told and retold, you can bet that "the year Unkie Bobber unwapped kissmus" remains one of the family's all-time favorites.

FUN LITTLE SURPRISES
LED TO BIG MEMORIES

Our family owned land near Boyne Mountain, Michigan, not far from a ski resort, and we built a pole cabin (above) there in the 1960s.

One Christmas Eve, after a day of cross-country skiing, we tucked the children in bed, then began to fill all the stockings for the next morning.

Suddenly I had a mischievous idea. Next to our heating stove was a coal pail filled with charcoal briquettes. I was sure the kids would get a laugh out of finding them in their socks the next morning, wrapped in aluminum foil.

While everyone else slept, an eager son, Fred, found his sock by prowling around in the dark. He unwrapped one foil-wrapped nugget and took a bite, expecting a treat. His coughing and sputtering became the alarm clock for the rest of us. I didn't know if I should laugh or cry.

Fred recuperated enough to join us all in a good laugh. In fun, he still tells of the "cruel" Christmas stocking joke. Perhaps the experience taught him to wait for morning light with the rest of the family on Christmas Day.

VELMA BEAVON • DAYTON, MT

I SWEAR IT WAS SANTA

NEVER FEAR, HE WAS HERE

How would Santa Claus know my brother and I lived in the house on 61st Street in Milwaukee if we weren't going to be there on Christmas Eve? Santa came to houses where children lived, and we were going to visit our relatives in Nenno, Wisconsin.

I was 4 years old and my brother was 2 that Christmas Eve. As we walked to the streetcar that cold night, the snow crunched beneath our boots and my anxiety increased with every step. But my parents seemed unconcerned as we boarded the streetcar that would take us far from home.

I fell asleep on the way to the farm homestead where my mother was born and my grandparents still lived. After being greeted, kissed and hugged at the kitchen door, we were trundled off to bed.

Later that night our cousins woke us up and took us to the adjoining bedroom, where the light from downstairs came in through the floor vent. Kneeling and looking down, we saw Santa and Aunt Annie trimming a Christmas tree!

I whispered, "Where is Uncle John?"

"He's sleeping," my cousin replied. "Can't you hear how loud he's snoring?"

Uncle John's snoring was infamous, and my imagination supplied the familiar sound. Then we tiptoed back to bed.

On Christmas morning, the house filled with aunts and uncles and more cousins. Grandmother stuffed an orange, cookies, nuts and hard candies into shoe boxes for my brother and me. It was some consolation for missing Santa.

We went home that evening, clutching our

THEIR GIFTS were few, but these kids cherished what they received on Christmas morning in 1930.

boxes. Would they be our only gifts?

My brother and I should have known better. When Daddy opened the front door, we looked in amazement at a beautiful tree with toys underneath.

We each got a tricycle and a top that spun when we pushed down the handle. Puzzles, crayons and coloring books added to the display. How did Santa do it? We had seen him last night! How could he be in so many places at once? I couldn't believe it. I asked my mother how it was possible.

Mother said it was magic. Magic indeed! It took the form of our loving Aunt Lizzie, who lived with us. While we were on our way to the country, she took the tree and trimmings out of the shed, along with the presents, and put everything together. Then she took a later bus and was at the farm when we awoke. How tired she must have been!

That Christmas I learned that Santa Claus is another name for love.
SHIRLEY MARY BROOKS • BRADENTON, FL

ST. NICK ON THE RADIO
I'll never forget the thrill of hearing Santa's booming voice one snowy night before Christmas—especially since that voice came from our radio!

My brother and I, along with all the other kids in our neighborhood, had written letters to Santa and given them to my mother, who "forwarded" them to the North Pole. We were assured that Santa would not only receive our letters, but respond to each one in person.

On the appointed evening, we all huddled in front of our radio. Santa called each of us by name and acknowledged receiving our letters, although he warned that he might not be able to deliver everything we'd asked for.

When asked if we'd been good, we all nodded vigorously. We were so caught up in all the magic that we forget Santa couldn't see us. Or could he?

Years later, I found out that my father, an electronics buff, had played Santa for us. He'd hooked up a microphone to the radio speaker and talked to us from the cellar, where he read our letters with a flashlight.

My mother told us, laughing, that she thought he was just as nervous and excited as we kids were that night!
BEVERLY SHERESH • BONITA, CA

LISTEN! WAS THAT SANTA? The wonder of the Christmas season for a child is captured in this 1956 picture of Milt Skillman in front of the family Christmas tree in Mount Pleasant, Michigan.

MAGIC FOOTPRINTS
I remember one particularly magical Christmas morning during my childhood in Kalamazoo, Michigan, in the 1960s. My younger siblings and I jumped out of bed and rushed downstairs. To our amazement, we saw big white footprints across the living room right up to our Christmas tree.

Our dad explained that Santa's boots had "magic Christmas snow" on them, and that no matter where the jolly old man went, the snow would never melt. He also said he'd heard Santa's reindeer stomping their hooves up on the roof. I knew he was trying to convince us kids, especially me, that Santa Claus did exist.

I was almost ready to believe in Santa again. But being the oldest, I was suspicious and put my finger in the "magic snow." It tasted strangely like flour.

I kept Dad's secret and didn't tell the others that Dad had stepped in the flour and walked across the floor to the keep the magic of Santa alive for his children.
CHRISTINE PEAKE • DELTON, MI

SHORT-PANTS SANTA

Holiday spirits wreaked merry havoc with the jolly old elf's visit.

MILLIE DESENFANTS • SHELBYVILLE, IN

Christmas was always exciting at our house in Lafayette, Indiana—but in 1953 it was going to be even better. Our three boys and one girl, ages 3 to 9, had their letters off to Santa and were thrilled about his arrival.

About a week before Christmas, their daddy got some happy news. Our good friend Don Beaver, who'd been the best man in our wedding, called to say he'd rented a Santa Claus suit to surprise his brother's children. Don, who had no kids and was close to our four, said he would be glad to come to our house, too. We'd keep the kids up on Christmas Eve for a real encounter with Santa Claus!

Don said he'd arrive about 9 p.m., and we agreed to put the toys in pillowcases behind the shrubbery by our front stoop for him to find. We put flashing lights on our shrubs. With the tree in our picture window, all was lovely.

To complete the scene, it began snowing Dec. 23 and didn't let up until 4 o'clock on Christmas Eve, leaving pretty 3- and 4-foot drifts. But soon the city plows were out and the main streets were cleared for traffic—and Santa.

After supper, we dressed the kids in their pajamas and let them stay up late and watch the holiday shows on our new television. Soon we were all settled in—not for a long winter's nap, but for a longtime friend to arrive in his red and white suit.

It turned out to be a much longer wait than we had anticipated. Nine o'clock came and went. Our two youngest fell asleep on the couch, so we gently picked them up and tucked them in their beds. The two older ones sat up with us, sleepy-eyed, with quizzical looks on their faces.

We figured the blowing snow had delayed Don, but we learned later that we weren't the only ones on Santa's schedule. Don had offered his kindness to others, too. We'd never known him to imbibe much, but in the spirit of the holiday, he was offered a drink at most stops and did not refuse.

Finally, near 11 p.m., we heard Santa outside calling, "On, Dasher! On, Dancer!"— and then silence. My husband sprang from his chair to see what was the matter.

It turned out Don had either fallen off the stoop or slid and landed headfirst in the snowbank behind the shrubs. My husband helped him find the shoe he'd lost and pick

ILLUSTRATION: CHERYL A. MICHALEK

ST. NICK'S FOOTPRINTS! "When our youngest, Jimmy, was 5, in 1966, he was having doubts about the existence of Santa," says Mal Telloian of Tumwater, Washington. "So my wife and I made footprints from ashes on newspaper on the hearth. It worked!"

up all the scattered toys. When Santa finally appeared in our doorway, he was a mess!

The rented suit was too short, with pants barely below his knees. He was trying to empty his shoe of snow and get his foot back in. The crooked beard and wet, wrinkled suit only added to his eccentricity. As a finishing touch, he was wearing a pair of blue and white argyle socks I had knitted for him the previous Christmas.

We made his visit as short as possible. The boys' mouths were hanging open as they stared at this character who was ho-ho-ho-ing all over the place. We very politely helped Santa out the door in hopes the boys would not smell his breath. We put the wet toys under the tree, then hustled our sons off to bed.

Before he fell asleep, our 7-year-old called out to us, "I wonder how old Short-Pants Santa got Don Beaver's socks!" What a night.

"I'll never forget the Christmas when the flu sidelined the gentleman who always visited our children as Santa Claus. My husband, George, and I were at a loss about how to explain the jolly elf's absence and asked a few friends for suggestions.

Dec. 24 came, and we still hadn't come up with a story. That evening, the doorbell rang and in walked Santa Claus! What astounded us even more was what happened next.

Within half an hour, the doorbell rang again. It was a neighbor who'd heard of our dilemma and suited himself up as a Santa substitute. Then a knock came at the back door. Another St. Nick—a third thoughtful friend.

The kids were thrilled to have been visited by Santa and two of his helpers that Christmas Eve. We were deeply touched to realize what wonderful people there are in this world."

Evelyn Falk • Hales Corners, WI

MOM AND SANTA. Like this woman, the author's mom took a turn as Santa—and showed her kids the real Christmas spirit.

Secret Santas

SANTA WHO?

Our father died in 1938, and Mother was left to raise four children between the ages of 7 and 14. She managed to feed and clothe us by working as a seamstress.

As Christmas approached that year, we knew things were going to be different, but I don't think any of us realized how hard it was going to be on our mother.

We did all the usual things that year—sent cards, hung wreaths, baked cookies, bought a Christmas turkey and even went as a family to buy a tree. When Christmas Eve finally arrived, we dragged the big box of holiday decorations up the cellar stairs, put the tree in the stand and started to trim it.

Mother hung a few things on the tree, but we could tell she was feeling sad. Her heart just wasn't in it. After a while, she left the room and went upstairs.

A short time later, she reappeared—dressed as Santa Claus! We kids didn't know what to think.

As it turned out, Mother had played Santa Claus for a number of years at the Christmas party where she worked. That was where she'd gotten the costume.

Although she was tall and thin, she looked very much like jolly old St. Nick. A white wig, a beard and a pillow padding her stomach did the trick.

"You kids finish the tree," she told us. "I'm going to take a little walk."

She returned about two hours later, and that walk did wonders for her mood. She gave us homemade cookies and milk and wished us a merry Christmas. We went to bed happy that night, with no idea what Mother had been up to.

The next morning, after we'd opened our

presents and returned home from church, a steady stream of visitors stopped by the house. Our home had always been a place where the neighborhood children were welcome, so it wasn't unusual for them to stop by on Christmas Day. But this time, there was something very different in the air.

The little ones couldn't wait to talk to Mother, and the older ones seemed to have a knowing, conspiratorial look in their eyes.

"Oh, Mrs. Kaelin," the younger kids exclaimed excitedly, "we saw Santa Claus last night! He came to our house and hugged us and talked to us!"

It was then that I realized all the nudges and winks I'd seen neighbors exchange with Mother outside of church that morning had special meaning.

Yes, on a night when it would have been easy for Mother to remain at home with her grief, she found a unique way to cheer herself up. She'd visited every home on our street where there were young children, talked with each of them and gave out big "Santa" hugs.

Although the parents and older siblings recognized her, no one gave her identity away. Despite her sadness, Mother had found a way to give joy to others. And in the process, she'd brought joy into her own life.

All in all, it was a truly memorable Christmas.

ELAINE WOJENSKI • BURLINGTON, NJ

SIS SCRAMBLED
TO SAVE CHRISTMAS

There were eight children in our family in 1924, and times were hard. We were a family of cotton farmers living in East Texas. But a bad year depleted the small income farmers normally received from their crop, making a tough situation even more dire.

An extremely dry summer kept the cotton bolls from maturing, so the yield was very small. In addition, Grandmother Newsom had been ill for months and Mama and Papa had to go to her home to sit up with her all night, depriving Papa of crucial hours needed to tend to the cotton fields.

We knew we needed to pull together, so we older kids took on as much farm work as we could. But it wasn't enough. A windstorm came one day when we were in the fields and nearly blew us away, along with whisking away the bolls from the cotton stalks.

When the Christmas season arrived, there was very little money to buy gifts for the smaller children in the family who still believed in Santa Claus. Papa was distraught over the gloomy situation and could see no way to remedy it.

I awoke on Christmas Eve overcome with sorrow that the little ones would miss out on the joy of Santa Claus coming to deliver gifts for them. I was 15 and the oldest child, and decided to hatch a plan.

I asked Papa to let me gather any produce we could find on the farm and take it to Mount Vernon, 7 miles away, to sell and get money to buy gifts for the little ones. Papa was brokenhearted. In tears, he told me to do what I could.

In the henhouse, I gathered the eggs laid that day and found we had some cream to sell, along with a pound or two of butter. I caught a couple of chickens and tied their feet together to take to town, too.

I called my aunt, 2 miles up the road, and asked if I could go to Mount Vernon with her family in their wagon. Toting chickens, eggs, butter and cream, I walked to Aunt Johnnie's.

In Mount Vernon, I went to the place where produce was sold and presented my wares. The produce man gave me $3.65 for the lot.

With this wealth, I began bargaining with the grocery man and dime store clerks to get as much candy, fruit, nuts, firecrackers, tops and tiny 5-cent pocket knives as I could buy.

This was 1924 and prices were low. By the time I spent the money, I had enough trinkets and goodies to make Christmas a joyous occasion for all of us. Everyone would be able to get a surprise, even Mama and Papa.

On Christmas morning, the shouts, laughter and good cheer made the whole project worth a fortune to me. My brothers and sisters didn't know of my secret endeavor and believed Santa made a trip down our chimney. Papa was finally jolly and lighthearted. A glow of happiness washed over me that wonderful Christmas.

Despite the hardships, we children never felt deprived during those meager and difficult times. We didn't know what it was like to have money, so we never missed it. We had so much more than money. We had Mama and Papa, whose love, patience and faith gave us a foundation that would sustain us throughout life. And we had each other. Family—that's what Christmas is all about.

ALICE BANKS • ARLINGTON, TX

A JOLLY TIME

WINTER WOODSMEN. "On Sunday afternoons, I took my sons (from left), Chuck, Billy and Gary, on walks in the woods," says Robert Siple Sr. of Central Bridge, New York. "We lived in the country outside of Middleburgh. There was plenty of snow on the ground during this 1969 outing."

BELL ON HIS BELFRY. "My mom, Charlotte Fauss, is holding my 2-month-old brother, John, on Christmas Day 1956 in Lincoln, Nebraska," writes David Fauss of Roseburg, Oregon.

SIMPLE GIFTS. "The mounds of Christmas presents my grandchildren receive now would have been unbelievable to me as a teen in the 1950s," writes Virginia Meseraull of Berrien Springs, Michigan. "We dressed in our best for this picture. Each of us kids received two gifts that year. My brother, Donald, got his usual gift—a dress shirt—but he's still smiling!"

PAJAMA GAME. "In 1967, we lived in Joliet, Illinois. Our parents, Ray and Mary Jo Williams, lined us up for a photo in our Winnie-the-Pooh pajamas, which were gifts from our aunt and uncle in California," says Jim Williams of Chicago. "Pictured, from left, are Mary Beth, Johnny, Janice, me and Joey."

PAPA NOEL. "While going through my mom's things, I found this picture of Santa taking a break in the basement of Pomeroy's department store in Reading, Pennsylvania," writes Robert Bear from Knoxville, Tennessee. "I didn't know it then, but that Santa Claus was my dad!"

SLIDE CAR. "My grandpa August T. Berg is standing next to the snowmobile he built," writes Gwen Berg of Bloomington, Minnesota. "The photo was taken in the mid-1930s in McIntosh. The machine was powered by an airplane engine. You can see the wooden propeller on the back."

A White Christmas

SNOW IN SOUTH TEXAS

My father grew up in Kansas City and my mother in North Texas, so both were familiar with snow. In 1921, they moved to San Antonio, Texas, where the Chamber of Commerce motto was "Where the Sunshine Spends the Winter."

I grew up in that wonderful city. Some of my school chums had come from up north and told stories of the fun they had playing in the snow. One of them even brought his sled along; it hung in the garage, rusting.

Many of the boys' magazines of the time carried stories about Alaska and Canada and how men used snowshoes there to traverse the snow.

I read the book *White Fang* about a dog that pulled a sled in Alaska. Every winter, I wished for snow so I could capture some of the fun depicted in the stories and pictures, and the tales my school chums told.

But it was not to be, for it did not snow in San Antonio, I was told.

One December night in 1927, my dad looked outside, then stepped onto the front porch. He called for me to join him.

I recall Dad pointing up to the sky, which was a peculiar gray color and completely covered with thick clouds.

"If this was Kansas City, it would snow tonight," he said.

I didn't think too much about it since it *never* snowed in San Antonio.

The next morning, my mother awakened me early and told me to look out the window.

It had snowed heavily during the night, about 5 inches, and it was still snowing! I flew into my clothes, put on my heaviest coat and headed outside.

I was the first kid out and ran to all the neighboring houses to rouse my friends. About 30 minutes later, we were engrossed in snowball fights. My friend with the sled got it out and we pulled each other up and down the sidewalk.

Finally our fingers and noses got so cold we couldn't stand it anymore, and we went inside. None of us had warm clothing, and our parents were afraid we might catch colds. We were allowed to play outside several times that day and really enjoyed it.

That snow, which lasted for several days before melting, was a memorable experience for a young boy in San Antonio, where it never snowed.

GEORGE MCGINNISS • GULF BREEZE, FL

PRAYERS FOR A YULEMOBILE

A few years ago, when our boys were 10 and 6 years old, they both dreamed of our getting a snowmobile. We told them quite frankly that we couldn't afford one. So they agreed they'd talk to God about it.

Two weeks before Christmas, we returned home one evening to find our answering machine blinking. We were astonished to hear a message telling us we'd won the county fair raffle. Our prize, believe it or not, was a new snowmobile.

As the Bible says, God delights in giving good gifts to His children.

BRENDA KNABLE • BAGLEY, MN

KING OF THE WORLD. This photograph, which was taken in the 1970s, proves just how timeless the perfect snow day can be.

"Silly snow play was the theme of the afternoon when this photo of my youngest sisters was taken in our front yard in Kankakee, Illinois, in 1948. Linda piled on top of the twins, Rosemary and Barbara."

Jackie Cross • Bonfield, IL

A GRAND HOLIDAY

GRANDPA KNEW LITTLE THINGS CREATE BIG MEMORIES

He was our grandfather, but we called him "Papa." This special man was a combination of Teddy Roosevelt, Heidi's grandfather and Santa Claus. In fact, Papa resembled Santa Claus, and we loved to sit in his ample lap and run our little hands over his whiskers.

Our grandparents lived a block away from us when I was growing up in Washington, D.C. There were seven kids in our family, and we each took turns going to their house for Sunday dinner—it made an individual treat during those Depression years.

Dinner always started with Papa's delicious chicken soup, even during D.C.'s renowned summer heat. "The hotter the day, the hotter the soup!" was his credo. Dessert never varied—it was Nabisco cookies, and the guest got to take a whole box home to share with the family.

Holidays were incredibly exciting, with Papa adding a special touch that assured a fun time. Papa would order a huge 30- or 40-pound turkey, which our mother would roast all night long in a slow oven. He also provided other goodies, such as peanut brittle and Seckel pears that had been stored in their basement. Often we got little licorice men, which always brought shouts of joy from the younger Gilberts.

We found out years later that it was Papa and his unmarried sister, Aunt Aggie, who helped our parents play Santa Claus during our childhood in those tough Depression times of the '30s.

It was Papa who provided the money for the high-tops my brothers wore and the patent leather shoes my three sisters and I received. Papa would also bring bags of nuts, a treat enjoyed only during the holidays. And my sainted grandmother would listen with all the patience in the world as we displayed our gifts from Santa.

When dinner was over, we piled into Papa's car and drove to downtown D.C. to look at the decorated windows in the big department stores. We'd jump out of the car, bundled against the cold, and peer at the magic before us.

GREAT GRANDPA. Annette Gilbert (shown with her grandfather) says her "Papa" had a special way of making all their family gatherings memorable.

Then we'd hustle back into the car for the drive back, where Mother, who had remained home with the smallest Gilbert, would have hot chocolate waiting.

Papa sprinkled so much magic over our lives. I thank him for his very special place in a warm and loving childhood.

ANNETTE GILBERT • OLNEY, MD

CHRISTMAS AT MY GRANDPARENTS' HOUSE

My earliest recollections of Christmas go back to a house high on a hill in St. Albans, West Virginia. It was my grandparents' home and the source of many wonderful memories.

Every Christmas Eve the family gathered for a *big* Christmas dinner my grandmother prepared entirely by herself. We would all gather in a large room in their basement, which had sawhorses with sheets of plywood on top for makeshift tables. My grandfather was responsible for gathering chairs, stools and nail kegs to sit on.

It was not uncommon to sit down to a meal with 50 or more people. All family members, friends, cousins and anyone else in the neighborhood (or that my grandparents had seen in town in the past few weeks) were welcomed. Of course, as our family grew, so grew the number of places set and number of plywood sheets and sawhorses.

This wondrous occasion was wrapped in so much love, and the true meaning of Christmas was always discussed. Along with big helpings of turkey, dressing, mashed potatoes and strawberry custard, we were served words of love and wisdom to last us a lifetime!

PATSY YOUNG • ST. ALBANS, WV

LITTLE MAGIC CAN DO WONDERS

Christmas was a special time in the Ozark Mountains, where I grew up in the 1930s, but the one I remember best was in 1931, when I was 5 years old.

My parents had broken up and I was living with my grandparents, a wonderful couple in their mid-40s, and their son and youngest daughter. My aunt was only 6 and my uncle was in his early 20s.

This made a real family for me. Although I missed my parents, I had a good home there for many years.

I think everyone else realized what I was going through in the beginning and tried to make me happy.

This particular Christmas occurred during typical winter weather. Sundown hardly made a dent in the already dark afternoon, and a cold chilly night promised snowfall before morning.

We'd been talking about Santa's visit during the day, and as evening approached, the anticipation was almost tangible.

My aunt and I looked forward to Christmas goodies, and even with the Depression, my grandparents always had candy, fruit and small presents, including a toy or two for Santa to bring.

The Christmas tree was in the room next to the living room. We didn't have electricity, but there was plenty of tinsel, strings of popcorn, and red and green paper chains covering the limbs of the red cedar that my uncle and I had cut on a nearby hillside.

After Christmas dinner, when it was dark outside, my grandfather suddenly turned his head to listen.

"I think I hear something bothering the stock in the barn lot," he exclaimed. "I'm going to see about it."

He took down a shotgun from over the doorway and lit a kerosene lantern. Bundling up in a heavy coat, Grandfather went out into the night.

He was gone for some time when my uncle said, "I hear something on the porch. Maybe it's on the roof."

We listened, a little fearful of what might be happening.

Then we heard the outside door to the room with the Christmas tree slowly creak as it opened.

The door between that room and the living room was ajar. Looking through, we could see a figure dressed in red and white, with a white beard. Carrying a large sack, he slowly entered the room.

He went to the tree we had decorated, placed his sack on the floor and began removing packages. Then he threw the empty sack over his shoulder and left.

"Why, that was old Santy!" my uncle said, running to the window and looking out.

"He's gone already, but I think I just heard his reindeer."

In about 20 minutes, Grandfather came back from checking the livestock, remarking that he hadn't heard a thing. Hanging up his shotgun and removing his outer clothing, he joined us around the fire.

My aunt and I pestered him with our tale about the stranger in red and white who'd left things under our tree.

Naturally, Grandfather didn't believe us and had to go and check the tree for himself. After that, he said he surely wished he'd been there and asked why we hadn't called him.

Neither my aunt nor I slept much that night. But our Christmas celebration was the usual fun time of opening presents, eating oranges and enjoying a family dinner.

My mother was able to get away from her job, some three hours' drive away, and this made the rest of the day really special.

I don't know how long it was before I figured out what happened that night, but it was a while. And that was good, because youngsters must have their dreams, and at that point in my life, I needed some dreams.

My grandparents have been gone for many years, but I'll never forget their kindness and all they did to help a young boy get through some trying times.

RUSSELL WEST • EL DORADO HILLS, CA

SPARKLE IN HER EYES. Mary Long was overwhelmed by the surprise husband Delbert gave her for Christmas in 1952.

'CAN'T WE OPEN JUST ONE?'

That Christmas Eve plea took on a special meaning in 1952.

GARY LONG • CHAMBERSBURG, PA

December 24! Christmas was just about here. We spent the morning in our classrooms finishing up some last-minute assignments. How long before we got out?

The nuns at St. Matthew's attempted to make the subjects more interesting. Where's Bethlehem? Find Jerusalem on the map. Can you spell "Nativity"?

By 11:30 a.m., I was free and even had time for last-minute shopping—an aluminum pot for Aunt Gert; a small bottle of Green Irish Tweed perfume for Mom; and for Dad, Zane Grey's *The Last of the Plainsmen.*

At our house, Christmas began shortly after supper on Christmas Eve, when the air was electric with anticipation, and the sweet aroma of fudge, cookies and pies filled the house.

Our tree, always a Scotch pine, was trimmed with red lights, red shiny balls and Ivory Snow laundry detergent flakes that had been whipped and layered on the branches to look like new-fallen snow.

It became tradition to place our presents under the tree right after supper. Mom straightened the house while my brother, sister and I completed a few chores. Mom then got out the cookies, fudge and other treats, covered them with waxed paper and put them out on the dining room table.

After the work was done, we would get ready for church. After Mass, we'd return home, exchange gifts, eat cookies and drink some eggnog.

This year, 1952, seemed different. The Korean War was raging and a lot of service members weren't home for the holidays. The hope for "peace on earth" seemed so remote.

Still, people did their best to keep the holiday spirit alive. Dad seemed especially giddy and full of joy. He always wanted to open the gifts before church, but this year he was even more intense.

"Come on, Mary, it won't hurt to open them before we leave," he told Mom.

His pleas fell on deaf ears, and he even tried singing a few carols in the hope Mom would give in. We all went about our routine and by 10 p.m., we were ready for church.

In one last attempt, Dad suggested that if we couldn't open all our gifts, at least we could each open one. The kids wanted to, he said.

Mom gave him a friendly scowl, then laughed. "OK, but just one."

We dug through the packages and found something for everyone. Dad got a necktie he'd never wear, Aunt Gert opened an apron and I got a pair of shoes. Then, finally, it was Mom's turn.

She started to open a package with her name on it, but before she could, Dad stopped her. He reached into his pocket and pulled out a small box and handed it to her.

"I waited 30 years for you to get this," he said tenderly.

The room got silent and all eyes focused on that small box. I noticed a tear form as Mom slowly opened the hinged satin box to reveal a single diamond set in a gold band.

Back in 1922, Dad couldn't afford an engagement ring; in 1952, he couldn't wait until after church to give it to her.

More than 50 years later, progress has taken away the old neighborhood and replaced it with a ramp to an interstate highway, but traditions still continue. The wonderful aroma of cookies baking still fills the house and our tree is trimmed in red, even though Scotch pines are harder to find.

Long after Dad died, Mom would touch her engagement ring, close her eyes and smile.

And at our house, someone always still pleads, "Can't we open just one gift early this year?"

Think twice before you say no. I will.

CHRISTMAS PLEA ANSWERED

I first met my future husband while we were working in Los Angeles aircraft factories during the early years of World War II. When he joined the Air Force and I went to the Women's Army Corps, we lost touch.

Both of our parents' homes were in Illinois, and in 1947 I received a Christmas card from him. In it, he wrote, "Please write to me." But when I looked at the envelope, I saw he had forgotten to include his return address!

I wrote to all three rural routes using the postmark. But, one by one, the letters all came back.

One night, there was a thunderstorm while we slept. A loud clap of thunder woke me, and for some reason, a name—Roseville— was in my head. I got up to look at a map. Sure enough, there was a Roseville, a town near Macomb. I still don't know why, but I was convinced: *That's where he is.*

I wrote one last letter, sent it off...and today, my husband and I give thanks every day for our children, grandchildren and great-grandchildren. I believe an angel was whispering in my ear the night of that thunderstorm.

DOROTHY ANDERSON • GOOD HOPE, IL

FEELING THE **WEIGHT** of the Great Depression in '36 were Ruth and Al Danielson (far left) and daughter Lavona. "Mother's sheer grit and a bit of feistiness helped her recover and live a long life," says Lavona.

YULETIDE MIRACLES

IN THE NICK OF TIME

Despite a job transfer and a move from Blue Island, Illinois, to Joplin, Missouri, my family's financial picture got worse, not better, as Christmas approached in 1936.

My father's employer had promised better times as a result of the transfer. While that hadn't happened, we were grateful that Dad was working during the Depression.

I was 10, and my parents asked me what I would like for Christmas. I explained that I had seen a watch that I would dearly love, but since it cost $2.95 they could surprise me with something more affordable.

A traditional turkey dinner was out of the question that year, but my enterprising mother learned of a restaurant that was selling ham bones for 10 cents each.

She immediately set out for the restaurant in the pouring rain, despite having a cold and fever, to purchase the basis for our Christmas dinner. After waiting an hour outside the restaurant, she finally was able to buy one ham bone.

When Christmas morning came, the aroma of bean soup filled the air, and there was a small package for me under the tree.

By this time, Mother was so weak she couldn't get out of bed, so I took my present into her bedroom so that she could share my opening it.

I couldn't believe my eyes. It was the very watch I had seen!

The next day, my mother was delirious with fever. Calling a doctor was out of the question because we didn't have the money to pay one.

I carefully took off my watch and gave it to my dad, telling him to take it back to the store and get a refund so that he could get medicine for my mother. That is the exact moment when the minister of our church arrived—he had sensed something was wrong when he saw that our family had not attended Christmas services.

He took one look at my mother and left immediately. He returned with a doctor who diagnosed Mother as having pneumonia.

As I was thanking our minister, I offered him my watch. He hugged me and told me that the doctor and the medicine were gifts. But I knew it was a Christmas miracle.

LAVONA DANIELSON • LAS VEGAS, NV

A PRAYER ON CHRISTMAS EVE

The Great Depression was in full swing at Christmastime in 1929 in Chicago. The winter cold was unbearble, and our allotment of coal was barely keeping us warm in our basement flat.

On top of that, Mom was in bed with double pneumonia, and the doctor, on his late-afternoon rounds, told Dad that the hours before dawn would be the most crucial for her.

During the night, I tossed and turned and woke with a start. I jumped out of bed and saw my father hunched over the kitchen table. It didn't look good to me.

He saw me and asked why I was out of bed. I told him I couldn't sleep because Mama was so sick. He said he had the same problem, but that it would be best if I went back to bed.

So I crawled back under the covers and prayed for Mom to get better, soaking the pillow with my tears. I must have fallen asleep from pure exhaustion.

When I woke up, Dad told me to go and wake my brother, and then we should go into the living room. There we both sat, feeling very worried.

When Dad came out of the bedroom, he was carrying Mother in his arms, and she was smiling! She had passed the crisis and was on her way to recovery.

That year, we had no Christmas tree or decorations, but when Dad brought Mom out, wrapped in her blankets, and said, "Merry Christmas, kids," we all hugged each other and cried with happiness as the winter morning sunlight made its way through the cold basement windows.

JANE NICOLL IDT • NORTH LAS VEGAS, NV

TRADITIONALLY CHRISTMAS

Gifts by Avon...A Joy to Select...A Joy to Give...A Joy to Receive.
AVON CALLING gives you all the excitement of Christmas shopping with all the comforts of home. Do welcome your Avon Representative when she calls.

AVON
cosmetics
RADIO CITY, NEW YORK

You'll be loved for giving the favorite Wake-up Radio!
CHOICE OF COLORS...NO EXTRA COST...NEW MODELS FROM $27.95

Gift wrapped ready for your card

GOD'S LITTLEST CAROLER

Farms, ranches and orchards made the foothills of San Francisco's South Bay a wonderful place to live, especially at Christmas. My three boys didn't have snow or sleds, but they had hills to climb, fields for kite-flying and fresh country air.

In 1962, Christmas was special, as we'd just had a baby girl, Suzanne. Our youngest boy, Ricky, 5, spent hours gazing at her. "Mom," he'd say, "if she gets any more beauty-fuller, I'll just die!"

Every night, Ricky thanked God for sending Sue, saying she was "the best Christmas present in the whole wide world."

On Christmas Eve, we snuggled around the fireplace. I read "The Night Before Christmas" and we watched a holiday movie. I was answering Ricky's question about caroling, explaining that people used to do this to spread the joy of Christmas, when his brothers started yelling:

"It's snowing! It's snowing!"

Our entire neighborhood was blanketed in white. The hills glowed in the moonlight. It was unbelievable. We had snow, in sunny California! My boys jumped all over the yard, the excitement and wonder almost more than they could handle.

Suddenly, Ricky slammed through the front door. "Mommy, I just got a great idea!" he said. "I want to sing Christmas carols to God and our neighbors! Can I, Mommy? I have to sing carols to thank God for this great Christmas. He'll hear me better outside, and I'll stay just on our street!"

"But it's dark and cold, and I don't want you wandering around alone," I said. Billy, 11, and Louie, 8, had just come back inside. "Your brothers will go with you." "No way!" they yelled. "What if our friends see us?"

"No one will see you, because I want you to stay in our front yard," I said. "God will hear you well enough from there. So hush up and bundle up."

Ricky beamed with pride. Billy and Louie mumbled as they stomped out the door behind him.

The three of them stood in the snow and the moonlight. Bundled up in coats, hats and gloves, they looked like figures in a Norman Rockwell painting—except that the two taller boys looked like they were facing a firing squad.

I was sure it'd be over after one lisping melody. Suddenly Ricky stepped forward, threw his little arms wide, tossed his head back, looked skyward and let 'er rip. "Thy-a-lent night! Ho-oh-lee night!"

Sue jolted awake, screaming. Dogs began yelping. Birds screeched and flew away. But never in my life have I heard man or beast make purer sounds of love and joy. This little man made sure God heard every word.

As Ricky belted out one Christmas carol after another, porch lights popped on up and down the block. One neighbor must have suspected mayhem, because a police car cruised past our house. I expected Billy and Louie to trample each other fleeing the scene of the crime, but they didn't.

As a small crowd of smiling neighbors formed in front of our house, my heart swelled with pride. Billy and Louie were singing with their brother.

They faced the front of the house, stocking caps down over their faces, coat collars pulled up high, hands cupped over their ears. They had no idea what was going on behind them—or that they were part of a wondrous Christmas none of us would ever forget.

DORIS BENNETT
SANTA CLARA, CA

ILLUSTRATION: KEVIN RECHIN

Belly Laughs

Eddie Waymel tries in vain to cover up his giggles as he sits on Santa's lap at a department store in Chicago, Illinois, on Dec. 16, 1960. The adorable 4-year-old couldn't seem to say what he wanted for Christmas. Perhaps he was in awe of the jolly old elf. Santa probably knew just what was in Eddie's heart—and on his list.

CHAPTER 5

CHRISTMAS IN THE MILITARY

When the country was at war, countless American men and women left their loved ones behind to defend liberty and uphold justice stateside and overseas. But the grim realities of war and the challenging circumstances didn't stop these service members and their families from celebrating the most wonderful time of the year. Both at home and abroad, they created their own miracles, showing compassion to strangers in countries where they were stationed and delighting in unexpected holiday reunions with kin near and far.

"The war in the Pacific was at its peak on Christmas in 1944," remembers Harry Von Handorf of Lakeside Park, Kentucky. "I was in the Navy's 117th Seabees on Saipan, where there was an orphanage. Some of the children were native Chamorros and some were Japanese.

"We invited about 20 of them, ages 8 to 13, to have dinner with us at the chow hall we had just built. The men in the carpenter shop made little wooden toys, and we shared our Christmas goodies from home. It was a pleasure to see the children's smiles.

"After the meal, the children sang for us. The last song was 'Auld Lang Syne.' We didn't understand the words but we recognized the tune. There wasn't a dry eye in the place. Although we were in a bitter war, we could still celebrate Christmas with those children. It was a Christmas I'll never forget."

Here's a salute to the strong people who kept the holiday spirit alive while fighting for victory in a million different ways. Read on to relive Christmas as seen through their eyes.

SEASON OF GIVING

Soldiers brought hope to refugees in Belgium and learned the true meaning of Christmas.
JOHN JARVIE • KEARNY, NJ

My holidays were always filled with family and friends, overdecorated trees with many gifts under their branches, and an abundance of food. But I never really knew what Christmas was about until 1944, in Belgium.

My Army unit had moved through biting winds and snow into an area of doubtful alliances (it was a former SS resort). We scrounged around for anything to make us more comfortable—blankets, bedsprings, stoves, you name it. Me? I found a box of Christmas ornaments and stowed them on the Army truck.

On Dec. 16, the Battle of the Bulge intervened and kept us moving in and out of action, obliterating all thoughts of the

holiday. But by Christmas Eve, we stopped at a refugee camp that sheltered hundreds of mothers and children—all very sad, weary and hungry.

My lights suddenly went on! *This is the reason you kept those Christmas ornaments*, I thought. *Now find a tree.*

I approached a friendly sergeant with my idea. He was all for it, so we jumped into a jeep and drove until we spotted our tree. Back at the camp, we suggested that each man in our company contribute a sock full of rations for the refugees. Word quickly passed through all the companies, and everybody gave.

The next day, the tree was up and fully decorated. We invited folks from the refugee camp, and they walked into a celebration they never would have imagined. Our guests looked at the tree in utter amazement. The branches were laden with found ornaments, packs of cigarettes, gum and radar tinsel.

We handed each kid a full Army sock that reached to the floor. The youngest children clung to their mothers or bigger siblings. They seemed a bit overwhelmed, but the older kids enjoyed themselves. Some of the soldiers played carols on guitars while others sang. We talked to the refugees with the help of some of our bilingual soldiers.

The U.S. Army feeds its troops well, and

CPL. JARVIE (opposite, top) learned the true meaning of Christmas during World War II, when his Army unit hosted a celebration for hungry refugees, including hundreds of children (opposite, bottom, and below).

our dinner that Christmas was no exception. We wanted to give our meals to the refugee mothers, but it wasn't allowed. All leftovers had to be thrown out. The hungry mothers simply pulled the carefully discarded food from the trash, and I knew from the grins on my buddies' faces that those mothers rescued hundreds of complete dinners that day.

I'll never forget that Christmas, when all of us soldiers truly gave from our hearts.

Around the 17th century, Europeans decorated their trees with apples, cookies and candy. The first glass ornaments were made in Germany in the latter part of the 19th century.

THE LONG RIDE HOME

DAY WAS MERRY AND BRIGHT

In 1962, I was coming home to Cincinnati for Christmas from training at Fort Leonard Wood when my flight out of Knoxville, Tennessee, was delayed.

To my surprise, a gentleman at the airport announced that he was driving to Cincinnati and asked if anyone would like a ride. I said, "Yes, sir!"

It was a nice ride, with the radio playing lots of Christmas music, including Jackie Gleason's beautiful *White Christmas* album. The man dropped me off in downtown Cincinnati, and I took a cab home.

I never forgot that kind man, and I think of him every time I play Jackie Gleason's *White Christmas*. I hope I thanked him enough. He made it a special holiday for my parents, my twin sister and me. That's me in uniform at home (below) in '62.

JERRY DOEKEL • CINCINNATI, OH

BUSIN' IT

During the Korean War, while recuperating from a wound at Camp Gordon (now Fort Gordon), Georgia, I took a few days of Christmas leave to go home to Rocky Mount, North Carolina. A soldier at the camp offered me a ride to Laurinberg, about halfway to my home, and dropped me off at the bus station.

The ticket agent said there was a two-hour wait for a bus to Fayetteville, the next leg of the journey, and that the bus to Rocky Mount would pick me up around 10 p.m. That would get me home at midnight.

I had been waiting about 10 minutes when a bus came up showing Fayetteville on the front. I asked the driver if this was my bus, but he said it was a chartered bus and did not carry regular passengers.

I sat down again, but in a few minutes the driver returned and said he would take me to Fayetteville. I've always assumed that my crutches and leg brace had a profound effect on him.

When we got to Fayetteville, the early bus to Rocky Mount was waiting. The driver had called ahead and asked for the bus to be held for me. I thanked him several times for his generosity in helping a crippled soldier get home for Christmas.

BENNETT COCKRELL • ROCKY MOUNT, NC

ROUND-TRIP KINDNESS

In December 1945, while stationed at Gowen Field in Boise, Idaho, I received a furlough to go home to Alliance, Ohio, for the holidays.

When I arrived at Union Station in Chicago, servicemen were wall to wall, and there was much pushing and shoving to get through the gates to the trains.

I was pushed through a gate, and the conductor checked my ticket and tried to hand it back to me. I reached for it but missed, and a gust of wind blew my ticket back into the terminal. I couldn't retrieve it, so I went ahead and boarded the train. When the conductor checked the tickets, I explained what happened, and he kindly let me go through.

After I was home a couple of days, I went to the Alliance station and asked about my

PROUD WAVE. Judith Perry in 1959 (above), and at an event in 2010.

and laughing uproariously. I realized that I had fallen prey to their prank. I felt I had disgraced my new uniform.

The cab had cost more than I expected, so I had only two candy bars and 15 cents for my 12-hour journey home. I took a seat to wait, and the two sailors came and sat beside me, flirting and saying things like "Wish you were on my ship, sailor" and "The Navy should issue a WAVE with every sea bag to keep us warm." Silently, I burned. I retreated to a busy ladies' room to spend the next 45 minutes sitting on my luggage.

Finally it was time to board my train. Near dawn I asked the conductor what time the train would stop at Blanchester. He said, "I'm sorry, miss, that's not a scheduled stop. You'll get off at Cincinnati." This meant the train would pass within a block of my house and I'd have to get someone to drive 45 minutes on treacherous roads to pick me up.

But then the conductor asked about my uniform and said the engineer's son was also in the Navy. He kindly made the long trip to the front of the train to see if anything could be done to help me get home. I was praying for a miracle.

He returned to say the engineer couldn't stop the train, which was already behind schedule. But if I were willing to jump off into a snow bank, he added, the engineer could slow the train down as it passed Blanchester. I said I would be most grateful.

The conductor took my luggage and me to the last car, where I thought about the fact that I was wearing a skirt and 2-inch heels. He told me not to jump until he gave the OK. When he unlocked the chain, I very nearly changed my mind. I was holding my bucket hat and clutching my shoulder bag to me when he ordered, "One, two, jump!"

I landed safely, and the conductor tossed my luggage after me. I waved and shouted, "Thank you!" The conductor gave me a snappy salute and yelled, "Merry Christmas!" The train picked up speed so quickly that he was gone before he could hear my grateful "Merry Christmas!" back to him. As the sun came up I trudged home, where my sleepy mother scolded me for jumping off the train and for having no boots!

After that leap from the train, I was ready to take on any adventure life threw my way!
JUDITH PERRY • CHESAPEAKE, VA

return ticket. They said they would see what they could do.

Later, I received a call from the Alliance ticket agent, asking me to pick up my return ticket. Someone in Chicago had found it and turned it in to the agent there.

I wish I knew the kind soul who did that for me. I have thanked that person many times in my prayers.
WILLIAM WRIGHT • CANTON, OH

JUMPING AT HER CHANCE TO GET HOME

In 1959, after high school graduation, I left my small hometown of Blanchester, Ohio, to enlist in the U.S. Navy WAVES. After boot camp, my orders sent me to the staff of the naval training center in Bainbridge, Maryland. I was told I could take five days of holiday leave. I was so proud and excited: I was going home for Christmas, wearing my dress blues!

By the time my cab arrived at the train station in Baltimore, it was cold and had been snowing for hours. When I entered the busy terminal, two young sailors stood up and yelled, "Atten-hut!" I came to attention and stood frozen for several minutes. When I glanced sideways, the sailors were seated

LETTERS HOME

NOTE GOT INTO RIGHT HANDS

In November 1943, my boss at Grumman Aircraft in Port Washington, New York, suggested we send cigarettes to the soldiers overseas instead of exchanging gifts. His cousin, a head nurse in an overseas hospital, would distribute the packs to injured soldiers.

I put my name, address and a Christmas greeting on three packs of cigarettes. In April '44, I received a note from an airman, Clinton R. Putnal, and we began exchanging friendly letters.

Clinton was in the medical corps in Santa Ana, California, and in February '45, he was asked to accompany a patient across the country to Vermont. He asked for a six-day delay before returning to California and

stopped in New York to see me. I was not home when my mother and uncle picked him up at the railroad station.

Clinton was upstairs freshening up when I got in, and my mother told me, "You look so pale, like a ghost. Please go put some lipstick on." This was such a surprise coming from my mother, who added, "Don't you dare jump into his arms. Act like a proper young lady."

I was about to meet the airman I'd been writing to for months. Well, without even thinking, I jumped into his arms as soon as I saw him. He held me so tight, and I didn't want him to ever let me go.

That night, Clinton asked me to marry him. He already had my engagement ring and wedding band with him. Less than 70 hours later, at 10 a.m. on Feb. 20, 1945, we were married (left) in Mineola, New York. By noon, our train left for Santa Ana.

ANN DETTORI PUTNAL • CANTONMENT, FL

BUNDLES OF JOY

It was in 1944, while I was in boot camp at the Great Lakes Naval Training Center in Illinois, that one of the fellows received a picture of his girlfriend in a bathing suit.

The alluring photo of "Julie" eventually made the rounds of our barracks, and someone got the idea that each of us should write a thank-you letter to her for brightening our day.

Every member of Company 1748, even those soldiers who seldom wrote to anyone, composed an appreciative letter, and they went out in one mailing. Julie was about to be flooded with mail from 99 sailors.

Instead of getting mess hall duty during the week, I lucked out and was assigned to the post office. One day, when the mailbags came in, we received several bundles of letters, all from the same address. They were Julie's replies.

It turns out that Julie had called in her girlfriends to help out, and they personally answered each and every one of our letters with a nice letter from "home."

JOSEPH DROBNY • MARQUETTE, MI

CIVVIES FOR CHRISTMAS

My husband, Elden Brame, served in the Navy in Oklahoma—an unusual place for a Navy man, which became a family joke.

As comedian George Gobel once quipped about his World War II service as a flight instructor in Oklahoma, "The Japanese never got past Tulsa." Elden served in the U.S. Naval Personnel Separation Center in Norman near the end of World War II.

This postcard (above) showing a sailor enjoying his gift of civilian clothes was on the cover of a Christmas menu Elden mailed home the day after their holiday meal. Inside, the commander's greeting noted that it was the first peaceful Christmas in five years and added that the men in Norman had been "devoted to the sending of thousands of men back home—where we hope they will enjoy many peaceful days ahead."
MARY ANN BRAME • DALLAS, TX

MAIL TRAIN RIGHT ON TIME

My mother told me this story from World War I many years ago.

Christmas 1917 was coming, but because her brother Archie Clikeman (top right) was missing in action and presumed dead, the family was not going to celebrate the holiday.

The townspeople of Parker, South Dakota, always joked that the small-town postmaster read all of the postcards whenever the mail train came into town. On that Christmas Eve, he lived up to his reputation.

The family was always grateful that the postmaster, instead of waiting for the rural mail to go out the day after Christmas, called my grandmother and told her that Archie was being held as a prisoner of war. Archie even wrote on the postcard that he was well.

Of course, my mother said, that turned out to be the best Christmas ever. Archie came home after the war and lived to a ripe old age.
KAY JOHNSON • PARKER, SD

BRUSHES WITH FAME. Big-name entertainers like Bob Hope (above), Jerry Colonna (top left) and Raymond Burr (left) visited the 8th Army headquarters in Seoul, South Korea, while Ken Herst was stationed there.

Hope for the Holidays

USO visits included star-studded shows and a thoughtful act by Raymond Burr.

KEN HERST • SPRINGFIELD, VA

Two Christmastime visits from celebrities at our 8th Army headquarters in Seoul, South Korea, left lasting impressions for me.

On Dec. 19, 1964, Bob Hope and his USO troupe put on a Christmas show, bringing reigning Miss World Ann Sydney and opera singer and actress Anna Marie Alberghetti (opposite, bottom left).

Mr. Hope was also accompanied by his USO regulars, including comedian Jerry Colonna (top inset, above), singer and actress Janis Paige, and Les Brown and His Band of Renown. What a fantastic show that was!

In the middle of a number by Miss Paige, who was clad in a most revealing outfit, a heavy snow squall passed over us. Being the trouper that she was, Miss Paige never missed a beat or a note. The moment her number ended, she was wrapped in a fur coat.

Mr. Hope was presented with a large pot (above), painted with the 1st Cavalry insignia, for fermenting the traditional vegetable dish kimchee. I doubt it gained a place of honor on his mantel along with his other awards.

The following Christmas, as the war in Vietnam progressed, Mr. Hope and his entourage headed there to entertain the troops. We were told that actor Raymond Burr (opposite, bottom inset) was coming to our base that year. We joked that we couldn't wait to hear him sing and dance.

Mr. Burr arrived by jeep, without security or an entourage. He set up shop in the mess hall with a large pad of paper in front of him. He then proceeded to chat with all the soldiers, one on one, and took down the names, addresses and phone numbers of their loved ones back home.

When Mr. Burr arrived back in the States, he telephoned every one of the soldiers' homes on Christmas Day with the heartfelt messages from the sons, daughters or other loved ones serving 13,000 miles away.

I gained a new respect for Raymond Burr after that. I never watched *Perry Mason* on television the same way again.

CELEBRITY DROPS IN

When I was 9, in 1927, my family owned a farm in Hicksville, New York, several miles away from the Mitchel Field Army air base on Long Island.

On Dec. 27, as a haze covered the fields at dusk, we heard a plane circling. The sound got louder and louder, and then we heard a crash. A pilot had landed his Curtis Falcon in our field and taxied right into the machine shed (above). A pole from the mowing machine had gone through the side of the plane, just missing the pilot, Maj. Frederick L. Martin, and his passenger, Roy Ives.

Neither of the men were seriously injured, but we called our family doctor, who tended to a cut on the major's face and nose.

When the excitement was over, we all ate supper together. Maj. Martin, who had become famous for leading the Army's first flight around the world in 1924, gave my mother the plane's ID plate as a souvenir. It was truly a night to remember.

EVELYN McGUNNIGLE • WALSH BATH, NY

I'LL BE HOME
FOR CHRISTMAS

After a year of separation, a young couple defied all the odds to be together at Christmas. **BERNADETTE PORTER** • VILLA PARK, IL

At Christmastime 1945, the excitement of the season was doubled because the boys were coming home from war. One long year before, Bob and I had gotten married, on Dec. 9, 1944. Five days after our wedding, he received his orders to ship out.

In early 1945, Bob was aboard a German cruise ship, the *Blum Fontaine*. One night, during the 43-day trip, he was talking with another soldier. The fluorescence in the black water was quite beautiful. Bob stared down into the depths and said, "I'm praying I'll be home for Christmas."

"Are you crazy?" said the soldier. "We don't even know where we're going."

Bob said, "I'm praying, crazy or not."

Their destination was the Pacific island of Iwo Jima; our Marines, 4,163 of them, had fought to take it. Bob's 506th Fighter Group was to occupy the island. Bob wrote to me every single day and I to him.

Now, the long, lonely year was over. He had been many thousands of miles away. It was hard to believe Bob was coming home, but how? Men needed points to go home. Flyers with 70 points had left earlier. Bob, a master sergeant, had 60 points.

For reasons we never knew, the naval destroyer *USS Independence* came by Iwo Jima. The crew called for anyone still on the island. Points did not matter; they were all heading home.

The captain challenged the men. "If you boys tighten your belts and do not waste food, we can be home for Christmas. If we're not careful, we'll have to stop for supplies."

Of course, there was nothing the men wanted more than to be home for Christmas. Because of their determination and the captain's plan to travel straight through, they made the trip in 16 days.

On Dec. 23, the *Independence* reached its California port, which was filled with ships. This was no problem, since the only place available was an empty dock too large for many ships but made for a huge destroyer. The men were offered a two-week pass; discharges would come after Christmas.

Bob took the pass and hurriedly sent me a Western Union telegram before getting back on ship. It said: "Darling, expect to arrive at Fort Owens, Massachusetts on the 24th. Suggest you leave Chicago to arrive Boston the same date. Register hotel manager at North Station will meet you there."

Serendipity (or fate) was with Bob and me throughout our attempted reunion. The *Independence* coming when it did, picking up anyone left on Iwo Jima, was a miracle to us. The captain's challenging plan to sail straight through to reach home by Christmas was also a surprising success.

By train, the men got to Fort Devens, Massachusetts, later joining hundreds of soldiers lined up to take the train to Boston. This crowd would never fit on one train!

Just then, a cabbie arrived, shouting, "I'm going to Boston, $10 each, with room enough for six."

Bob ran to the cab and somehow made it as one of the six. This, too, was unlikely. Bob wondered how I was managing my trip and hoping I would be lucky enough to have the same good fortune.

At home, in Berwyn, Illinois, my bag was packed. People thought I was foolish, since there were so many unknowns. My friend Laura took me to the station in Chicago to catch a train to Boston.

The train station was jam-packed, with people standing shoulder to shoulder. A Coast Guard man asked if I was going to meet someone special. I answered, "Yes, my husband."

A fellow Coast Guardsman said, "There won't be a seat on the train for you." Then another servicemen said, "I'll carry her

HOME AT LAST. Bob and Bernadette Porter, reunited, in December of '45.

luggage and hold her arm. They'll let us both on if they think we're together."

We climbed aboard, but there was no seat for me, so I turned my suitcase on end and sat on it. It was a long ride from Chicago to Boston, but I was delighted just to be on my way. The unbelievable had happened again. Today, I wonder, *How did all these things fall into place?*

In Boston, our train came in under a hotel. Hundreds of men in uniform were milling about. I walked to the Travelers Aid folks for help. They read my telegram and explained that I could not meet the manager. They suggested that perhaps it meant that I should go to the Hotel Mangor, upstairs, and meet my husband there. It seemed likely that the Western Union worker misunderstood the message when he or she wrote it down.

I went upstairs to register. The hotel clerk was very sorry, but there were no rooms available. I decided to wait in the lobby. It was about 9 p.m. on Christmas Eve, and at least I was there!

About an hour later, the clerk came over to me and told me a room would be available in a few minutes. I could not believe it!

I waited in the room till about 10:30, when there was a knock at the door. It was Bob! We were both shaking so much that it took quite a few minutes to settle down, or even know what to say to each other.

After we calmed down and got through our hellos, we wanted to go to midnight Mass. With directions in hand from the same hotel clerk, we walked through the busy crowds to church.

It was Christmas Eve, and Bob was home— safe and sound. As we entered the warm, gently lit church, Bob looked at his watch. It was midnight, and as we knelt down, the organ began to play.

STRIKING A POSE. Daniel Monahan (on left) stands with another serviceman next to a missile in front of their barracks in West Germany in the early 1960s.

Tales from the Table

SNEAKY SERGEANT

I had arrived at my 39th Artillery Army (atomic) unit in West Germany in September 1962, and I don't think we saw the sun more than three days that fall. Now it was late Christmas morning and I was one homesick lad from sunny Southern California.

Some of us were loafing in the day room when our staff sergeant came in and barked, "Four volunteers, now! You, you, you and you!" This young sergeant, a gung-ho type, could make life miserable for even a high-tech outfit like ours.

Groaning, we walked to the sergeant's car as he said, "Get in. That's an order! No questions!"

We were surprised when he drove us off the base and even more surprised when he took us home and introduced us to his wife. They both made us feel very welcome. The sergeant opened up his bar and his wife gave us a home-cooked turkey dinner with all the fixin's—served on real china, not the sloppy metal trays we were used to in the mess hall.

His wife even gave us little presents of homemade cookies and candy to take back. What a wonderful treat for four lonesome GIs who were far away from home!

DANIEL MONAHAN • CLARKSTON, WA

MAKING A FOOD RUN

Members of our 75th Division of the Army were engaged in a fight for our lives during the Battle of the Bulge on Christmas Day 1944. Of course, there was no Christmas meal, just a K ration if you had it. The fight lasted for weeks in a snowy, wooded area with few trails, so it was tough for the cooks to get us food or water.

I believe it was Dec. 29 when someone decided we would get a nighttime Christmas dinner. No lights were allowed on the front line; you ate by feel. The cooks placed the insulated cans of food along a trail and left quickly when a German patrol was sighted.

The riflemen all went to their foxholes, deciding it was too dangerous to eat. As a technical sergeant in charge of the 3rd Platoon, I went to retrieve some turkey for them. The first can I reached for must have been creamed corn, or so my hands told me. The next try was mashed potatoes. Then I got gravy, gelatin and finally turkey.

I took all I could carry and started back to pass out the food, which was a mess by the time I got there. Some of the men later told me that the food was such a treat they tried to save some for later...but it froze!

JOSEPH MCCLURE • HUNTINGDON, PA

HOLIDAY EATS WEREN'T SO SPECIAL

On Christmas Day 1944, as an aircraft radio operator with the 2nd Transport Squadron, I was stationed at the U.S. Air Force base in Luliang, China (below). For the holiday, each member of the squadron contributed $1 to fund a purchase of canned chicken for a special dinner.

Early in the morning, I was told to report for a flight. Arriving at Myitkyina, my pilot, co-pilot and I were told we would transport 38 fully equipped Chinese soldiers to a distant base. As we went to our plane, the base cook presented us with a marvelous fresh-baked loaf of bread as a Christmas gift, to be appreciated later. It was placed on the navigator's table in the cabin, just forward of the troops.

We had been warned to fly low out of Myitkyina to avoid antiaircraft fire from nearby Japanese troops. This caused a great deal of turbulence from the thermal waves rising out of the warm forest.

We had a safe trip, and soon 38 soldiers disembarked, each one carrying his metal helmet containing whatever he had eaten before the bouncy flight. Making matters worse, we discovered while flying back to Luliang that the precious loaf of bread had vacated our plane along with the troops.

To add to our consternation, we rushed to

our home base mess hall only to find that the rest of the squadron had eaten all the canned chicken. We didn't even get the tough water buffalo roast we sometimes had—just our normal C rations!

LEON DYKSTRA • JENISON, MI

NO ACCOUNTING FOR TASTE

While I was serving in Korea (above) in 1950, we had to have our holiday dinner a few days before Christmas.

Our mess sergeant was a cheat and a conniver, but only when it was to the benefit of his boys, as he called us. His questionable conduct resulted in a fantastic dinner for us.

After our fine meal, we spotted an English soldier on guard duty at a bridge adjacent to our position.

A few of us approached him and offered to take his post long enough for him to join in on the greatest meal of his life.

In a good limey accent, he said he would actually prefer some "pork luncheon meat." We thought he was off his rocker, but he rewarded us with a big grin when we gave him five 5-pound cans of Spam. We'd never known anyone who could smile about that canned meat.

LARRY STOVERN • DULUTH, MN

No Greater Wish

In December 1945, my only brother, Leo G. Nash, was in the Navy. He had enlisted a few years earlier, at age 17.

I was just a little girl who desperately wanted her brother home for Christmas, and I had been praying for weeks that Santa would bring him in his sleigh on Christmas Eve.

When my dad took my little sister Peggie and me to see Santa, he held each of us on his lap and asked, "And what do you two little girls want Santa to bring?"

I answered immediately: "We want our brother home from the war. Please put him in a big box tied with a big red ribbon, behind the Christmas tree. And make sure the box has airholes, so he can breathe."

Santa looked up at my father, who shook his head no. My parents knew Leo Gene was not scheduled for a furlough for the holidays.

"Now, that's a pretty tall order to fill," Santa said thoughtfully. "I think the Navy needs your brother. Would you each like to

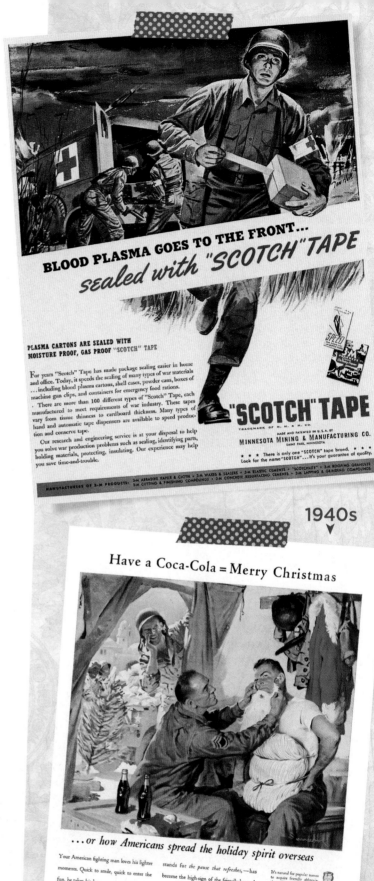

have a beautiful new baby doll? One in a pink dress and one in blue?"

Little Peggie was wide-eyed with the delightful prospect of a new doll. A big smile spread across her pretty face and she nodded yes, but I gave her a good, firm poke in the arm and said, "No, we don't want dolls. We want our brother."

"Yes, we want our brother," Peggie echoed dutifully.

Santa knew he was in a tight spot and said in his kindly voice, "I'm sure you would like new dolls."

At that, I yelled, "You're not the real Santa! You're just one of his helpers!" and yanked off his beard.

A collective gasp went up from the parents and children waiting in line. My father picked us up, one girl under each arm, and carried us off. He never said a word.

What we hadn't realized was that Leo Gene did get a leave, and he arrived home on Christmas Eve after almost six days traveling by train from Seattle to Chicago. Joy of joys!

But he had used up his leave trying to get home and should have returned to duty Christmas Day. There was a terrible ice storm, and travel was at a standstill, so it took him another five days to get back, and he was AWOL. The *Chicago Tribune* ran a photo of the throngs of people stranded in Union Station. My brother cut out the photo and the article and took them to his superior officer as proof of his situation, but it didn't help. He was busted from coxswain to seaman. He said it was worth it, though, because he hadn't made it home the year before.

And so, that Christmas, Leo Gene wasn't in a big box with airholes. He was in his sailor suit, standing next to our decorated tree. My two little sisters, Peggie and Kathleen, and I jumped into his arms and hugged and kissed him. My brother was home for Christmas, even if it was only for 24 hours. The real Santa had, indeed, come through.

KENLYN NASH-DEMETER • SUGAR GROVE, IL

TREES TO CHERISH

ESPECIALLY JOYFUL YULE

Because of the scarcity of so many items during World War II, we made our Christmas ornaments in 1945 by cutting and fitting tin can lids together and brushing pinecones with starch.

In this Christmas morning photo, our 22-month-old son, Douglas, intently examines a new toy. His doting mother, Yvonne, and equally proud father, an Air Force lieutenant, look on in front of the hand-decorated Christmas tree.

With V-J Day behind us, it was an especially joyful Christmas at our small military-area house in Warner Robins, Georgia, near Robins Field.

EMMIT MOORE • EASTPOINTE, MI

SAILOR MAN. Andrew Soucy, shown in his Navy days, hopes that someone from the family mentioned in his story at right will see this and consider it a second thank you.

A VISIT WITH ALL THE TRIMMINGS

While waiting for a train in Columbus, Ohio, we 80 sailors were given a four-hour liberty to browse around the city in December 1943. Several of us started out to explore and were soon met by several young girls who introduced themselves and asked if we were interested in decorating a Christmas tree. We agreed and took a short walk to the home of one of the girls. Her parents greeted us warmly, and after we chatted with them for a while, we were shown the tree.

With the help of all the girls, we quickly trimmed the tree. The family treated us to drinks and goodies and we had a wonderful visit. I often wonder if these nice people remember us as fondly as I remember them.

ANDREW SOUCY • GARDNER, MA

A TREE FOR HOMECOMING

My brother Jim Holzem, serving as an Army paratrooper in the Pacific, was in the thick of many World War II battles. He said he never really expected to survive, but survive he did, even after a daring parachute jump behind the lines of a Philippines prison.

When the war ended, Jim was sent to Japan as part of the occupation force, but he wrote that he expected to be home by Christmas. Mother went out and bought the biggest tree she could find and decorated it with all the lights it would hold.

We waited and waited. Christmas of 1945 came and went, but Mother was determined to leave the tree up until Jim came home. Pine needles were falling all over the rug, and the tree began to look like a brightly lighted skeleton.

Finally, Jim wrote that he'd arrive Jan. 28. We sat by the phone waiting for his call, but Jim, not wanting any big fanfare, decided to walk the mile home from the train station.

When Mom saw my brother walking down the street, she ran down the block to welcome him with open arms and tears in her eyes.

Dad yelled to turn the tree lights on, so Jim's first sight as he walked in the door was a scraggly old tree. But the shine from any tree at all would have been nothing compared to the shine in our eyes when we saw Jim home at last!

BETTY WOODARD • ST. JOSEPH, IL

THANKS "FIR" THE MEMORIES

On Christmas 1944, I was at a naval base in the Philippines when my inventive father sent me a Christmas "tree" in a small wooden cheese box.

The box actually contained a number of small Douglas fir boughs, with instructions on how to make a tree from a short piece of broom handle.

I drilled holes into the broom handle, fastened it to a block of wood, then stuck the boughs in the holes.

It made a small but pretty good tree. And the best thing was, the boughs had been so tightly sealed in the box that they still gave off that wonderful aroma.

Guys came from all over the island just to see and smell that tree to bring back memories of home.

GEORGE BOSTWICK • HOOD RIVER, OR

CHRISTMAS IN THE SOUTH PACIFIC

On Christmas Eve 1945, the carrier *USS Bon Homme Richard* was off Leyte Gulf in the Philippines, between "magic carpet" trips of returning troops from the South Pacific back to the States.

There were mixed emotions from the crew. The war was over and we were eager to get back to our families.

The signal gang (below) was able to make the best of the situation, however. We made a Christmas tree from coat hanger wire, then decorated it with Christmas cards and gift wrapping from the packages we received from home.

The tree, set up in our sleeping quarters, became quite a holiday attraction for a lot of homesick sailors.

BILL KEARNS • BOSTON, MA

WISH BOOK.
The author found
the 1942 Sears
catalog couldn't
fulfill all her wishes.

BROTHER'S LAST GIFT

The love shown by her older brother—
this was the true gift. **HELEN HAAS** • ELEVA, WI

As I remember, it was September 1942, and the nation had been at war for almost 10 months.

My older brother, Oliver Marion Ramsey, who had graduated from the U.S. Naval Academy five years earlier, was aboard the *USS San Francisco* in the South Pacific. The fight between the U.S. fleet and the Japanese forces for supremacy of the seas there was turning ugly.

At Christmastime, Marion, as we called him, always remembered his three younger siblings and parents back on the farm in Wisconsin. In one of his weekly letters home, he asked for our Christmas wish lists. We could ask for three things each. This was thrilling, because presents were few in those days—and now was our chance to ask for what we truly wanted.

At 13, I was giddy with my choices. After much paging through the Sears, Roebuck catalog, I chose a pair of shoes, a toy and some candy, knowing that Marion had access to a Sears catalog on his ship.

Earlier in the year, Marion had sent the family a battery-operated radio, also ordered from the catalog, since we had no electricity on the farm. Our family gathered around that small radio for the war news, hoping to hear something relevant to my brother. To prolong the life of the battery, my father had decreed that the radio was to be used only for news. In my youthful self-absorption, I took little notice that my mother might slip quietly into another room as we listened. Now, in retrospect, I know she went there to pray and weep.

In his letters home, my brother never wrote about the war or expressed anxiety. Only once did he hint at it, writing, "We've jumped out of the frying pan into the fire."

He could have been referring to the time

around Oct. 13, when a major battle in the Guadalcanal campaign was on. Or perhaps he meant the time the *San Francisco* was disabled in battle and he was transferred to the *USS Atlanta*. But this time, Marion was a part of the Rear Adm. Norman Scott's flagship command crew.

And then, an early-morning clash on Nov. 13, in the third naval battle of Guadalcanal, enemy fire sank the *Atlanta*, killing my beloved brother and many other men. They were buried at sea.

News of our loss didn't reach us until Nov. 27, which was Marion's birthday. That's the day my father went into the small town of Fairchild to do some errands. Word spread around town, and someone told my father that the train stationmaster wanted to see him. He went to the station and was handed that life-changing telegram: "We regret to inform you…" Even now, 68 years later, I have tears in my eyes as I write this.

Later, in mid-December, a large package arrived from Sears—our Christmas gifts from Marion. What a bittersweet moment. Those much-anticipated gifts were here, but the beloved and precious giver was forever gone.

HER CREATIVE TOYS SPARKED SMILES IN DIRE TIMES

A Saturday job at Woolworth's in Elizabeth, New Jersey, turned into a full-time position when I graduated from high school at 17 in June 1942. I became responsible for selling the toy counter merchandise, which another employee ordered.

By 1943 the toy selection was not very plentiful. Many of the materials used for making toys had been redirected to items for the war.

That Christmas Eve, the toy counter really looked sad, and so did I, with nothing to offer for children who came in. Then I remembered something I had seen in the storeroom. I had nothing to sell, so leaving the counter was not a problem.

Sure enough, there they were—long boxes, lots of them, on the shelves—3-foot-tall boy and girl Easter bunnies, their large ears protruding from caps and bonnets.

Dare I? Indeed I did! I chopped off all their ears (carefully) and filled my counter.

Word spread quickly. Soon my boss, a rotund Southern gentleman, came huffing and puffing to the counter and said, "Miss Alice, where did you get those dolls?"

"Mr. B," I said, my voice and knees shaking, "they aren't dolls, they're Easter bunnies with their ears chopped off."

He looked at the counter, filled with our new "dolls," and gave me a great big smile.

Needless to say, the repurposed rabbits sold like hotcakes, I was not fired, and a lot of kids in my hometown got some unusual dolls that unforgettable Christmas of 1943.

ALICE CARROLL • BASKING RIDGE, NJ

STAFF SGT. John E. Sharpe (far right, middle row) with soldiers in Germany. Above, his daughter, Barbara, age 2.

GIFTS OF LOVE

A PRESENT FROM DADDY

It was February 1945, and my father, Staff Sgt. John E. Sharpe, was in Germany. I would turn 5 on April 9, and we hadn't seen Dad since I was 3 and my brother, Charles, was 1.

We hadn't received any letters from him in three weeks, and my mother, Mildred, was terribly worried. Every day I waited for the postman on the front steps of our home in Chattanooga, Tennessee. Finally, he brought us a package of letters and gifts.

"Look, Barbara!" my mother said. "There's a letter for you from Daddy. Let's read it."

"Dear Princess," the letter began, "I was so sad to learn that you were so unhappy on Christmas because you thought I would be home with you. I would have been there if I could have, but we can't get any leave to come home to see our families. But I make

you a promise that if I possibly can, I will be there next Christmas. This war is coming to an end, and I can't wait. I want you to know that if I can't be there, Santa Claus will be there for me.

"I have sent you a present for your birthday and one for Charles. Do not open until your birthday, OK? If I am not with you on Christmas, have your mother read this letter to you. Remember that I love you bushels and baskets. Love forever, Daddy."

A few weeks after our birthdays, my father was shot while saving the life of a fellow soldier. My mother was notified that he was missing in action, but it wasn't until the end of the summer that we received a telegram confirming he'd died April 24, 1945.

My aunt came to live with us, but our home was a sad place. My mom, devastated by our dad's death, finally got out of the house and went to work, but it seemed like ages before she became our sweet, smiling mother again.

Then came Christmas Eve 1945.

Charles and I were in our beds when we heard something on the roof that sounded like bells and footsteps. A few minutes later, Mom called both of us to come to the top of the stairs.

"Look!" I yelled. "It's Santa!" There in the front hall stood St. Nick.

"Hi, Barbara and Charles!" Santa said. "Have you been good little children? I know your father couldn't be here with you, so I am here for him. Well, I have to go—there are so many little children for me to see. Merry Christmas! And go back to sleep so I can come to leave you presents later!"

The visit from Santa was our last Christmas present from our father. Later, my mother told me that the package Daddy sent early that year had included a note to our teenage neighbor, asking the young man to do him this favor if he didn't get home.

Because Charles was so young when our father died, he had very little memory of him, and I mostly knew Daddy from photographs and stories shared by my mother and other relatives and friends. He was a well-loved and respected man.

BARBARA SHARPE MARTIN
POWDER SPRINGS, GA

THE MIRACLE OF THE RING

In February 1946, after 2 years of submarine service in the Pacific, I was on leave from the U.S. Navy. While I was home, my mother gave me a ring with a rubylike gemstone. During that leave, she passed away. From that day on, the ring became a real link between my mother and me. I took it off only to clean it.

I was discharged from the Navy in 1947. By 1952, I was working as a firefighter for the city of Dayton, Ohio, and for a landscaping company on my days off.

About the middle of July, while driving home from the landscaping job, I glanced down at my right hand and discovered the red stone in my ring was missing.

I panicked. I started to cry and became so overwhelmed with grief that I had to pull over and park the car. At home, my wife tried to console me by saying, "Put the ring away for now. When we save up enough money, we can take it to a jeweler and have the stone replaced."

Later that year, the owner of the landscape company called and asked if I would come in after Thanksgiving to help set up a shipment of Christmas trees for display.

When I arrived, the trees, tied in bundles of four, had to be unloaded in an area where we typically load up our tools on the trucks to go out on the day's work. I took one bundle from the pile, placed it on the ground and started to cut the twine.

As I cut the last piece of twine at the top of the trees, my knife hit the ground and I thought I felt a piece of gravel. Suddenly I saw a flash of red. I parted the stubble of dry grass and there was the lost stone from my ring! It was a miracle.

We took the ring to a jeweler to have the stone remounted. It's been reworked one more time since then, so the stone will not get lost again.

That wonderful gift from my mother holds the fondest of memories, and I will forever cherish it.

RICHARD J. PHILLIPS SR. • ENGLEWOOD, OH

RICHARD PHILLIPS still wears the ring his mother gave him.

UNEXPECTED REUNIONS

BEST PRESENT. Dean Harding McGarity with her husband, Steven, at his mother's house in 1945. See her story at right.

THE CHRISTMAS PROMISE

On Christmas Eve in 1944, the war in the Pacific was raging. I said goodbye to my husband, Steven Turner, at the train station in Los Angeles, California. We had been married only a year. A chief petty officer and photographer and in the Naval Air Forces, he was off to San Diego for his next assignment aboard an aircraft carrier.

Amid a horde of people—men in uniform and women crying, hugging and calling goodbyes—I stood, holding back tears and panic as he stepped on the train. He turned at the last minute and shouted above the din, "I'll be home for Christmas, I promise."

"Promise," I mouthed. Steven smiled his devoted smile and nodded.

I went home to Vicksburg, Mississippi, and took up my job at the local welfare office. I lived with three other "war brides" in an old antebellum home presided over by a kind elderly lady.

I waited for his letters—letters that often told of distant islands under a different sun, of Japanese suicide plans that missed their mark, of loneliness and longing.

The "brides" and I felt blessed to have one another, sharing our fears and loneliness, offering comforting words when letters didn't arrive, keeping one another company at the movies or on long walks, keeping a radio vigil when news came of battles in far-off places.

Then one glorious day, the war was over—Japan had surrendered! We laughed and cried and ran down the street, shrieking with joy and even hugging strangers. Then we settled down to wait.

Time passed, and the letters came telling me about Japan and the POW camps they flew over, dropping food and supplies. This was good work, I knew, but I longed for my husband to come home.

The days rolled on. Before I knew it, it was December and then Christmas Eve. I stayed late at work, packing food baskets that would be distributed the next day to some of our clients. I returned to an empty house. The "brides" had gone to their homes for Christmas. I would go south the next day to have dinner with my family.

My landlady and I ate a solitary meal together. She shared her memories of Christmases gone by, but all I could think of was the previous Christmas Eve and saying farewell to Steven. Finally, sadly, I climbed the stairs and went to my room. Later, listening to the radio, I heard Bing Crosby crooning "I'll Be Home for Christmas." It made me weep.

It was almost midnight and still I could not sleep. I moved over to the window seat and looked out onto the street. The icy moon seemed to light up the world.

A taxi turned the corner, came slowly down the street and stopped in front of the house. Curious, I leaned against the window. A tall figure emerged from the back. The driver came around the car and shook his hand. In an instant, I knew it was Steven.

Forgetting my feet were bare, I ran down the stairs, out the front door and down the sidewalk, not even feeling the cold concrete beneath my toes. He turned, opened his arms and picked me up. I was laughing and crying. He asked the cabbie, "Will you please bring my bag into the house? This lady has begun to go barefoot in freezing weather."

Then he whispered to me, "I promised, remember?"

And the year we'd spent apart suddenly vanished like a melting snowflake.

DEAN HARDING MCGARITY • DUNCANVILLE, TX

BROTHERS IN ARMS

A second consecutive Christmas in war-torn Europe was destined to be a dismal reality for this lonely soldier barely out of his teens.

Seated at my well-traveled typewriter in the chaplain's makeshift office—an abandoned house in a small village in Luxembourg—I helped the chaplain by typing letters of condolence to families back home. This stirred up memories of family and prayerful thoughts of my three brothers serving in World War II.

We were aware of 3,000 U.S. troops arriving that afternoon to replace early casualties in the Battle of the Bulge, and it was not unusual for a soldier to seek out the chaplain before departing for foxhole duty. Thus, one weary soldier who burst into the room received no more than a casual greeting.

When the soldier called my name, a quick turn around startled me into disbelief. The GI was my brother Follis! In one happy moment, loneliness turned to joy. What are the odds of us being reunited on the Western Front after not having seen each other for three years?

Follis was granted a special reprieve to spend a day with me, and when the Special Services Company noted his many skills and qualifications, it requested his assignment. This enabled us to share the next 10 months together and made some bad times more tolerable.

Christmas of 1944, burdened by the grim realities of war, was surely a time of wishes. I'm grateful mine was granted.

FESTUS PAUL • DECATUR, IL

1940s

"I'm going your way, Soldier!"

In uniform or in "civvies" their goal is the same — and Greyhound speeds the war job of both

It takes many men in uniform *behind the lines* to keep one soldier *fighting at the front*. It takes a whole nation working at top-speed to keep all that vast force fed, clothed, equipped, financially supported.

This whole giant effort requires transportation on a scale never approached before in history—*especially is this true of the movement of manpower by motor bus, to the tune of three-quarters of a billion passengers in a single year!*

The man with the kit of precision tools must get to a bomber plant served only by motor bus—the non-com from the air corps is checking a new plane at the same plant. The girl who works at the arsenal—the WAAC rejoining her unit—the selectee headed for an induction center—the mother visiting her son in camp—the businessman, the farmer, the nurse, the teacher—all have essential places in wartime America.

Greyhound is proud to carry millions like these—determined to keep its fleet of buses fully in service for America, in spite of severe wartime restrictions.

All of you who have taken occasional discomfort like good soldiers—responding willingly to suggestions for making the most patriotic use of wartime travel. *Thank you—please keep it up!* And when Victory is won, look to Greyhound for brand-new standards of highway travel comfort, convenience, scenic enjoyment. They're coming, sure as sunrise!

TO KEEP WARTIME TRANSPORTATION SERVING AT TOP EFFICIENCY: *It is best to plan necessary trips for the less-crowded Spring months—and for midweek days. Whenever possible, avoid travel during the crowded midsummer months, on week-ends, and on holidays.*

GREYHOUND

WARMTH ON THE PIEDMONT

GI gets a bit of Southern comfort at Christmastime. **VERN REIS** • TACOMA, WA

In 1953, I was stationed at Fort Gordon, Georgia, with a group of GIs from my home state of Washington. The soldiers who had the resources to travel back home at Christmastime were given time off. Those of us who couldn't afford to go home were assigned 12-hour shifts of guard duty and furnace watch. Both of those jobs were equally unpleasant and grueling—walking for miles in freezing, pitch-black nighttime conditions and doing the dirty, backbreaking job of firing coal furnaces.

Being away from home for the holidays was one of the loneliest feelings I had ever experienced, especially since Christmas had a deep religious and cultural significance for my Germanic family.

Three days prior to Christmas, I received a package of my mother's traditional baked goods and a surprise letter: an invitation to spend Christmas with our family friend, Elsie Wilson. She lived in the Piedmont region's rolling hills in central North Carolina.

During the Korean War, my family was one of many around Tacoma that hosted servicemen sent to Fort Lewis. Elsie, a widow who'd lost her husband and children in a car accident, stayed with us for a short time while visiting her soldier brother.

Fortunately, I was able to obtain a three-day leave for a Christmas visit with Elsie and her new family. A long journey on a crowded bus ended in front of a rural country store in Wilsonville, near Charlotte, where three elderly men in bib overalls were sitting on wooden boxes.

When I asked for directions to the George Wilson residence, one of the gentlemen stood up with his thumbs in the straps of his overalls and proceeded to slowly point out the residences of every Wilson in the village. He ended by pointing to a home directly across the street as he informed me that the Wilsons I was looking for lived "over yonder."

A SOLDIER'S WELCOME. Vern Reis, pictured in his Army uniform, was out of his element as a lonely GI from the West Coast stationed in Georgia in the early 1950s. But he discovered that the Christmas spirit can be found most anywhere.

When I arrived at Elsie's home, I was welcomed with a warmth and hospitality that I have never forgotten. All the things I had ever heard about Southern hospitality became a reality, and although some of the holiday customs were somewhat different from those in the Northwest, the true spirit of Christmas was the same.

MY MOST MEMORABLE CHRISTMAS

While flying combat missions out of England in 1944, my bombardier and I were invited to have Christmas dinner with an English family at their home in Northampton.

I suggested we bring a gift to thank them for their hospitality, but didn't know what to take. We had just begun to get a Sunkist navel orange with our breakfast each morning, and I thought the fruit might be appreciated. So we both decided to save our orange each day to give the family. A few of our friends gave us some of their oranges, too, so we had about 15 by the time we went to dinner.

We arrive and handed the bag to the lady of the house. She was overjoyed with the unexpected gift! She fetched a decorative bowl, put all but two or three of the oranges inside and placed it on the mantel. She and her husband then peeled the oranges set aside, saving the peelings, and then carefully cleaned each section. The lady then asked her husband to round up the neighborhood children and bring them over to the house.

When the children arrived, the husband and wife gave each child a section or two to eat and then let them smell and touch the peelings. My army buddy and I thought this was a little strange and asked them why they did that.

They explained to us that they felt compelled to share the oranges with the neighborhood children because most of them had never even seen an orange, let alone tasted one!

We knew then that we had made the right choice for our present, and I certainly felt happy that I was fortunate enough to have witnessed an outstanding example of the true spirit of the season. I will never forget the Christmas of 1944.

ROBERT J. FISHER • MISSION, TX

ORANGES: RDAEB

PREHOLIDAY CELEBRATION

Every Dec. 22, Mom cooked a huge feast to celebrate several significant events. On that date in 1918, my father had come home after serving in World War I. A year later, in 1919, my brother, Bernard, was born.

Years passed, and on Dec. 22, 1945, Bernard came home from the Army after serving in World War II. This date was our preholiday gala every year.

VERA NAIMAN • STATEN ISLAND, NY

SERGEANT PLAYS SANTA

Just 10 days after we married, in April 1960, my husband, Don, received a draft notice. After basic training, he was assigned to Fort Bliss in Texas. I joined him there in late November.

Our first Christmas dinner was unlike anything either of us had ever experienced growing up in southern Indiana. Don had invited three of his Army buddies to join us for dinner only a few days before. I wondered what magic might turn our meager grocery budget into a nice holiday dinner for five.

The next day, Don was assigned kitchen duty. The mess sergeant, full of the Christmas spirit, hinted that since many soldiers were on leave, there was extra food that should probably be used up—whole chickens, butter and potatoes. He said it would be a shame to waste it.

On Christmas day, in our tiny apartment kitchen with only two chairs, all five of us enjoyed a bountiful holiday dinner. We had fried chicken, mashed potatoes and gravy, green beans and hot biscuits with butter. For dessert, I made a Jell-O mold in the only container available—a metal cake pan.

It may not have been the usual holiday fare, but nothing could have tasted better for five youngsters spending Christmas a long way from home.

LAURA RAMSEY • WASHINGTON, IN

MILITARY MERRIMENT

HOLIDAY INN. "That's me next to my pup tent in the winter of 1952-'53 on a weeklong bivouac at Fort Knox, Kentucky, over the Christmas holiday," says Richard Grunewald of Mosinee, Wisconsin. "A few days before Christmas, we had a rare mail call. The lucky recipients opened boxes of assorted baked goods. You can imagine the ribbing I took when I opened a box from my girlfriend that contained an electric razor."

SERVICE FAMILY. "Seated at the piano at Christmastime during World War II is my grandmother Mary Mairose of Cincinnati, Ohio," says Diane Mairose Feeney of Greenwood, Indiana. "On the piano are the portraits of the children who were serving our country (from left), Norbert, Richard, Angela, Jack, Leo and Frank. The other children, not pictured, were my father, Arthur, who ran the family grocery store, and Rosella, a nurse and nun. My grandfather Frank Mairose's picture is the inset at the bottom."

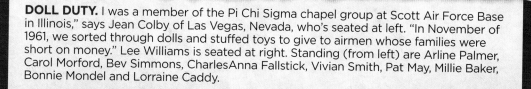

DOLL DUTY. I was a member of the Pi Chi Sigma chapel group at Scott Air Force Base in Illinois," says Jean Colby of Las Vegas, Nevada, who's seated at left. "In November of 1961, we sorted through dolls and stuffed toys to give to airmen whose families were short on money." Lee Williams is seated at right. Standing (from left) are Arline Palmer, Carol Morford, Bev Simmons, CharlesAnna Fallstick, Vivian Smith, Pat May, Millie Baker, Bonnie Mondel and Lorraine Caddy.

I'LL BE SEEIN' YOU SOON !

LEAVE CAMP ON. *Dec. 11th, 5:30*

ARRIVE *Dec. 12th A.M.*

WILL BE ABLE TO STAY .... *2* .... DAYS

BE SURE YOU HAVE THE OL' FEATHER BED READY !

© WIPCO 1942

HAPPY FOR A HOMECOMING. "My father, Ralph J. Lee, of Bloomington, Illinois, sent this 1942 postcard to my mother, Mary Gleason Lee, while he was serving in the military at Fort Leonard Wood, Missouri," writes Deborah Rowe of Charlotte, North Carolina.

Songs for Soldiers

PEACE FOR A SHORT TIME

As prisoners of war at Stalag Luft IV, near Kiefheide, West Prussia, Germany, we were allowed out of our barracks for a short time on Christmas Eve 1944.

The harsh setting of barbed wire and armed sentry posts was softened by huge starlike snowflakes lazily drifting down.

All of a sudden, over the soft shuffle of feet, rising gently at first, then swelling as everyone began to join in, came the sweet sound of 7,500 male voices singing "White Christmas." It was a most unforgettable moment.

We sang Christmas carols for the entire hour, raising our spirits tremendously.

The following day, another surprise came in the way of an American Red Cross food parcel with turkey and plum pudding for everyone. Most of us ended the day by giving thanks to the Lord for His bounty.
LOWELL SLAYTON • BUFFALO, WY

SOUNDS OF FREEDOM

During World War II, my dad, Robert Howie, of Chetek, Wisconsin, was part of the 5th Army under Gen. Mark Clark.

After the 5th Army liberated a town in France a day before Christmas Eve in 1944, the mayor asked the commanding officer if he had anyone in his unit who could fix the town's pipe organ, which had been shot up by the Germans. The organ took up one whole end of a church.

The commanding officer assigned the task to my dad and Army buddy Bernard Pinnow of Bruce, Wisconsin.

They set to work fixing the instrument. They determined they could use shell casings from one of the big guns as a collar fit over the holes in the pipes. They welded them to the pipes to seal off the air.

The mayor then had the church organist tune the organ. The organist started playing at noon on Christmas Eve and continued playing until late that night. The beautiful music from the church could be heard clear into the French countryside.

People began gathering from everywhere to celebrate the holiday with the soldiers with church services, food and song. My dad said he couldn't believe how good he felt to be a soldier that night.
TAM HOWIE • LUCK, WI

JAZZED-UP CHRISTMAS. "My first Christmas away from home was made more festive by this dance band of fellow Air Force cadets and the pretty local girls who came to enjoy the music at Elon University in North Carolina," says Arthur Lovell of Essex, Connecticut. "If you closed your eyes, you would think it was Glenn Miller's band. Shortly after this, we all left for flight training and then points unknown."

Christmas Cheer

During Christmas week of 1943, when most of our fellow Marines stationed at Quantico, Virginia, were on leave for the holidays, a few of us were left to "guard the barracks." We were spending a quiet Sunday when the photo lab boys showed up with their canine mascot to bring cheer to us lonely girls and take a picture to show our folks back home. That's me on the right, closest to the window. I suspect the boys were kind of lonely, too.

LUCILLE GREENBERG • WEST PALM BEACH, FL

CHAPTER 6

A TIME FOR TOYS

We all had that one Christmas toy we wished for with all our hearts—or that came as a total surprise. From dolls and board games to bikes, model trains and other treasures, there is nothing that makes Christmas morning more magical than to be a babe in toyland.

"When I was 6 years old, my heart's desire was to have a doll with hair that could be combed and styled," writes Ellen Mast of Ottawa, Kansas. "My parents were doing their best to keep our farm going, but with a baby on the way, dolls were not in their budget.

"On Christmas Eve, we went shopping together for groceries at the local supermarket. Out of the blue, the store manager walked up to my parents and handed them a large, unopened gift box. He said the store had sponsored a drawing, and this prize had never been claimed.

"On Christmas morning, my parents handed me this mystery box. I opened it...and inside, wearing a dress of blue satin and white lace, was a 3-foot-tall princess doll! Best of all, she had a mass of blond hair, crowned with a beautiful tiara.

"Over the years, this doll has endured many hours of play—and countless different hairstyles. But she remains a treasured reminder of a little girl's dream come true."

Often, recollections of an adored toy remain alive and vivid, holding a special place in our childhood memories. Unwrap more stories of tots and the toys that brought them hours of unbridled fun on the pages that follow.

A SURPRISE IN THE ATTIC

A dollhouse hidden in her grandparents' attic yielded hours of fun—and a Christmas surprise!

MARIAN SPEERLESS • SULLIVAN, WI

As a 6-year-old living on a small farm outside East Troy, Wisconsin, in 1947, I had a few chores to do, like gathering kindling and feeding the chickens. But most of the time I played, read and used my imagination.

Because we were poor, I wore my cousins' hand-me-down clothes and played with their old unwanted toys, mainly dolls. One doll had no fingers on one hand and the other only shut one eye when I laid her down, but I loved them both dearly.

Once a month, we would pile into my father's '37 Ford and drive to the big city of Milwaukee for needed items we couldn't get in East Troy.

On those trips, we would also visit my maternal grandparents. While the adults visited, I would venture into the attic of their bungalow to play dress-up with old clothes.

One day, I noticed something covered with a quilt on a table. When I lifted the edge of the quilt for a peek, I found a magnificent dollhouse! It even had real carpeting in the living room.

I played with the dollhouse on that day and every visit afterward for three months.

Then, in November, I went into the attic and saw the dollhouse was gone. It had disappeared as magically as it had appeared.

Soon it was December and then Christmas Day. I asked my father if I could go with him to Milwaukee to pick up my grandparents. He said, "No, you'd better stay and help your mom and sister."

That afternoon, when it was time to open our few (but much anticipated) presents, my mother said there was a special gift for me from Grandpa. My father carried in a large item covered by a familiar quilt and set it on the kitchen table.

I lifted up the quilt and immediately began playing with the beautiful dollhouse. There was stunned silence behind me.

When I turned, I saw bewilderment on my parents' faces, and my grandfather looked very sad.

In exasperation, my sister asked me, "Well, aren't you even surprised?"

"No," I said quietly. "I've been playing with this in Grandma and Grandpa's attic most of the summer, but then it disappeared at Thanksgiving time."

Now there was laughter, and my grandpa said, "I put it back in the garage to finish it for you."

For me! Just for me, and it was brand-new!

Crawling up into my grandfather's lap, I gave him a huge hug and said, "Oh, Grandpa, thank you so much. It is the most wonderful dollhouse."

"You're very welcome, Marian," he said lovingly, holding me tightly in his arms. "And merry Christmas."

SOUTHERN CHARM. "This Southern-style dollhouse (right) appeared on Christmas morning in 1942, when we lived in Summit, New Jersey," says Paula Evans Hauser Tompkins from Warrington, Pennsylavia. "That's me, looking very pleased about my gift. My mother, Beryl Hauser, and my aunt Margaret Coulborn made the the furniture and curtains for the dollhouse."

STITCHING UP A CHRISTMAS MEMORY

It was a few days before Christmas in 1954. I was 4 years old and fell off a chair, splitting open my chin. My mother called our pediatrician, Dr. Matthews, who came rushing to our house. "She'll need to have stitches," he told her.

My mother told me that if I was brave, I could open up the special Christmas present Gran and Grandpa had sent from their home in Toronto.

Dr. Matthews put three stitches in my chin right there on the kitchen table, and I didn't shed a single tear. When he was done I got to open the present, an Eaton's Beauty doll—the exact one I had asked Santa for at Eaton's department store (left). I was thrilled!

I don't remember any pain associated with my tabletop surgery, but I certainly remember that beautiful brunette doll.
SANDRA WALTON • MAPLE RIDGE, BC

Writer and illustrator Johnny Gruelle patented the soft, huggable Raggedy Ann doll in 1915, but brother Raggedy Andy didn't come along until a few years later.

ALL DOLLED UP

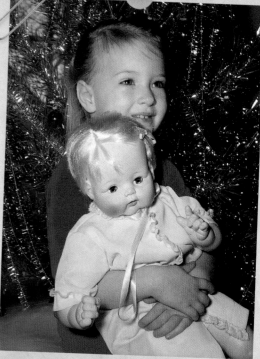

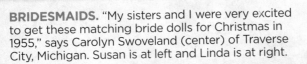

BRIDESMAIDS. "My sisters and I were very excited to get these matching bride dolls for Christmas in 1955," says Carolyn Swoveland (center) of Traverse City, Michigan. Susan is at left and Linda is at right.

DOLLFACE. "This is a picture of my cousin Darla Faye Lampton Barrow sitting in front of my family's aluminum Christmas tree in 1962," writes Jim Crawford of Newburgh, Indiana. "She is holding her new Christmas doll at my parents' home in Newburgh."

TABLE'S FULL. "As an only child, I'd get lots of toys each year, but no new doll—only new homemade doll clothes," writes Ruth Higgins of Avon Lake, Ohio, seen at age 2 in 1924. "The chalkboard unfolded into a desk."

PATTI PLAYPAL, a popular doll of the 1950s, was nearly as tall as her new friend Doreen Dragonetti, sharing a 1959 Christmas moment with her dad, George, in Wantagh on New York's Long Island. Her mom, Elsie, of Wayne, Maine, shared this adorable picture.

DINNER FOR DOLLS. "This photo is from Christmas 1951, when our daughter Martha was 3 and her sister Susan was 7," writes John E. Thompson, Seminole, Florida. "It was taken at our farm home in West Branch, Iowa. They are now Susan Kinsey of Springdale, Arkansas, and Martha Resotko of Steuben, Maine."

HAPPY HALF-DOZEN. "The Christmas of 1962 was a happy and fun time for our family," Holly Schroeder remembers. "The three oldest of our children, Jeff, Cheryl and Randy (back row), all got new bikes. The younger ones, Ricky, Scott and Tim, got their share, too, and everyone was pleased."

PEDAL PUSHERS

SELFLESS "SANTA"

I longed for a bicycle during the Depression, but my parents told me it was out of the question that Christmas, since Daddy had lost his business.

On Christmas morning, my parents and brother and I crept downstairs to see if Santa had come. When Daddy turned on the lights, I gasped as my eyes fell on the shining, sparkling two-wheeler that I had dreamed of.

A year or two later, when I had come to the conclusion that my parents had been Santa all along, I learned the true story of my wonderful two-wheeler.

My brother Jack had been earning his own money on a magazine route. He had earned enough points to get himself a sturdy wagon for his deliveries.

My precious brother had seen just the kind of bike I wanted in a catalog. He was only about 10 years old, but with complete unselfishness, he turned in all of his hard-earned bonus coupons for my two-wheeler.

Tears well in my eyes when I think of that gift and my brother's act of love for me.
EILEEN ADAIR • BEAVERTON, OR

BICYCLE BUILT WITH LOVE

In the mid-1950s, my parents could not afford the bicycle I wanted, so I went to see Santa Claus at the Arnold Constable store in New Rochelle, New York. He asked if I had been good, and I told him I wanted a blue and white bike with two wheels and a basket.

When the big day arrived, there, to my surprise was a shiny blue and white two-wheeled bicycle!

After 35 years of my retelling the story, my

mom finally told me that my dad had labored over the restoration of that used bike, which he had intended to use himself to get to work. To this day, I can't thank him enough.

ANDREW BISSINGER • FALL RIVER, MA

BIG WHEELER

I remember when I got my first bike. I'd wanted one for so long—especially one of those new balloon-tire jobs. But it was the Depression, and my folks couldn't afford a new bike.

Not wanting to disappoint me, Dad found a used one. Unfortunately, it was about one step above an old-fashioned 1900 model with the large front wheel.

Unknown to me, he repainted it, and I found the bike next to the tree on Christmas morning. I was devastated, but I somehow managed to show a little bit of enthusiasm for the gift.

When spring came, I was almost ashamed to ride it. But all that changed when the guys saw I had the fastest bike on the street. Suddenly, everyone wanted to ride *my* bike, and the value of that gift increased to at least a million dollars.

CLYDE TROSSEN • SOUTH BEND, IN

SANTA LIVED NEXT DOOR. "We spent Christmas 1960 with our grandparents, and these bicycles (above) were not in our apartment when we left," says Dianne Roberts of Richmond, Kentucky. "But when we got home—well, this picture of my brother Terrell and me tells the happy ending. It was 30 years before we found out that the 'Santa' who put the bikes there was our neighbor, Paul Fuller."

What a Christmas present!
...and only $7⁵⁰
complete with all playing equipment

The Brunswick Junior Playmate Pocket Billiard Table is the best juvenile Christmas investment you can make. Children and grown-ups alike, all love games. In Billiards you have one that affords healthful recreation...mental and muscular coordination...endless, tireless amusement...all-year, all-weather play.

It gives parents added control over the children by making the home more attractive...thus keeping them within the family circle during their most formative and impressionable years. Every member of the family will enjoy the game...*and Billiards is easy to learn.*

The Junior Playmate is strong...sturdily constructed...of quality materials. Children won't drop it in a week like a cheap toy but will play on it for years....

Five other sizes, $13.50, $18.50, $37.50, $60.00 and $100.00 (prices slightly higher west of Denver and in Canada).

For sale at leading department, hardware and sporting goods stores, everywhere. You'll identify it immediately by its rich mahogany finish and the gold and black Brunswick trademark on the rail, which is shown below.

Brunswick
JUNIOR PLAYMATE

A complete line of Junior Playmates and other home tables are shown in "The Home Magnet" catalog, which we will gladly send on request. The more expensive tables can be bought on a deferred payment plan from Brunswick Branches located in all principal cities.

THE BRUNSWICK-BALKE-COLLENDER CO., 627 South Wabash Avenue, Chicago, Illinois. In Canada, Toronto

▲
1929

The pause that refreshes

Drink **Coca-Cola**

◄ **1953**

TO SEE YOU SMILE

POSTMAN REALLY DELIVERED

Like most little girls, I loved to play with my dolls, especially my baby doll "Lovey."

Since Christmas 1926 was not far off, I spent hours looking at the Sears, Roebuck & Co. Christmas catalog. I wrote a letter to Santa, asking for a buggy for Lovey. And each day, I asked my mother if she thought Santa got my letter. She assured me that he had.

Mother had ordered the buggy from Sears and was secretly making doll clothes for Lovey.

Concerned about the buggy's arrival, she started watching for Sam, the mail carrier, the week before Christmas. On the last mail delivery day before Christmas, Sam checked carefully, but the package still had not come from Sears.

Mother sat down with me and told me that Santa was so busy that he needed the whole week after Christmas to distribute all of his gifts. She told me she wasn't sure when he'd visit us.

When Sam returned to the post office after his delivery that day, he discovered the package had just arrived.

He felt so sorry and told his wife, Bessie, how disappointed I'd be. Bessie looked Sam in the eye and said, "I think we must make a visit to the Johnsons."

And that's what they did, driving far into the country to deliver the precious package.

When I woke up on Christmas morning to see if Santa had come, there was the buggy I wanted so much, with Lovey inside, dressed in new clothes!

I was one happy little girl (above), and my parents were so grateful that Sam and Bessie made a special effort just to make sure I could have a delightful Christmas.

REBECCA CROUCH • HIGGINSVILLE, MO

THE YEAR SANTA CAME BACK

In 1932, I was a lonely 6-year-old living on a farm near Rockdale, Texas. Mother had died four years earlier, and Daddy (shown below) did the best he could to take care of me.

Just before Christmas, my best friend, Betty Margaret, and I visited Santa Claus. We both had a special wish. I told Santa my name and whispered my secret wish in his ear. He assured me it would be granted if I'd been a good girl.

Betty Margaret was next. She whispered in his ear and was about to leave when she turned to him and said, "Please, Santa— would you make them both blue?"

The next day was Christmas Eve. Daddy cut a cedar tree, and we decorated it with chains made from bright construction paper. It was beautiful.

That night, I went to bed early. I closed my eyes tight, but it took a long time to drift off.

In the morning, I was up at first light to see what Santa had left. Daddy, who slept in the living room, wasn't awake yet.

I found hard candies, an apple, an orange, a new pair of shoes and a kaleidoscope. But where was my other present?

Maybe Santa had left it on the porch. I opened the door and looked outside, but there was no blue bicycle anywhere.

I started sobbing as if my heart would break. I'd been a good girl—I knew I had!

Daddy woke up with a start, thinking something had scared me. He took me in his arms, and I calmed down enough to tell him about the secret wish I'd told Santa's.

"Daddy, you know I've been a good girl all year, and Santa *promised*!" Tears ran down my cheeks.

Poor Daddy had a pensive look on his face as he fixed our oatmeal. I felt ashamed that I'd made him so sad.

A little while later, I saw Daddy open his old hump-backed trunk and get out the ledger where he kept seed money for spring planting. Then he put it back, closed the lid on the trunk and stared into the fireplace. I wondered what was making him so sad.

It was almost lunchtime when Daddy saddled "Old Bill" and we rode the 5 miles to Uncle Alex and Aunt Nettie's. Since we lived alone, a turkey dinner with all the trimmings was a real treat for Daddy and me.

I spent the night at Aunt Nettie's. It was turning out to be a good Christmas, but I wanted to see Betty. I wondered if Santa had left a blue bicycle under her tree.

Late the next day, Daddy came to take me home. It was dark when we reached the house, and I was surprised to see a lamp shining in the window and smoke coming from the chimney.

Daddy pulled Old Bill up to the porch and lifted me from the saddle. "You run on in and get warm while I put up Old Bill," he said.

I opened the door, and the first thing I laid eyes on was a beautiful blue bicycle standing by the Christmas tree.

"Daddy! Daddy!" I yelled. "He came back! Santa came back and brought my blue bicycle. I knew he didn't forget his promise!"

Daddy came through the door and picked me up in his arms. Without saying a word, he hugged me real close. And although he was smiling, I saw a tear trickling down his cheek.

LUELLA TUMA MULLINS • HUNTINGTON, TX

SACRIFICE GRANTED A WISH

My doll, Bonnie Lee (above), has aged gracefully since 1947. I love her iridescent blue eyes, which turn from side to side. Her curly hair has faded to a lighter brown with time. If I tip her forward, she still cries.

I woke up early on Christmas Eve when I was 11, and there was Bonnie Lee, sitting on a small chair. I couldn't believe she was mine.

Bonnie Lee cost Mom a week's salary, but she knew how important the doll was to me. I'd cut her picture out of the Montgomery Ward catalog and kept it under my pillow. It was quite a sacrifice for Mom, because Daddy died in July of that year and she must have had many more things to spend her small income on.

I still appreciate Mom's sacrifice. When I look at Bonnie Lee, I remember vividly the moment when I first saw her by the tree.

ELVIRA CASTILLO • CHICAGO, IL

THE NEED FOR SPEED

UNLICENSED DRIVERS. "Grandpa and Grandma got as much enjoyment in giving these Champion pedal cars to their first grandchildren in 1953 as our son, Jimmy, and his cousin, Patsy Porter, had driving them inside and outside their grandparents' house in Detroit, Michigan," writes Robert Snyder of Redlands, California. "I remember the cars were light blue, and that we had to scurry out of the way of these unlicensed drivers."

BIKE BRIGADE. "There were smiles all around during Christmas in 1962," says Tom Dukowitz of St. Cloud, Minnesota. "Of the 10 kids in my family, the seven youngest, including me, received bikes that year."

DESKTOP DASH. "This is me in 1962 or '63 with my car dashboard toy, which had to be one of my favorite Christmas gifts ever," says Glenn Sweigart of Fort Myers, Florida. "The blinkers, wipers and a few other things worked, and it made an engine noise. I must have driven my mom crazy. The DeLuxe Reading Corp. of Elizabeth, New Jersey, manufactured the battery-powered Playmobil Dashboard, which also had a working horn and the horizontal speedometer used in cars of that era."

IT HAD MAGNE-TRACTION! "That's me holding one of our Christmas gifts in 1956," says Ross Adams of Stow, Ohio. "The Fairbanks-Morse Train Master locomotive was one of the most desirable Lionel offerings that year. It had lights, a horn, a dual motor, Magne-Traction and forward, neutral and reverse controls. The best part is that we still have it after all these years. My brother, Don, pictured on the right, has helped preserve our trains, which still make regular trips around the tree at Christmastime on the same layout our dad, Don Sr., built for us in '55. The trains are now valuable collectibles, and the memories are priceless."

All Aboard!

MEMORABLE MODEL RAILROAD

I grew up in a tiny one-bedroom apartment on the west side of Detroit. Even though it was only Mom, Dad and me, it was rather crowded. However, being an only child did have its benefits. Although my parents were on a tight budget, they always made sure to page through my Firestone holiday book and give me the one special thing that I had circled for Christmas.

In 1948, my holiday treat was an American Flyer electric train. I placed the small round track on our living room floor to watch the train trundle along it. Eventually, my dad constructed a plywood table for it, which we concealed in a large closet where it wouldn't be in the way.

Finances improved for my family by the mid-1950s and we moved to a larger three-bedroom place with a basement, which meant more toy train room. My dad and I added a second American Flyer, and that's when a couple of toy trains became his full-time hobby.

In addition to the two trains, he created a small town with houses, stores, a hospital and a school (pictured below). A large board mounted on the wall contained switches that controlled lights in all the structures. People, cars and animals populated the wonderful miniature town. I loved all of it, of course, but it was truly my dad's baby.

I still display a portion of that set every year at Christmas. Even though it's just a small circular track with the first American Flyer, it brings back such great memories of my dad. The hours he spent creating this amazing gift were only a portion of the many things he gave me over his lifetime.

GLENN FODEN • COLDWATER, MI

DAD'S TRAIN CITY

Do you think your electric train setup was something? Take a look at this magnificent layout (above)! It was crafted by my father, George Reynolds, in 1929 at our home in Milton, Pennsylvania.

My father started building the Christmas train layout in our dining room the day after Easter. I was 2 years old at the time. This photo, taken by our neighbor Mr. Ishiguro, shows me sitting next to my older brother, Andrew, in awe of the elaborate spectacle before us.

Dad was an electrician and also built the Ferris wheel seen on the left. It was run by a small electric motor. The two Lionel trains were standard gauge.

My brother and I got to enjoy the setup for 10 years. The trains were later given to neighbors after World War II. By that time Andrew and I had moved out of state to raise our own families. How I wish I had those trains today!

JAMES REYNOLDS • MENOMONEE FALLS, WI

LOCOMOTIVE RETURNS HOME

On Christmas Day 1933, when I was only a month old, my oldest brother, who was 7, received a Lionel train set with a black and green locomotive. Three years later, my other brother got a Lionel Blue Comet locomotive and tender.

By the time I was old enough to get a train, World War II was in full force and such items were not available. Still, I spent many happy hours playing with my brothers' trains, which were set up only when we were out of school for the Christmas holidays. They went back in their boxes after New Year's Day.

As time passed, marriage, work and family forced aside my interest in trains. But then our oldest daughter married a young man who happened to be interested in trains and had a collection.

This rekindled my interest in our old trains. My cousin had operated his family's feed, hardware and toy store after his father's death, so I called to ask if he could help me find a locomotive like the one we had.

He said he had ours! Someone in the family had taken it to the store years earlier for a new set of drive wheels. My cousin couldn't find any replacement wheels for it, so he put the the piece on the shelf in the shop at his home.

I rushed over to get the locomotive. When I got it back home, I told my wife that if it was really the one we had as kids, it would have a pointed red Christmas tree bulb inside the front of the boiler. It did!

I still run the train occasionally, just to keep it limbered up. The rest of the time, it enjoys a place of honor in a glass display case.

SANFORD SMITH • SPARTANBURG, SC

WINDOW SHOPPING
was a treat for all ages.
Francaise Lardy admires
dolls in at a store in
Washington, D.C. Below:
Holiday rooms beckon at
Marshall Field's.

ALL THE
BEAUTIFUL TOYS

The Christmas season in 1937 began shortly after Thanksgiving, when my grandmother took my sister and me to downtown Chicago.

I wriggled on the elevated train's scratchy varnished straw seats, my nose squashed against the window to look down at the city and into people's backyards.

Stepping carefully out of the oily-smelling cars (I was terrified of the live rail), warily watching for pigeons above, we descended the metal stairways. Walking down State Street, oblivious to the gusts of wind blowing off Lake Michigan and freezing our legs, we stopped at each department store window to see fairy-tale illustrations come alive, with only the glass to separate us from Cinderella, Snow White or Santa and his elves.

Our destination was Marshall Field & Co., where my sister and I could ride the escalators all the way up to the ninth floor and back down again, gazing wide-eyed at the decorations on each level. The store in our hometown of Waukesha, Wisconsin, had no such thing.

The most enchanting place in Marshall Field's was its toy department, where all my dreams were on sale. Fluffy, long-haired white cats with brilliant green glass eyes. Fat, cuddly teddy bears begging for a hug. Chemistry sets with rows of mysterious little vials lettered with strange symbols (could I really make an explosion by mixing two colored powders?). Electric trains, lights flashing, whistles sounding, whizzing through tunnels cut into forested hills, past tiny villages and farms.

And the dolls! Dolls in peasant costumes with twirly skirts, high boots, billowing white blouses and tight bodices. Plump baby dolls nestled in cradles. Smiling Sonja Henie dolls with little white skates. Shirley Temple dolls with the blond curls I longed for. Lenci dolls from Italy with real hair and poignant little-girl faces.

And finally, ruling serenely from her throne, the Princess Elizabeth doll, in a white satin dress and red velvet cloak trimmed with realistic-looking ermine tails, and a jeweled tiara atop her curls. The princess had an opulent wardrobe of silk and satin, encrusted with duplicates of the crown jewels.

Everything we did that day was magical for a 7-year-old.

BARBARA THWAITES • STATE COLLEGE, PA

DOLL HEAVEN. "My daughter, Karen, admired a doll in the toy shop window (top) in 1960," says Pauline Crowley of Virginia Beach, Virginia. Karen likely had high hopes of receiving a special Christmas present, as did Helen Gaines Hoge of St. Charles, Illinois, and her sister Jeanne. In the bottom photo, the girls are seen wishing for a Dolly Madison dollhouse in Kline's department store in 1943.

ALL-TIME FAVORITE GIFTS

STOCKINGS WERE FULL

Our family lived in Ponca, City, Oklahoma, during Christmas in 1949. That year my four sisters and I (from left above, Patsy, Janet, me, Joyce and Carole) happily posed in the new bathrobes and slippers our mother made for us from pink and blue flannel.

Our Uncle Elmo made the stockings from bright red oilcloth. He was a career Marine, and we seldom saw him. It's a wonder he didn't misspell more names than just Carole's! But he helped out Santa by filling the stockings with coloring books and small toys. The other special gift from Santa was the metal dollhouse on the left.

MARILEE WEBER CAMBLIN • PORTLAND, OR

A HASTY DELIVERY

The Christmas of 1954 stands out as one of the most magical when I was growing up in Camden, Maine.

I was 6 years old and wrote Santa, asking him to please bring some nice blocks and baby rattles for my new baby sister. I also told him I had been very good and would really like a sled with red runners.

Daddy sent my letter by putting it in the fireplace. Santa's helpers, the elves, were very magical, he said, and could read my letter through the smoke signals that came up through the chimney.

I woke up on Christmas morning and saw that Santa had left blocks for my sister and a beautiful doll for me. He also brought me a wonderful hutch (handmade by my father) for my doll dishes. But where was my sled? I did not want to show my disappointment because of all the other lovely gifts.

During breakfast, our neighbors phoned, telling us they could see a sled stuck in our chimney. I could hardly believe my ears!

I quickly put on my Brewster snowsuit and boots and ran out the front door. Looking up, I could see the sled with red runners. Poor Santa had to leave it there so he could continue delivering toys.

Daddy got out his ladder and proceeded up the slippery rooftop to rescue my sled.

Years later I figured out that "Santa" was Dad. He always created many memorable experiences like this for my sister and me.
SHARON SALLINEN • ROCKPORT, MA

BEAR BROUGHT COMFORT
My husband gave me a stuffed bear (below, left) named Vic (short for Victory), during World War II. It was my first Christmas away from home, and we were visiting his parents. When I could no longer hide my tears on Christmas Eve, I retired, not wanting to ruin the holiday celebration for others. When I felt my husband slip Vic next to me, I hugged him and fell asleep.

Vic continued to give comfort to others over the years. Although I lost my husband after 58 years, Vic still watches over me.
ETHEL KNOPP • OKLAHOMA CITY, OK

OLD WEST SIDEKICKS
Roy Rogers, Hopalong Cassidy and Gene Autry were my heroes in the 1950s. So when Mom asked me what I wanted from Santa, I said a holster and six-shooter.

When Christmas morning came, I got up early, checked under the tree and found nothing. A bit downhearted, I went out to do my chores. I looked under the tree again after breakfast to give Santa one more chance. But still, nothing.

My older brother and I both knew why Santa hadn't come: Our family really couldn't afford gifts.

Suddenly Mom appeared in the doorway and said, "Look what Santa left!" She held a shiny new gun and holster set.

Before I could react, Mom said, "You both have to share it." I didn't know my brother had wished for the same thing. We took turns holding the gun and wearing the holster, but one of us was always left out.

We finally put our heads together and decided one of us would wear the holster, with a corncob or piece of wood stuck in it for a gun, and the other would stick the six-shooter in his belt. Now we were real rootin'-tootin' cowboys. We also learned a rewarding lesson in how to share.
GARY SCHROEDER • GARBER, IA

A BOY'S LIFE
Dry weather was all I needed to try out the shiny bicycle I received for Christmas in 1958. My family lived in a house near the American Legion Country Club outside Mount Union, Pennsylvania.

In the photo below, I appear to be deep in thought as I examine the bike, which was one of my favorite Christmas gifts. Perhaps I was trying to figure out how Santa got the bike down the chimney!

A gasoline-powered Comet Sabre 44 model airplane was another great gift.

Barely showing in the basket behind the bike is the cover of a *Boys' Life* magazine. It sure was a boy's life on this Christmas.
PAUL L. PROUGH JR. • MOUNT UNION, PA

Wishes for Santa

The lead-up to Christmas was exciting, agonizing and ultimately worth it.

MARY LOUISE TOOLE JENNINGS GUTHRIE • AUGUSTA, GA

Christmas has always been a time of joy, magic, loved ones and friends. But as I look back through the years, I'm certain the Christmas of 1927 was the very best.

The week before had dripped by slowly, despite all the hustle and bustle of getting ready for the holiday. My brother and I had paged through the big Sears catalog and picked out what we wanted Santa to bring. Even though we'd been told Santa was having financial difficulties, we were confident the gifts we wanted would be under our tree.

Our older sister, who was a teenager, was not nearly as excited about Santa's visit. She was more concerned with rolling her hair, trying on my visiting aunt's high heels and dresses, and putting on rouge and lipstick.

On Christmas Eve, we filled the wood box, brought in bits of wood and bark to start a fire, and ate our delicious supper of oyster stew with Oysterette crackers and Mama's fried apple tarts. After our baths, we sat by the toasty fireplace as Daddy told us about holidays on the farm during his boyhood.

We were eager to go to bed so Santa would come. But our sleep was restless. Every now and then we would wake up, sure that the noise we'd heard was Santa's sleigh and reindeer outside our windows. Our parents assured us it was only branches scratching against the house in the night.

At 4 a.m., we peeped out from the covers and could see in the dim firelight that Santa had indeed come. The stockings, which had hung limply when we went to bed, were now lumpy with surprises, and we could vaguely make out some mysterious shapes next to the fireplace. Mama and Daddy told us we must wait until 6 to get up. What torture!

When we finally rushed out of bed, there by the fireplace were two big, beautiful scooters exactly like the ones we'd hoped for. They were green with red handles, balloon tires and even brakes—a necessity as we planned to speed down the hill. Santa had brought my brother and me a couple of other small gifts, and our sister was happy to find the presents she had wished for, too.

All three of us took our stockings from the mantel and found candy, nuts, fruit and small toys inside. But the scooters— just what we'd picked out in the Sears catalog—were what truly delighted us.

By this time, our grandparents, several aunts and uncles and other relatives had arrived at our house and a big breakfast was ready at the square dining table.

When we went in the dining room, the Christmas tree—a pine from the nearby woods—was shining in all its glory, with bits of tinsel, pretty decorations and tiny candles clipped to its branches. What a beautiful sight!

After our blessing, we had a homemade country breakfast of hot biscuits, grits, homemade sausages, ham and fresh eggs. The grown-ups exchanged small gifts, and then we hurried out to try our scooters and visit our friends to show them what Santa had brought.

During the next year or so, my brother, sister and I flew up and down the road many times on those scooters. We've given and received many gifts over the years—some much more expensive. But my brother and I will always remember those scooters as our all-time favorite present and that Christmas as the best one of all.

SANTA CLAUS' TOYLAND

Santa Claus' Toyland was on the top floor of Turner's department store in Kokomo, Indiana, in the 1940s. I remember there always being snow on the ground when we'd visit right before Christmas. We'd park three or four blocks west of downtown. Bundled up and trudging through the snow, I could hardly keep from running in anticipation.

The streets were decorated with wreaths and colored lights. The downtown square looked like a winter wonderland. Christmas music swelled around the square as shoppers hurried from one store to another, searching for that big surprise for Christmas.

Turner's was full of shoppers when we arrived. We rode the elevator to the top floor and stepped out into the brilliance of Toyland. The whole floor was decorated with toys and presents of all kinds.

Santa Claus was at the far end of the floor. A line of children waited their turn to sit on his lap and spell out all their wishes for Christmas. Eager parents stood watching as each child took his or her place on Santa's lap, hoping for a clue as to what their child wanted for Christmas.

I remember sitting on Santa's lap. I had memorized the items I wanted and, in my eager childlike voice, quickly went over the list. Then Santa gave me a candy cane and told me he would see what he could do.

MELVIN ARMSTRONG with his baby sister, Sharon, in 1942.

With that, I slid off the jolly old man's lap, and that's when the real fun began—the tour of all the toys! I headed straight for a display with miniature cars and trucks being towed around on a board painted with a roadway and some houses in the background. I watched in amazement as these vehicles circled the display.

We were at war in the early '40s, and rationing was serious. We were not poor, but we sure weren't rich. Toys were at a premium.

I wanted a brand-new car or truck so badly, but the money just wasn't available. I knew in my heart, however, that Santa would come up with something just as wonderful.

As I ventured through Toyland, I realized that the magic of the holiday was just as valuable as any gift, and that notion brought me comfort for years to come.

MELVIN E. ARMSTRONG • GALVESTON, IN

TOTS LOVE TOYS

PINK PUP. "Our bright-eyed baby explores the goodies under the tree on her first Christmas in 1959," write Rita and Ed Clarke from Larchmont, New York. "This is Carol, our first daughter, and she is reaching for her stuffed dog Pinky, which gave her great joy for a number of years."

LOOK WHAT WE GOT! "We Winge children (from left), Diane, Rusty and I, are showing our gifts on Christmas morning, circa 1947, in Uleta, Florida," says Lolly Webster, now of Southern Pines, North Carolina. "The popgun likely belonged to Rusty, though."

HAPPY LI'L PARTNER. "Christmas 1953 was very exciting for my husband, Greg (left), then 5 years old," says Cheryl Kozell of Waterford, Michigan. "Thanks to a good year at work, his parents, Vincent and Elma, were able to give Greg not only this cowboy outfit and mechanical horse, but a metal tractor and fire engine, both of which he still has today."

IT'S A GIRL THING. "This photo is from Christmas Day of 1964 at our house in Dorchester, Massachusetts," says Laura Thomas of Upton. "That's me on the left with my two older sisters, Nancy (middle) and Peggy, showing off our favorite presents received that year. I was a big fan of *The Flintstones* and so excited to receive my Pebbles doll on Christmas morning."

BOYS' TOYS. "My dad, Leonard Johnson, snapped this photo on my second Christmas in 1940 at our home in Springfield, Pennsylvania," says Ron Johnson from Safety Harbor, Florida. "That's me on the far right. With me are my brothers (from left), Bob, Leonard Jr. and Warren. The carbide cannon (foreground) was passed down through the years. I received it when I reached my teens."

DARE TO DREAM

A young boy's ardent hope for the perfect present would either sink or swim.

THOMAS WISE • STILLWATER, MN

My parents must have toiled mightily to make Christmas magical for their four children. Money wasn't plentiful along Ninth Avenue in Hopkins, Minnesota, in the late 1950s and early '60s—and it was even less so in the decrepit dwelling at No. 118.

My father was a grocer and my mother a cake decorator. The family budget didn't allow expensive clothing or trips out to restaurants, let alone distant vacations.

But like many heroic parents of that era, George and Ruth Wise sometimes managed to produce a miracle almost as wondrous as Christmas itself.

Alice Smith Elementary School was built to accommodate the wealthy elite in my hometown, but its district boundaries inadvertently included my family's shabby neighborhood.

Thus, I spent the balance of my days mingling with society's golden children.

On a day-to-day basis, the economic lines that separated my parents from those of my peers were not evident to me or my playmates. I was just one more fifth-grade kid hanging around the playground or scaring up a game of kickball.

But Christmas always arrived for me like an annual cold-water bath when our teacher assigned the inevitable essay: "How I Will Spend My Christmas Vacation."

While my young colleagues busily sketched details of family trips and other upcoming adventures, my most-desired activity was to climb the massive pine tree in our front yard and throw snowballs at passing cars.

I might have remained agreeably ignorant of all the marvelous toys that awaited my lucky classmates if it weren't for the Muntz TV in our living room. Every day, new and wonderful gadgets were displayed on the tiny round black-and-white screen.

But there was one item so special, so extraordinary, that I couldn't resist the urge to dream.

That item was the Remco Frogman, a sleek wonder of plastic technology. He

THE U.S. NAVY COMMANDO

ON LAND
HELMET : WALKIE TALKIE : RIFLE

measured about 2 feet from head to flipper tips and sported twin yellow tanks that concealed a battery-driven propeller that served as his means of locomotion.

His adjustable arms and legs allowed him to perform amazing maneuvers in the family pool. And although there was no such pool at my house, that past summer, I had swum to the big dock at Shady Oak Beach. And after watching *Sea Hunt* on TV, I'd begun to consider myself an accomplished aquanaut.

I'd become obsessed with the toy, even though my parents said they couldn't afford it and suggested I not talk about it.

I resigned myself to another Christmas of underwear and socks. Nevertheless, one day a mysterious package bearing my name materialized under the tree.

The big morning finally arrived and my brother, Chuckie, and I ran about the house, waking the family at 5 a.m. I opened the stuff that was from "Santa" first, wanting to put off the inevitable disappointment as long as possible.

Shortly, there was one package left, the mysterious one. I tried to read my parents' eyes, but they gave away nothing.

Heart in throat, I tore the paper away and revealed—no, it couldn't be—but it was...a Remco Frogman!

Dad installed four D batteries, and I raced to the bathtub and filled it to the top. For the remainder of the day and the rest of my vacation, my marvel raced from one end of the tub to the other and bumped his head. Then I reversed his direction, and he raced to the other end.

I'd remove him from the water, still dripping, and run him around the house, imagining all the adventures we'd share.

The long winter passed into spring and finally summer. I carried my Frogman to Shady Oak Beach. I'd waited a long time for this moment and intended to savor it.

My family stood in silent expectation as I got him ready for launch. In my excitement, I threw the plastic switch that activated the propeller. And to this day, I don't know why I mistakenly did that. I should have first attached the plastic float that tracked the activities of the Frogman in the event he swam beyond my reach.

As I tried to attach the float, the propeller struck my finger. More startled than hurt, I dropped the Frogman into the water and watched with horror as he swam in an unerringly straight course for the cool depths in the center of the lake.

I was inconsolable. The best Christmas present anyone could ever receive had taken the first opportunity to bolt!

As disappointed as I was, I still had an immense amount of gratitude for the joy I experienced when I opened that present. On that Christmas evening of my ninth year, I had gone to bed feeling the warm glow of contentment that my classmates must have known all their fortunate lives.

I believed the world was indeed a magical place where a young boy's dreams could come to pass.

WONDER IN WATER. Being a big fan of the TV show *Sea Hunt*, the author, pictured on the opposite page as a young boy and above with his son, Gregory, dreamed of water exploration with the Remco Frogman.

THE RIFLEMAN. Thomas Torresson Jr. (above in 1928, with his foot on the running board) was supposed to get a BB gun for Christmas, as the blond boy at left did, but lucked out and got a real Winchester rifle.

A SURE-AS-SHOOTIN'
GREAT HOLIDAY

When this 12-year-old became the man of the house in 1928, he took a step up in caliber.
THOMAS TORRESSON JR. • TOMS RIVER, NJ

Christmas 1928 was right around the corner, and like many 12-year-old boys, I had my heart set on a BB gun. Of course, I'd made sure my folks knew all about my wish so there'd be no mistake under the Christmas tree.

But with only two weeks to go until the big day, Dad announced he had to go to Mobile, Alabama, on business. He told Mom it was OK for me to have a BB gun, but she'd have to buy it because he didn't have time.

My dear mother (who admittedly didn't know the difference between a cap pistol and a Colt .45) decided to take me across the river to Macy's in New York and let me select the BB gun I wanted. As we walked through the sporting goods department, my eyes fell on the one gun that was every youngster's impossible dream—a Winchester Model 06.

This was no BB gun, but a real .22-caliber rifle. Oh, what a beauty! Before my guardian angel had time to interfere, I pointed to the Winchester and said, "That one!"

As the clerk was filling out the sales slip, Mom said, "I suppose he should have some BBs also, shouldn't he?"

The clerk had a funny look on his face, but he wasn't about to lose the sale. So he told her that "they" came in boxes of 50. Soon, a carton of .22 shorts was added to the sales slip.

On the way home to New Jersey, I clutched my prize to my chest and felt my conscience gnawing at me. What would Dad say about my deceit? Should I say anything to Mom? But I couldn't do it. I really wanted that 06!

Just before Christmas Eve, Dad sent a telegram saying he couldn't make it home for Christmas. Mom was devastated, and we five kids fell into a state of gloom. For the first time in our young lives, Daddy wouldn't be there on Christmas morning.

I was the oldest son, so Mom designated me "man of the house." After the younger kids went bed, she and I placed the gifts under the tree with tears in our eyes.

All the while, I couldn't help but feel that Dad wasn't coming home because God was punishing me for the sneaky trick I'd pulled on Mom. I was trying to work up the courage to confess my deception when we heard a noise at the side door. It opened—and there was Dad, who had somehow managed to catch the last train after all!

My siblings came running down the stairs, and Dad was overrun with youngsters, a wife hugging him and the former "man of the house" bawling openly. It took some time for Mom and Dad to get us calm and into bed.

On Christmas morning, the rule was no one was allowed in the front room until Dad came down and turned on the tree lights and the gas log in the fireplace. When he let out a hearty "Merry Christmas!," we all rushed in.

As we ran to our piles of presents, I heard Dad ask Mom if she got the BB gun. She smiled and proudly pointed at the 06.

Dad looked astonished, but then a slight smile crossed his face. "Boy," he chuckled at last, "we'll have a great time with this!"

And we did.

A BOOK LOVER'S
CHRISTMAS

From shopping for gifts to putting up the tree, I loved Christmas and all the traditions that came with it.

Every year when Mother put out the wrapped presents, it was torture looking at them, wondering what toys were inside.

About a week before Christmas when I was 12, a blizzard closed my school in the Kingsbridge section of the Bronx.

I came down with a really bad cold after playing in the snow and was confined to bed. My parents worked during the day, so I was left alone.

I had done some snooping in my family's apartment that year and discovered one of my presents was the latest Nancy Drew novel—one of my favorite childhood book series. What better time to read it than sitting in bed with a cold!

After they left for work, I got the book down from its hiding place and enjoyed reading all day, then put it back before they were due home.

That book had been a delightful way to pass time, but I knew I had to act surprised when I unwrapped it on Christmas Day.

I also knew a secret. My father had saved money from every paycheck and bought my mother an expensive wristwatch. He had wrapped it in a small box, then in other bigger boxes to disguise what it really was.

My mother was very curious and kept nagging me to tell her what was inside the box—especially when I told her not to shake it, as there was something in there that could break. I was dying to tell her and finally did, warning her that she'd better act surprised on Christmas morning.

When I opened the Nancy Drew novel, I didn't tell my parents that I snooped, but I was sure my father knew. After Christmas, he kept asking me when I was going to read the book, since I could hardly put a new novel down once I started reading.

I kept answering, "Soon."

Today, when I hear Bing Crosby's "White Christmas"—the recording my father loved to hear—it takes me back to the wonderful Christmases of my youth. I can almost hear my parents' voices as the warmth of those precious memories washes over me.

JOAN HINMAN • SALEM, MO

LIKE FATHER, LIKE DAUGHTER. Joan Hinman and her father, James de Graat (left), shared a mutual love for Christmas. Here they stand on a pile of snow in New York City after a huge snowfall in 1947. The tree (right) at the author's house in '47, adorned with a silver star on top.

The Best Gift Ever

My husband, Preston Reeves, was just 18 months old when he received this Jet-Flow Drive Station Wagon for Christmas in 1952. As you can tell by the look on his face, this pedal car was the most exciting thing he had ever seen.

He was so excited that he could hardly contain himself and had to give his new toy a big hug!

Preston has fond memories of riding his slick new wheels through the red iron ore dust that covered his family's driveway in Birmingham, Alabama.

My in-laws eventually gave away the pedal car, which they'd bought from the Sears Christmas catalog. But Preston was a lucky boy that year. He also received a new tricycle, a big firetruck and a cowboy outfit with guns, holsters, a hat and boots.

The snazzy new pajamas, slippers and robe he's wearing in this photo were gifts that year, too. His favorite toy the next year was a metal service station.

As a child, he loved cars and trucks—real ones included. His father, a police officer, took him for many memorable rides in his patrol car, No. 56.

My husband enjoys working on his own cars as a "shade tree mechanic" in his spare time, and I'm grateful that he passed his love of automobiles on to our son.

GINGER CRICK REEVES • PINSON, AL

CHAPTER 7

FESTIVE FLAVORS

A t the heart of all holiday get-togethers is great-tasting food. And of all the meals you look forward to throughout the year, there is none that stirs up as much joyous anticipation as Christmas. From a glazed turkey slowing simmering in the oven to a parade of cookies and candies that will make even Santa stick around for dinner, the Christmas feast is the pinnacle of all celebrations.

Some turn into affairs that almost transcend even the big day itself. This was certainly the case for Ali Koomen of Mesa, Arizona. "Christmas dinner at my great-grandparents' house in Hinckley, Illinois, started with hors d' oeuvres. After we finished the 'ants on a log' or rumaki, we'd sneak off to play and wait for the magic words—'suppertime!'

"What a feast it would be—turkey and ham, roast beef and chicken. There was always a fantastic array of salads and almost every veggie known to humankind. We had marvelous things like carrots glazed in butter, brown sugar and cinnamon, or an unbelievable sweet potato casserole that tasted like a dessert. My favorite was fresh green beans and onions stir-fried in bacon grease and topped with real bacon pieces. Seconds and thirds were always expected.

"After dinner there were dozens of types of cookies and pieces of homemade candy and rows of varied pies—enough to make a baker blush. There were also cakes of every sort.

"You wouldn't think we'd be able to eat another bite, but we would eat and eat until our belts were loosened and our top (and sometimes second) buttons were undone. Even those wearing elastic waistbands were groaning!"

Savor heartwarming and hilarious memories of favorite foods and enjoy the deliciously festive lineup of recipes on the pages that follow.

TIME TO BAKE
FRUITCAKE!

Baking fruitcakes with Mom kicked off the holiday season.
BARBARA SIMS • MOBILE, AL

Whenever I chop pecans for a fruitcake, I'm immediately taken back to my childhood in the 1940s. I'm 5 years old again, seated on a bench at our dinette table, carefully cutting pecans for Mama's famous fruitcake.

Making Christmas fruitcakes was a special day in our house, and I was eager to help. There were always spoons and bowls to lick... and an occasional candied cherry found its way into my mouth. I might even be too "sick" to go to school on fruitcake day.

The dinette table was covered with all the fruitcake makings. The big white enamel dishpan with the red rim had been scalded and scrubbed. It would be a gigantic mixing bowl.

The makings included 2 pounds each of candied cherries and pineapple—half red and half green. There was also a small amount of orange and lemon peel.

"Not too much orange or lemon peel," Mama warned. "It makes the cake too bitter."

And there was no citron. "Citron makes the cake taste store-bought," Mama said. Early on, I learned that a "store-bought" cake wasn't something to be desired.

Nothing Like Handmade

The sugar was measured and creamed with real butter, and the fruit was dredged in flour before being added to the batter. Only the freshest eggs were used.

Everything was mixed with loving care, and all the fruit and nuts were properly blended throughout the batter. A bottle of Watkins Vanilla Flavoring stood nearby as a reminder to add some at the proper time.

Besides cutting up pecans, I helped mix the ingredients. But when the batter got too stiff for a spoon, Mama mixed it by hand.

An assortment of baking pans stood at the ready on the enamel-topped kitchen table. There were round ones for the big fruitcakes, several smaller loaf pans and one rectangular dish. These were the "fruitcake pans", used only at Christmas.

They required special preparation. Brown paper grocery bags were cut to line the sides and bottom, then waxed paper was cut to cover the brown paper.

After each pan was filled with batter, Mama decorated the tops of the cakes with some of the candied fruit she'd set aside and some of the pecans I'd cut in half.

Waiting for the First Bite

All the cakes went into the oven at the same time, filling the house with its first holiday aroma. I don't know how long they baked, but to a 5-year-old, it seemed like an eternity.

When the cakes were finally the perfect shade of brown, they were carefully removed and arranged on the kitchen table to cool. "Fruitcakes have to be cold before they can be cut," Mama always reminded me.

That meant we couldn't have our first taste until after Daddy came home and we finished supper. It was worth the wait.

During the holidays, everyone bragged on Mama's fruitcake, and I always felt proud. After all, I'd cut the pecans.

Now I make my own fruitcakes. My husband loves them, but I don't think they're as good as Mama's. Those happy days spent baking her classic holiday treats will always live on in my memory.

When it comes to Christmas baking, colorful cookies often take center stage. But the holiday wouldn't be the same without a rich, fruit-and-nut-filled fruitcake. It's an oven-fresh delight that serves up old-fashioned goodness.

HOLIDAY FRUITCAKE
ALLENE SPENCE • DELBARTON, WV

PREP: 20 MIN. • **BAKE:** 2 HOURS + COOLING • **MAKES:** 16 SERVINGS

- 3 cups whole red and green candied cherries
- 3 cups diced candied pineapple
- 1 package (1 pound) shelled walnuts
- 1 package (10 ounces) golden raisins
- 1 cup shortening
- 1 cup sugar
- 5 eggs
- 4 tablespoons vanilla extract
- 3 cups all-purpose flour
- 3 teaspoons baking powder
- 1 teaspoon salt

1. Preheat oven to 300°. In a large bowl, combine cherries, pineapple, walnuts and raisins; set aside.
2. In another large bowl, cream shortening and sugar until light and fluffy. Beat in eggs and vanilla. Combine flour, baking powder and salt; add to creamed mixture and mix well. Pour over fruit mixture and stir to coat.
3. Transfer to a greased and floured 10-in. tube pan. Bake 2 hours or until a toothpick inserted in center comes out clean. Cool 10 minutes before removing from pan to a wire rack to cool completely.
4. Wrap tightly and store in a cool place. Slice with a serrated knife; bring to room temperature before serving.

NO NEED TO WRAP IT
Just before Christmas in the late 1940s, I excitedly read an ad for Dromedary Dixie Mix, a delicious fruitcake mix that, according to the ad, could be made in two minutes. As further enticement, the mix came with a free baking tin and lid (below).

As a school-aged cook, I thought the fruitcake would be a perfect Christmas gift for Grandma Waggett, who loved sweets. So, I made the fruitcake and proudly gave it to Grandma in its baking tin, embellished with the Dromedary logo.

Grandma, shown in the photo (above) with my little cousin Pat and me, enjoyed the fruitcake. She even kept the tin for many years.

SANDRA WAGGETT MILLER
LEXINGTON, KY

BOOTLEG BAKERS

Oleo smuggling was a crime, but Ma and Martha risked it for the sake of Christmas cookies.

HELENE BURNETT • BREMOND, TX

I'll never forget Christmas 1956, when I was 6 years old—not for the presents or decorations, but for the cookies. Holiday baking was always a major undertaking at our house, starting in early November. Each year, the list of recipients grew, and so did our shopping list.

That year, I overheard Ma talking to my oldest sister, Martha, in a hushed voice. I managed to catch a few words—"the price of butter," "saving money" and "Illinois." I knew better than to pry into anyone's private conversations, but my curiosity burned.

RISKY BUSINESS. Like the Wisconsin women pictured here, Helene's mother and sister turned to margarine smuggling.

What I didn't know was that butter was expensive and oleomargarine was not—but back then, and for many years after that, Wisconsin law banned the sale of colored margarine. If you were caught buying it in a neighboring state, you would be fined and your precious oleo confiscated.

The next Saturday morning, Ma, Martha and I climbed into our behemoth Pontiac four-door and pointed its silvery hood ornament south.

As Highway 41 rolled on, my mom and sister chatted about holiday plans. Cows and cornfields gave way to hogs and more cornfields as we crossed the Illinois border.

Soon we made a sweeping turn into the parking lot of a gray clapboard house-turned-store. "Park back here," Ma told Martha. "People won't be able to see our license plates."

Was there something wrong with being from Wisconsin? What were we doing here? Clutching their purses, Ma and Martha headed inside the store, leaving me in the car for a few minutes.

When they came out, a man followed behind them, pushing a dolly loaded with cardboard boxes. I read part of a word before they disappeared behind the car: "ole." The man stowed the boxes in the trunk and slammed the lid with a solid *whump*.

Ma and Martha settled back into the car, and Martha turned north out of the lot. Things were very quiet in the front seat. There was no chatting as we passed corn and hogs, no talking as we passed corn and cows.

Then we passed a black and white police car parked behind a roadside billboard, and Ma almost jumped out of her seat. "Do you think he knows?" she asked Martha in a high, scratchy voice.

"He won't pull us over as long as he doesn't suspect anything," Martha said. "Just be calm."

I could hardly sit still. Were we going to jail? What was ole, and why were we in trouble with the police?

"MAKING CHRISTMAS COOKIES was fun! Like the kids pictured above, I had a blast decorating gingerbread men just out of the oven. They came to life when I placed raisins for eyes, orange peels for mouths and Red Hots for buttons," says Mary Kasting of Indianapolis, Indiana.

Ten minutes later Martha was pulling into our driveway. She and Ma laughed with giddy relief. Dad came outside and Ma shouted to him, "We did it! We did it!" He only grumbled and carried the ole boxes into the house.

Anxious to finally see what this was all about, I clambered onto a kitchen chair, watching as Ma placed a paper-wrapped rectangle on the table. It turned out ole was oleomargarine. We had just hauled an entire illegal trunkful of margarine into America's Dairyland! Ma and Martha were smugglers! Only 6 years old, and I was a smuggler, too!

The next day, the smell of vanilla and other wonderful things filled the air as we set to baking. I've eaten my share of Christmas cookies since then, but none nearly as memorable as that exciting bootleg bakery of '56.

"My good friend Terri Moyer cherishes this 1944 photo of her grandmother (above) making Christmas cookies," says Carol Norwood, Myerstown, Pennsylvania. "Terri's lucky enough to have the original rolling pin and bowl she used."

BAKING BLISS

Kindle warm memories of Christmases past with the heavenly aroma of irresistible fresh-baked favorites. Here you'll find an appealing assortment of golden goodies that will rise to the occasion!

CELEBRATION CRANBERRY CAKE

JERI CLAYTON • SANDY, UT

PREP: 25 MIN. • **BAKE:** 40 MIN. + COOLING • **MAKES:** 9 SERVINGS

- 3 tablespoons butter, softened
- 1 cup sugar
- 1 cup evaporated milk
- 2 cups all-purpose flour
- 3 teaspoons baking powder
- 1 teaspoon salt
- 2 cups fresh or frozen cranberries, halved

BUTTER CREAM SAUCE:
- ½ cup butter, cubed
- 1 cup sugar
- 1 cup heavy whipping cream
- 1 teaspoon vanilla extract

1. In a large bowl, cream butter and sugar until light and fluffy; beat in milk. Combine the flour, baking powder and salt; gradually add to creamed mixture. Stir in cranberries.

2. Pour into a greased 9-in. square baking pan. Bake at 350° for 40-45 minutes or until a toothpick inserted near the center comes out clean. Cool on a wire rack.

3. For sauce, melt butter in a saucepan. Stir in the sugar and cream; bring to a boil, stirring often. Boil for 8-10 minutes or until slightly thickened. Remove from the heat; stir in vanilla. Serve warm with cake.

COFFEE-GLAZED DOUGHNUTS

PAT SIEBENALER
RANDOM LAKE, WI

PREP: 25 MIN. + RISING
COOK: 5 MIN./BATCH
MAKES: ABOUT 4 DOZEN

- 2 packages (¼ ounce each) active dry yeast
- ¼ cup warm water (110° to 115°)
- 2 cups warm 2% milk (110° to 115°)
- ½ cup butter, softened
- 1 cup hot mashed potatoes (without added milk and butter)
- 3 eggs
- ½ teaspoon lemon extract, optional
- 1 cup sugar
- 1½ teaspoons salt
- ½ teaspoon ground cinnamon
- 9¼ to 9¾ cups all-purpose flour

COFFEE GLAZE:
- 6 to 8 tablespoons cold 2% milk
- 1 tablespoon instant coffee granules
- 2 teaspoons vanilla extract
- ¾ cup butter, softened
- 6 cups confectioners' sugar
- ½ teaspoon ground cinnamon

Dash salt
Oil for deep-fat frying

1. In a large bowl, dissolve yeast in warm water. Add the milk, butter, potatoes, eggs and extract if desired. Add the sugar, salt, cinnamon and 3 cups flour. Beat until smooth. Stir in enough remaining flour to form a soft dough. Cover and let rise in a warm place until doubled, about 1 hour.

2. Stir down dough. On a well-floured surface, roll out to ½-in. thickness. Cut with a floured 2½-in. doughnut cutter. Place cut-out dough on greased baking sheets; cover and let rise for 45 minutes.

3. Meanwhile, to make the glaze, combine 6 tablespoons milk, coffee and vanilla; stir to dissolve coffee. In a large bowl, beat the butter, sugar, cinnamon and salt. Gradually add the milk mixture; beat until smooth, adding additional milk to make a smooth dipping consistency.

4. In an electric skillet or deep-fat fryer, heat the oil to 375°. Fry the doughnuts, a few at a time, about 1½ minutes per side or until golden. Transfer to paper towels to drain. Dip tops in glaze while still warm.

CHRISTMAS BANANA BREAD
PHYLLIS SCHMALZ • KANSAS CITY, KS

PREP: 20 MIN. • **BAKE:** 70 MIN. + COOLING • **MAKES:** 1 LOAF (16 SLICES)

- ½ cup butter, softened
- 1 cup sugar
- 2 eggs
- 2 cups all-purpose flour
- 1 teaspoon baking soda
- ¼ teaspoon salt
- 1¼ cups mashed ripe bananas (about 3 medium)
- ½ cup chopped walnuts
- ½ cup semisweet chocolate chips
- ½ cup chopped maraschino cherries

1. In a large bowl, cream butter and sugar until light and fluffy. Add eggs, one at a time, beating well after each addition. Combine the flour, baking soda and salt; gradually add to creamed mixture. Beat in bananas just until combined. Stir in the walnuts, chocolate chips and cherries.

2. Pour into a greased 9x5-in. loaf pan. Bake at 350° for 70-80 minutes or until a toothpick inserted near the center comes out clean. Cool for 10 minutes before removing from pan to a wire rack.

MERRY CHRISTMAS SCONES
JOAN PECSEK • CHESAPEAKE, VA

PREP: 25 MIN. • **BAKE:** 15 MIN. • **MAKES:** 1 DOZEN

- 2 cups all-purpose flour
- 3 teaspoons baking powder
- ½ teaspoon salt
- 2 tablespoons cold butter
- 1 cup eggnog
- 1 cup chopped pecans
- ½ cup red candied cherries, quartered
- ½ cup green candied cherries, quartered

GLAZE:
- ½ cup confectioners' sugar
- 1 teaspoon rum extract
- 4 to 5 teaspoons heavy whipping cream

1. In a large bowl, combine the flour, baking powder and salt; cut in butter until mixture resembles coarse crumbs. Stir in eggnog just until moistened. Stir in pecans and candied cherries.

2. Turn onto a floured surface; knead 10 times. Transfer dough to a greased baking sheet. Pat into a 9-in. circle. Cut into 12 wedges, but do not separate.

3. Bake at 425° for 12-14 minutes or until golden brown. Combine glaze ingredients; drizzle over scones. Serve warm.

OK, MOM, WHERE'D YOU STASH THE COOKIES?

Each year after Thanksgiving, I would get busy baking cookies and making candy for Christmas, something I did on a daily basis.

Each day, I gave a few treats to my children, Nancy and John, and my husband, Tom, but that didn't seem to satisfy them. By the time the week of Christmas rolled around, there were no treats left to serve guests and family, and I didn't have time to spend hours in the kitchen making more.

One year, I decided to package the treats and hide them in the freezer out in the garage, where I was certain they would be safe. Wrong!

After dinner one night just before Christmas, I went to the freezer to get some goodies to serve, only to find every container was empty. When I confronted my family, I was met with sly grins. They thought they had put a good one over on me.

But the next year, I pulled one over on them.

For weeks, I did my usual baking and stashing. When my children came home from school, the first thing they asked was where I hid the cookies and candy. They said they knew I had been baking because they could smell the wonderful aroma wafting all through the house. They searched for the goodies, without success.

A few days before Christmas, I started serving the treats after supper, and only on Christmas Day did I reveal my hiding place. I told my son that every night, he had been sleeping not 10 feet away from it: a large locked suitcase on his closet shelf. The look on his face was priceless.

Of course, that meant the end of this particular secret place, but at least family and guests were assured daily goodies that Christmas season.

My children are grown and my husband has since passed away, so there's no longer a need to hide treats. But I wouldn't trade those memories for anything.

CAROLEE STRAUGHAN • REDDING, CA

SWEET TREATS FOR SANTA

Santa will say "ho, ho, ho!" when he sees cookies and other treats set out for him on a platter. From nostalgic cookie-jar classics to sweet Christmas novelties, these yuletide goodies are guaranteed to please!

CRISP LEMON COOKIES

DARLENE DIXON • HANOVER, MN

PREP: 30 MIN. • **BAKE:** 15 MIN./BATCH + COOLING
MAKES: ABOUT 4½ DOZEN

- 1⅓ cups butter, softened
- 2 cups confectioners' sugar
- 2 tablespoons lemon juice
- 2 teaspoons grated lemon peel
- ½ teaspoon vanilla extract
- 3 cups all-purpose flour
- ¼ cup sugar
- ¾ cup vanilla or white chips, melted

1. In a large bowl, cream the butter and confectioners' sugar until light and fluffy. Beat in the lemon juice, peel and vanilla. Gradually add flour and mix well.

2. Shape dough into 1-in. balls. Place 2 in. apart on ungreased baking sheets. Coat the bottom of a glass with cooking spray; dip in sugar. Flatten cookies with glass, redipping in sugar as needed.

3. Bake at 325° for 11-13 minutes or until edges are lightly browned. Remove to wire racks to cool. Drizzle with melted vanilla chips.

FILLED CHOCOLATE SPRITZ

MARILYN BLANKSCHIEN • CLINTONVILLE, WI

PREP: 15 MIN. + CHILLING • **BAKE:** 10 MIN./BATCH + COOLING
MAKES: ABOUT 2 DOZEN

- ¾ cup semisweet chocolate chips
- ¼ cup butter, cubed
- ½ cup packed brown sugar
- 2 eggs, lightly beaten
- 1 teaspoon vanilla extract
- 1½ cups all-purpose flour
- ⅛ teaspoon baking soda

PEPPERMINT FILLING:

- ¼ cup butter, softened
- ¾ cup confectioners' sugar
- 1 tablespoon milk
- ½ teaspoon peppermint extract
- 3 to 4 drops green food coloring

GLAZE:

- ⅔ cup milk chocolate chips
- 1 teaspoon shortening

1. In a microwave-safe bowl, melt chocolate chips; stir until smooth. Stir in butter, brown sugar, eggs and vanilla. Add flour and baking soda and mix well. Cover and refrigerate for 30 minutes or until easy to handle.

2. Using a cookie press fitted with the disk of your choice, press dough 2 in. apart onto ungreased baking sheets. Bake at 375° for 6-8 minutes or until set. Remove to wire racks to cool.

3. In a small bowl, combine filling ingredients; stir until smooth. Spread on the bottoms of half of the cookies; top with the remaining cookies.

4. In a microwave, melt milk chocolate chips and shortening; stir until smooth. Drizzle over cookies. Let stand until set.

CHERRY CORDIALS

DOROTHY BAYARD • HUBERTUS, WI

PREP: 30 MIN. + FREEZING • **MAKES:** ABOUT 2 DOZEN

- 1 jar (10 ounces) maraschino cherries with stems, drained
- ½ cup brandy
- 1 cup (6 ounces) semisweet chocolate chips

1. Place cherries in a small bowl; add brandy. Cover and freeze for at least 3 hours.

2. Place chocolate chips in a small heavy saucepan. Cook over low heat until chips begin to melt. Remove from the heat; stir. Return to the heat; cook just until melted. Immediately remove chocolate from the heat; stir until smooth.

3. Pat cherries dry. Holding onto the stems, dip cherries into chocolate; allow excess to drip off. Place on a waxed paper-lined pan. Refrigerate for 10 minutes or until firm. Store in an airtight container in the refrigerator.

CHOCOLATE-COATED PRETZELS

VIRGINIA CHRONIC • ROBINSON, IL

PREP: 15 MIN. + STANDING • **MAKES:** 5-6 DOZEN

- 1 to 1¼ pounds white and/or milk chocolate candy coating, coarsely chopped
- 1 package (8 ounces) miniature pretzels

Nonpareils, colored jimmies and colored sugar, optional

In a microwave, melt half of candy coating at a time; stir until smooth. Dip pretzels in candy coating; allow excess to drip off. Place on waxed paper; let stand until almost set. Garnish as desired; let stand until set.

VANILLA BUTTER CUTOUTS

COLLEEN SICKMAN • CHARLES CITY, IA

PREP: 30 MIN. + CHILLING • **BAKE:** 10 MIN./BATCH + COOLING
MAKES: 3½ DOZEN

- 1½ cups butter, softened
- 1½ cups sugar
- 2 eggs
- 1 tablespoon vanilla extract
- 4 cups all-purpose flour
- 1 teaspoon baking soda
- 1 teaspoon cream of tartar
- 1 teaspoon salt

1. In a large bowl, cream butter and sugar until light and fluffy. Add eggs, one at a time, beating well after each addition. Beat in vanilla. Combine the flour, baking soda, cream of tartar and salt; gradually add to the creamed mixture. Cover and refrigerate for 30 minutes or until easy to handle.

2. On a lightly floured surface, roll out dough to ¼-in. thickness. Cut with lightly floured 2½-in. cookie cutters. Place 2 in. apart on ungreased baking sheets.

3. Bake at 350° for 8-10 minutes or until edges are lightly browned. Cool for 1 minute before removing cookies to wire racks to cool completely. Decorate as desired.

LINZER COOKIES
JANE PEARCY • VERONA, WI

PREP: 30 MIN. + CHILLING • **BAKE:** 10 MIN./BATCH + COOLING
MAKES: 3 DOZEN

- 1¼ cups butter, softened
- 1 cup sugar
- 2 eggs
- 3 cups all-purpose flour
- 1 tablespoon baking cocoa
- ½ teaspoon salt
- ¼ teaspoon ground cinnamon
- ¼ teaspoon ground nutmeg
- ⅛ teaspoon ground cloves
- 2 cups ground almonds
- 6 tablespoons seedless raspberry jam
- 3 tablespoons confectioners' sugar

1. In a large bowl, cream butter and sugar until light and fluffy. Add eggs, one at a time, beating well after each addition. Combine flour, cocoa, salt and spices; gradually add to creamed mixture and mix well. Stir in almonds. Refrigerate for 1 hour or until easy to handle.
2. Preheat oven to 350°. On a lightly floured surface, roll out dough to ⅛-in. thickness. Cut with a floured 2½-in. round cookie cutter. From the center of half the cookies, cut out a 1½-in. shape.
3. Place on ungreased baking sheets. Bake for 10-12 minutes or until edges are golden brown. Remove to wire racks to cool.
4. Spread bottom of each solid cookie with ½ teaspoon jam. Sprinkle cutout cookies with confectioners' sugar; carefully place over jam.

FUDGY PINWHEEL COOKIES
MAUREEN DEVLIN • CHANDLER, AZ

PREP: 25 MIN. + CHILLING • **BAKE:** 10 MIN./BATCH
MAKES: ABOUT 2½ DOZEN.

- ½ cup butter, softened
- ½ cup packed brown sugar
- 1 egg yolk
- ½ teaspoon vanilla extract
- 1 cup all-purpose flour
- ½ teaspoon salt
- ¼ teaspoon baking powder

FILLING:
- 1 cup (6 ounces) semisweet chocolate chips
- 1 tablespoon shortening
- 1 cup finely chopped walnuts
- ⅓ cup sweetened condensed milk
- 1 teaspoon vanilla extract

1. In a large bowl, cream butter and brown sugar until light and fluffy. Beat in egg yolk and vanilla. Combine the flour, salt and baking powder; gradually add to creamed mixture and mix well.
2. Roll out dough into a 12x10-in. rectangle between two sheets of waxed paper; transfer to a baking sheet. Refrigerate for 30 minutes.
3. In a small microwave-safe bowl, melt the chocolate chips and shortening. Stir in the walnuts, milk and vanilla. Remove waxed paper from dough; spread with filling. Tightly roll up jelly-roll style, starting with a long side. Wrap in plastic wrap; refrigerate for 2 hours or until firm.
4. Unwrap and cut into ¼-in. slices. Place 2 in. apart on lightly greased baking sheets. Bake at 375° for 8-10 minutes or until set. Remove to wire racks. Store in an airtight container.

PECAN HORNS

DOLORES GRUENEWALD • GROVE, OK

PREP: 25 MIN. + CHILLING • **BAKE:** 25 MIN./BATCH • **MAKES:** 4 DOZEN

- 2 cups all-purpose flour
- 4½ teaspoons sugar
- ½ teaspoon salt
- 1 cup cold butter, cubed
- 1 egg plus 1 egg yolk
- 1 teaspoon vanilla extract

FILLING/TOPPING:
- 1½ cups ground pecans, divided
- ½ cup sugar, divided
- ¼ teaspoon grated lemon peel
- ¼ cup milk
- 1 egg white, beaten

1. In a large bowl, combine the flour, sugar and salt. Cut in butter until mixture resembles coarse crumbs. Combine the egg, yolk and vanilla; add to flour mixture. Shape dough into a ball. Chill dough for 1 hour or until easy to handle.

2. Meanwhile, for filling, combine 1¼ cups pecans, ¼ cup sugar, peel and milk; set aside. Divide dough into four portions; shape each into 12 balls. Flatten each ball into a 2½-in. circle; top each with a scant teaspoon of filling. Fold dough over filling; seal edges. Curve ends to form crescents.

3. Place crescents on ungreased baking sheets. Combine remaining pecans and sugar. Brush egg white over tops; sprinkle with pecan mixture. Bake at 350° for 17-20 minutes or until lightly browned. Remove to wire racks to cool completely.

APPLE CRISP CRESCENTS

BETTY LAWTON • PENNINGTON, NJ

PREP: 30 MIN. + CHILLING • **BAKE:** 20 MIN./BATCH • **MAKES:** 3 DOZEN

- 2 cups all-purpose flour
- ⅛ teaspoon salt
- 1 cup cold butter
- 1 egg, separated
- ⅔ cup sour cream
- ½ teaspoon vanilla extract
- 1 cup finely chopped peeled tart apple
- ⅓ cup finely chopped walnuts
- ¼ cup raisins, chopped
- ⅔ cup sugar
- 1 teaspoon ground cinnamon

1. In a large bowl, combine flour and salt; cut in butter until mixture resembles coarse crumbs. In a small bowl, whisk the egg yolk, sour cream and vanilla; add to the crumb mixture and mix well. Cover and refrigerate for 4 hours or overnight.

2. Divide the dough into thirds. On a lightly floured surface, roll each portion into a 10-in. circle. Combine the apple, walnuts, raisins, sugar and cinnamon; sprinkle ½ cup over each circle. Cut each circle into 12 wedges.

3. Roll up each wedge from the wide end and place point side down 1 in. apart on greased baking sheets. Curve ends to form crescents. Whisk the egg white until foamy; brush over the crescents.

4. Bake at 350° for 18-20 minutes or until lightly browned. Remove to wire racks to cool. Store in an airtight container.

RECIPE PHOTOS: RDAEB

ORANGE CRISPIES

RUTH GLADSTONE
BRUNSWICK, MD

PREP: 15 MIN. • **BAKE:** 10 MIN./BATCH
MAKES: 3½ DOZEN

- 1 cup shortening
- 1 cup sugar
- 1 egg
- 1½ teaspoons orange extract
- ½ teaspoon salt
- 1½ cups all-purpose flour
- Sugar or orange-colored sugar

1. In a small bowl, cream shortening and sugar until light and fluffy. Beat in the egg, extract and salt. Add flour; mix well. Drop rounded tablespoonfuls of dough 2 in. apart onto ungreased baking sheets.

2. Bake at 375° for 10 minutes or until edges begin to brown. Cool for 1-2 minutes; remove cookies from pans to wire racks. Sprinkle warm cookies with sugar.

CHOCOLATE CARAMELS

SUE GRONHOLZ
BEAVER DAM, WI

PREP: 5 MIN. • **COOK:** 1 HOUR 40 MIN. + COOLING • **MAKES:** 1¼ POUNDS

- 1 teaspoon butter, softened
- 1 cup sugar
- ¾ cup light corn syrup
- 2 ounces unsweetened chocolate, chopped
- 1½ cups heavy whipping cream, divided

1. Line a 9x5-in. loaf pan with foil and grease the foil with butter; set aside.

2. In a large heavy saucepan, bring the sugar, corn syrup and chocolate to a boil over medium heat; stir until smooth. Add ½ cup of heavy whipping cream; cook, stirring constantly, until a candy thermometer reads 234° (soft-ball stage). Add another ½ cup cream; return mixture to 234° (soft-ball stage). Add the remaining cream; cook to 248° (firm-ball stage).

3. Immediately pour into prepared pan (do not scrape saucepan). Let stand until firm, about 5 hours or overnight. Using foil, lift candy out of pan. Discard foil; cut candy into 1-in. squares using a buttered knife. Wrap individually in waxed paper; twist ends.

NOTE: Test your candy thermometer by bringing water to a boil; the thermometer should read 212°. Adjust temperature up or down based on your test.

GUMDROP COOKIES

CAROLYN STROMBERG • WEVER, IA

PREP: 20 MIN. • **BAKE:** 15 MIN. + COOLING • **MAKES:** 3½ DOZEN

- ¾ cup shortening
- 1 cup sugar, divided
- ½ teaspoon almond extract
- 1¾ cups all-purpose flour
- ½ teaspoon baking soda
- ¼ teaspoon salt
- 1 cup chopped fruit-flavored or spiced gumdrops
- 2 egg whites

1. In a large bowl, cream shortening and ¾ cup sugar until light and fluffy. Beat in extract. Combine the flour, baking soda and salt; gradually add to creamed mixture and mix well. Stir in gumdrops.

2. In a small bowl, beat egg whites until soft peaks form. Gradually add remaining sugar, beating until stiff peaks form. Fold into the dough.

3. Drop by heaping teaspoonfuls 2 in. apart onto ungreased baking sheets. Bake at 350° for 12-15 minutes or until golden brown. Cool for 1 minute before removing from pans to wire racks to cool completely.

Festa Italiana

MANGIA! MANGIA!

The dining room table at my grandparents' home in Utica, New York, was the place to be on Christmas Eve. Everyone was welcome—family, friends, acquaintances. If you sat around the old maple table that creaked with the abundance of the traditional seven-fish meal, you were family.

Grandma and Grandpa were the behind-the-scenes producers, the main actors and the presenters. On the table was a plastic cover protecting Grandma's handmade crocheted tablecloth. The plates, glasses and cutlery sparkled while our stomachs growled and our mouths watered in anticipation.

As a child, in the late 1950s and early '60s, I felt left out of the animated conversation because everyone spoke Italian.

"Mangia! Mangia!" Grandma and Grandpa urged—"Eat! Eat!" in Italian—and happily passed the platter of spaghetti tossed with bread crumbs and anchovies. Like an expert, I picked out the spaghetti coated only with the sauteed, seasoned bread crumbs, leaving the anchovies to swim with each other. My father would spear those from my plate if I happened to get any.

Homemade wine was poured and served with a sliced tangerine, as was their custom. My grandparents always loaded up a shelf in the refrigerator with soda pop for us kids.

Laughter and Italian floated about the dining room. So did the platter of bright green broccoli, dressed in olive oil with lemon wedges surrounding it. Next came the salad and the Italian celery that tasted like anise, along with Italian bread, fresh and crunchy, served with Italian cheeses.

Shrimp, anchovies, eel, smelt, perch, haddock and calamari were served, some with a dusting of bread crumbs or tomatoes, oils and garlic, all in Grandma's seasonings.

THE AIELLO FAMILY. John and Dolores Aiello pose with their children, author Mary Gautner and her brother, Jack, before leaving their home in Cleveland, Ohio, for New York. At left, a teenage Mary visits with grandparents Luigi and Antonetta Aiello in 1968.

Grandma never followed a recipe or a cookbook. Her seasoning technique and measurements were in her wrist and on her fingertips. If you asked her how she prepared her dishes, she would tell you in Italian. With a smile, my father would translate, "Oh, you add a little bit of this and a little bit of that." Whatever the pinch of this or that was, Grandma was the master chef of her own five-star restaurant.

Hours would go by. When the main courses were exhausted and the platters emptied, the table was cleared and the final course was served—homemade cannoli with espresso. For the cannoli, Grandpa made wooden rods and Grandma made the dough and wrapped it around the rods to dry. Then the filling was added. What a sweet, delicious end to a sumptuous meal! How we ever found room for dessert, I'll never know, but who could resist homemade cannoli?

As guests were still savoring the dessert, Grandpa carried a bowl of apples, pears and oranges to the table. He would tilt the bowl, and the fruit rolled down the table, with each person selecting what he or she wanted as it came rolling by. Then we passed around a basket of nuts with nutcrackers and picks.

Seven to eight hours passed from the beginning to the end of the Christmas Eve feast, but I never left my chair. When I was too tired to keep my eyes open, I cradled my head in my arms on the table and fell asleep.

This particular Christmas Eve ritual has died out in my family. It has been more than 40 years since that I last sat at the maple table. But I can still remember the sights and sounds, and the aroma of each dish. Every Christmas Eve, when I serve my own meal, I can still hear Grandma and Grandpa saying, "Mangia! Mangia!"

MARY GAUNTNER • PITTSBURGH, PA

CHRISTMAS STRUFFOLI

My Aunt Ange was an excellent cook and a fantastic baker of all Italian delicacies.

At Christmastime, my favorite treat of hers was struffoli—tiny pieces of batter rolled into little balls, quickly deep-fried, then drained and drenched in honey. She shaped these delicate pieces into a cone to represent a Christmas tree and then sprinkled each one with multicolored jimmies.

I still smack my lips when I recall this wonderful treat.

KATHERINE COSTA SENGER • FAYETTEVILLE, GA

▲
1952

OLD WORLD RITUAL. Oplatki (like the one shown at right) are thin, unleavened, tasteless wafers shared in private homes on Christmas Eve. Similar to communion wafers, each oplatek is embossed with Christmas scenes, usually of the Nativity or the Christ Child. "This is my family (above) on Christmas Eve in 1946," says Stephen Lukasik. "I am the younger son, on the left."

CULINARY TRADITIONS

EXCHANGE OF GOOD WISHES

Before the main meal on Christmas Eve, our family partook in one of the most ancient and beloved Polish traditions. This was to say grace and then pass the sacred oplatki (shown above right), a thin wafer embossed with traditional Christian designs.

Dad broke off a piece and then passed his wafer to Mom, wishing her peace, love, health and happiness for the coming year. Mom did the same thing, followed by each member of the family, oldest to youngest, breaking off a piece and sending the wish.

STEPHEN LUKASIK • DUPONT, PA

HOG WILD FOR PIG EARS

My mother, of German-Hungarian heritage, made a Christmas confection called pig ears, using leaf lard from hogs. It was a flaky pastry dough cut into strips and wrapped around a cone-shaped metal form, which had a long handle attached.

To make pig ears, the cone was dipped into hot lard and deep-fried until it was crisp and golden brown. When it cooled, it was sprinkled with powdered sugar flavored with cinnamon. This was our family's signature Christmas treat.

KARL WEINSCHROTT • CENTRALIA, WA

SWEDISH SMORGASBORD

This is Christmas dinner (at right) at our house in 1961. Every year I made it my goal to set an elegant table for this special feast. In deference to my husband George's heritage, Swedish side dishes always accompanied our holiday meal.

My mother-in-law patiently taught me how to make the traditional rye bread, Swedish coffee cake, cardamom cookies, beet salad and a rice pudding with lingonberries for dessert. A cold glass of root beer for the kids and a cup of coffee for the adults topped off the meal.

MARION THYREN • CALDWELL, NJ

COAL COOKERY. Even well into her 80s, Mary Ann Constanzer's Aunt Clara used her old coal stove to make traditional Polish family recipes (see Mary Ann's story at right).

FESTIVE CUSTOMS

When the first star appears in the heavens on Christmas Eve, our family celebration begins. In the Polish tradition, Christmas Eve is more festive than Christmas Day itself. The menu for the special feast consists of seven courses.

Except for the fat and meat of animals, the food served contains all that nature provides for us. I especially remember boiled eggs with homemade horseradish and beets, poppy seed and nut breads, pierogi (little dumplings filled with potato, sauerkraut, mushrooms, onions or cheese) and a variety of soups and fish dishes.

An extra place is set at the table for a stranger who would otherwise be alone that night. A Polish proverb states, "A guest in the home is God in the home."

The meal always begins with the breaking and sharing of oplatek, the sacred wafer. As we break the wafer and share it with each other, we also share wishes of peace, love, good health and happiness.

MARY ANN CONSTANZER
SOUTH CHINA, ME

WHAT A BIRD! Joyce Thompson, son Steve and her parents, Joe and Gert Foltz, took a moment to savor their beautiful turkey before digging in, as Joyce's husband, Bruce, captured the occasion. "It was 1953, and we were living in Eagle Lake, west of Racine, Wisconsin, at the time," remembers Bruce, now of Waukesha.

DOWN-HOME HOLIDAY

GRANDMA'S HOLIDAY FEAST

I grew up in a Polish family, in Cleveland, Ohio, after World War II.

Every Christmas, some 40 of us crowded into my grandma's small apartment for dinner. Everyone sat where he or she could find a spot, or just stood. I often sat under Grandma's small kitchen table, which was a good place to not get trampled on.

Grandma was known for her ham—a large, fresh ham, rubbed with brown sugar and decorated with pineapple, cherries and whole cloves, then slow-roasted until it was time to eat. Her daughters and daughters-in-law prepared side dishes like potatoes, yams, kishke, pig's feet, *potica*, rolls and more, all of it homemade.

But Grandma's ham took center stage. A generous slice of ham with pumpernickel bread and stone-ground Polish mustard melted in one's mouth.

LEONARD BANAS • BENTON CITY, WA

CHRISTMAS ON THE FARM

Preparing Christmas dinner on the farm in the '30s was an elaborate production. The day before, Mama and my sister, Willene, baked. On the list were peach, coconut cream, chocolate, pecan and dried apple pies, as well as chocolate and white cakes.

The rest of the menu for Christmas dinner was three chickens, dressing, canned corn and green beans seasoned with salt bacon, giblet gravy, ham from the smokehouse and lots of sweet potatoes with butter.

Food was left on the table most of the day so we could eat more whenever we wanted or treat friends who came by later to enjoy a piece of pie or cake.
IVA YEAGER • PANAMA CITY BEACH, FL

A SOUTHERN CHRISTMAS FEAST

When I was a kid in North Carolina during the '40s, Mother cooked all day long for Christmas Eve. There was fresh boiled ham, cooked collard greens, roast turkey with dressing and giblet gravy, sweet potatoes and potato salad, and chicken salad baked in the roaster.

Desserts included yellow layer cake

with cooked chocolate icing, fresh coconut cake, pineapple cake, icebox fruitcake, plus chocolate, coconut and sweet potato pies.

Our relatives gathered as often as possible during the holidays—and there was always plenty to eat.
SHELBY KEECH • TRENTON, FL

A WING AND A PRAYER. Ellen Baize and her sister (below) were thankful to be at Grandma's for the holidays in 1955. "Besides cooking the scrumptious dinner, she made our jumpers," Ellen writes from Fort Davis, Texas.

FREE TURKEY! "Every year, the rayon mill where Daddy worked gave its employees a turkey or ham for Christmas," recalls Ina Briggs from Elizabethton, Tennessee. "Mama was the best cook, and here she is in 1963, preparing the turkey for Christmas dinner. We'd also have sage dressing, gravy, and every vegetable she had preserved in the cellar, along with several different pies."

Dazzling Christmas Day Dinner

Create magical memories this season with a sumptuous and traditional Christmas Day dinner that loved ones won't forget. With this merry array of enticing foods adorning the table, your holidays are sure to be happy!

BROCCOLI SAUTE

JIM MACNEAL
WATERLOO, NY

START TO FINISH: 15 MIN.
MAKES: 10 SERVINGS

- 1 cup chopped onion
- 1 cup julienned sweet red pepper
- 1/4 cup olive oil
- 12 cups fresh broccoli florets
- 1 1/3 cups water
- 3 teaspoons minced garlic
- 1/2 teaspoon salt
- 1/2 teaspoon pepper

In a Dutch oven, saute the onion and red pepper in olive oil for 2-3 minutes or until crisp-tender. Stir in the broccoli, water, garlic, salt and pepper. Cover and cook over medium heat for 5-6 minutes or until broccoli is crisp-tender.

GORGONZOLA PEAR SALAD

MELINDA SINGER
TARZANA, CA

PREP: 15 MIN. • **BAKE:** 25 MIN.
MAKES: 12 SERVINGS

- 6 medium pears, quartered and cored
- 1/3 cup olive oil
- 1 teaspoon salt
- 12 cups spring mix salad greens
- 4 plum tomatoes, seeded and chopped
- 2 cups crumbled Gorgonzola cheese
- 1 cup pecan halves, toasted
- 1 1/2 cups balsamic vinaigrette

1. Preheat oven to 400°. Place quartered pears in an ungreased 13x9-in. baking dish. Drizzle with olive oil and sprinkle with salt. Bake, uncovered, 25-30 minutes, basting occasionally with cooking juices.
2. In a large salad bowl, combine greens, tomatoes, cheese and pecans. Drizzle with balsamic vinaigrette dressing and toss to coat. Divide salad among 12 serving plates; top each with two pear pieces.

ALMOND CRANBERRY SQUASH BAKE

RONICA BROWNSON • MADISON, WI

PREP: 20 MIN. • **BAKE:** 50 MIN.
MAKES: 8 SERVINGS

- 4 cups mashed cooked butternut squash
- 4 tablespoons butter, softened, divided
- 1/2 teaspoon salt
- 1/2 teaspoon ground cinnamon
- 1/4 teaspoon ground allspice
- 1/4 teaspoon ground nutmeg
- 1 can (14 ounces) whole-berry cranberry sauce
- 1/2 cup sliced almonds
- 1/4 cup packed brown sugar

1. In a large bowl, combine the squash, 2 tablespoons butter, salt, cinnamon, allspice and nutmeg. Transfer to a greased 2-qt. baking dish. Stir cranberry sauce until softened; spoon over squash.
2. Combine the almonds, brown sugar and the remaining butter; sprinkle over the cranberry sauce.
3. Bake, uncovered, at 350° for 50-60 minutes or until golden brown and bubbly.

FESTIVE NEW YORK-STYLE CHEESECAKE

GLORIA WARCZAK • CEDARBURG, WI

PREP: 20 MIN. • **BAKE:** 45 MIN. + CHILLING • **MAKES:** 12 SERVINGS

- 1¼ cups crushed chocolate wafers
- ½ cup chopped walnuts
- ⅓ cup sugar
- ½ cup butter, melted

FILLING:
- 2 packages (8 ounces each) cream cheese, softened
- 3 tablespoons sour cream
- ⅓ cup sugar
- 2 eggs, lightly beaten
- ½ cup evaporated milk
- 1 teaspoon lemon juice

TOPPING:
- 2 cups (16 ounces each) sour cream
- 5 tablespoons sugar
- 1 teaspoon vanilla extract

Assorted candies and chocolate syrup

1. In a small bowl, combine the wafer crumbs, walnuts and sugar; stir in butter. Press onto the bottom and halfway up the sides of an ungreased 10-in. springform pan. Freeze for 15 minutes.

2. In a large bowl, beat the cream cheese, sour cream and sugar until smooth. Add eggs; beat on low speed just until combined. Combine milk and lemon juice; add to cream cheese mixture just until blended.

3. Pour into crust. Place pan on a baking sheet. Bake at 350° for 35-40 minutes or until center is almost set.

4. Combine the sour cream, sugar and vanilla; carefully spread over cheesecake. Bake 10 minutes longer. Cool on a wire rack for 10 minutes. Carefully run a knife around edge of pan to loosen; cool 1 hour longer. Refrigerate overnight. Garnish with candies and drizzle with chocolate syrup. Refrigerate leftovers.

CLASSIC MAKE-AHEAD MASHED POTATOES

MARTY RUMMEL • TROUT LAKE, WA

PREP: 40 MIN. + CHILLING • **BAKE:** 50 MIN.
MAKES: 12 SERVINGS (¾ CUP EACH)

- 5 pounds potatoes, peeled and cut into wedges
- 1 package (8 ounces) reduced-fat cream cheese, cubed
- 2 egg whites, beaten
- 1 cup (8 ounces) reduced-fat sour cream
- 2 teaspoons onion powder
- 1 teaspoon salt
- ½ teaspoon pepper
- 1 tablespoon butter, melted

1. Place potatoes in a large saucepan and cover with water. Bring to a boil. Reduce heat; cover and cook for 15-20 minutes or until tender. Drain.
2. In a large bowl, mash potatoes with cream cheese. Combine the egg whites, sour cream, onion powder, salt and pepper; stir into the potatoes until blended. Transfer to a greased 3-qt. baking dish. Drizzle with butter. Cover and refrigerate overnight.
3. Remove baking dish from the refrigerator 30 minutes before baking. Preheat oven to 350°. Cover and bake for 50 minutes. Uncover; bake 5-10 minutes longer or until a thermometer reads 160°.

MAPLE-OAT DINNER ROLLS

HELEN DAVIS • WATERBURY, VT

PREP: 25 MIN. + RISING • **BAKE:** 25 MIN. • **MAKES:** 2 DOZEN

- 1 package (¼ ounce) active dry yeast
- ½ cup warm water (110° to 115°), divided
- ½ cup warm strong brewed coffee (110° to 115°)
- ½ cup old-fashioned oats
- ¼ cup sugar
- ¼ cup maple syrup
- 1 egg
- 3 tablespoons shortening
- 1 teaspoon salt
- 3 to 3½ cups bread flour
- 1 tablespoon butter, melted

1. In a large bowl, dissolve yeast in ¼ cup warm water. Add the coffee, oats, sugar, syrup, egg, shortening, salt, remaining water and 2 cups flour. Beat until smooth. Stir in enough remaining flour to form a soft dough.
2. Turn onto a floured surface; knead until smooth and elastic, about 6-8 minutes. Place in a greased bowl, turning once to grease top. Cover and let rise in a warm place until doubled, about 1 hour.
3. Punch down dough. Turn onto a floured surface; divide into four portions. Divide each portion into six pieces; shape each into a ball. Place dough in a greased 13x9-in. baking pan. Cover and let rise until dough has doubled, about 30 minutes.
4. Bake at 350° for 25-30 minutes or until golden brown. Brush the rolls with butter. Remove from pan to a wire rack. Serve warm.

TURKEY WITH APPLE STUFFING

NANCY ZIMMERMAN
CAPE MAY COURT HOUSE, NJ

PREP: 20 MIN. • **BAKE:** 3¾ HOURS + STANDING • **MAKES:** 10-12 SERVINGS

- 1½ cups chopped celery
- ¾ cup chopped onion
- ¾ cup butter, cubed
- 9 cups day-old cubed whole wheat bread
- 3 cups finely chopped apples
- ¾ cup raisins
- 1½ teaspoons salt
- 1½ teaspoons dried thyme
- ½ teaspoon rubbed sage
- ¼ teaspoon pepper
- 1 turkey (14 to 16 pounds)
- Additional butter, melted

1. In a Dutch oven, saute celery and onion in butter until tender. Remove from the heat; stir in the bread cubes, apples, raisins, salt, thyme, sage and pepper.

2. Just before baking, loosely stuff turkey with 4 cups stuffing. Place remaining stuffing in a greased 2-qt. baking dish; refrigerate until ready to bake. Skewer turkey openings; tie drumsticks together. Place bird breast side up on a rack in a roasting pan. Brush with melted butter.

3. Bake, uncovered, at 325° for 3¾ to 4 hours or until a thermometer reads 180° for the turkey and 165° for the stuffing, basting occasionally with pan drippings. (Cover loosely with foil if turkey browns too quickly.)

4. Bake additional stuffing, covered, for 20-30 minutes. Uncover; bake 10 minutes longer or until browned. Cover turkey and let stand for 20 minutes before removing stuffing and carving turkey. If desired, thicken pan drippings for gravy.

STRANDED STRANGERS WARMED THEIR HEARTS

In 1962, my family and I were spending our very first Christmas in our new house in Minneapolis. We were seated around the table, eating Christmas dinner, when the doorbell rang.

There on our front steps stood a Japanese family. They'd been driving around the city looking at all the beautifully decorated houses when their car stalled. It was 15 degrees below zero, and they couldn't get it started again.

I called my husband to the door, and we invited them to come inside and warm up. The man mentioned their young daughter was waiting in the car, so we told him to bring her in.

Hospitality Spoken Here

Then we asked if they'd had dinner yet. They said no, so we invited them to take off their coats and join us.

The husband, Yasuyuki Kaneko, could understand and speak English. His wife, Shoko, could understand but not speak it, and their daughter, Junko, did neither.

Yasuyuki had come to the United States because he was a doctor doing research at the University of Minnesota. He also said that he'd been a pilot during World War II.

My husband spent four years in the Navy during the war, so the two of them had an interesting discussion about the war and the terrible bombing that brought it to an end.

As it turned out, Junko was celebrating her eighth birthday that day. For dessert, I happened to have frozen Christmas ice cream molds that came with candles to be placed in the middle of each.

So, when dessert was served, we all sang "Happy Birthday" to little Junko.

Once dinner was over, my father called a road service to start our guests' car. Soon the vehicle was running again, and after much bowing and thanking us, our new friends were on their way.

About three weeks later, the doorbell rang, and there stood the same couple with gifts for us—five beautiful Japanese paintings. For the next two or three years, we exchanged Christmas cards and short notes, but I've since lost track of them.

When I think back over all the Christmas days I've spent, that one in 1962 is definitely the most memorable, and perhaps the most rewarding.

CELESTE LORIMER • MINNEAPOLIS, MN

HANDS ACROSS THE SEA. The Lorimer family (in background) was happy to invite the Kaneko family to join them for Christmas dinner.

REVERENCE for his parishioners' feelings guided Pastor Clarence Howell, shown with his wife, Leta, and their daughters Clara (in back) and Mary.

Pastor's Response Hit the Spot

In the early 1950s, I was dating a young lady whose father was the pastor of a small Baptist church in Hemphill, in east Texas.

While pastors were paid little, they often received gifts and perks to make up for their meager salaries. Among them were offerings of food from parishioners. Almost daily, a member of the congregation would stop by the pastor's home, leaving food.

It was a nice thing to do, but often the food was unidentifiable.

One day around the holidays, just before Clara and I were married, a parishioner dropped off a plucked and cleaned fowl that we couldn't identify. The consensus was that it was a goose, but I always thought it was a buzzard.

The Rev. Clarence Howell, my future father-in-law, was concerned about how to respond to church members who brought food that he was afraid to eat, particularly when he dumped it behind the garage.

If he told them it was delicious, he was obviously fibbing, which is frowned upon in the Bible.

He gave his situation some thought and eventually came up with a reasonable solution: He named the place where the undesirable food was discarded as "the spot." Then, whenever his members asked how he liked a dish they had brought, he'd respond, "It truly hit the spot. Thank you very much."

That eased his conscience and made everyone happy.

Over the years, my wife and I have often laughed about the food items brought to her father's house with good intentions that ended up in "the spot."

NEAL MURPHY • SAN AUGUSTINE, TX

GIFTS OF GOOD CHEER

Guessing at what gifts to give? Warm the hearts of everyone on your list this season with scrumptious, tasteful treats made at home. You'll find palate-pleasing recipes to tempt every set of taste buds.

APRICOT TEA BREAD

LYN ROBITAILLE
EAST HARTLAND, CT

PREP: 30 MIN. • **BAKE:** 40 MIN. + COOLING
MAKES: 2 LOAVES (12 SLICES EACH)

- ½ cup butter, softened
- 1 cup sugar
- 3 eggs
- 2 teaspoons vanilla extract
- 2 cups all-purpose flour
- 1½ teaspoons baking powder
- 1 teaspoon baking soda
- 1 cup (8 ounces) sour cream
- 1 cup chopped dried apricots
- 1 cup chopped pecans

TOPPING:
- ½ cup all-purpose flour
- ¼ cup sugar
- ¼ cup cold butter

1. In a large bowl, cream the butter and sugar until light and fluffy. Add the eggs, one at a time, beating well after each addition. Beat in the vanilla.

2. Combine the flour, baking powder and baking soda; add to creamed mixture alternately with sour cream, beating well after each addition. Fold in the dried apricots and pecans.

3. Spoon batter into two greased 8x4-in. loaf pans. For topping, combine flour and sugar in a small bowl; cut in butter until mixture resembles coarse crumbs. Sprinkle over batter.

4. Bake bread at 350° for 40-45 minutes or until a toothpick inserted near the center comes out clean. Cool loaves for 10 minutes before removing from pans to wire racks to cool completely.

PUMPKIN PIE COFFEE CREAMER

CAROL FORCUM • MARION, IL

START TO FINISH: 10 MIN.
MAKES: ABOUT 1 CUP

- 1 cup powdered nondairy creamer
- 4 teaspoons ground cinnamon
- 2 teaspoons ground ginger
- 2 teaspoons ground nutmeg
- 1 teaspoon ground cloves
- 1 teaspoon ground allspice

In a small bowl, combine all ingredients. Store in an airtight container.

MINT CHOCOLATE SAUCE

MARLENE WICZEK • LITTLE FALLS, MN

START TO FINISH: 20 MIN. • **MAKES:** ABOUT 5 CUPS

- 2 cups sugar
- 1 cup butter, cubed
- ½ cup water
- ½ cup light corn syrup
- 4 cups (24 ounces) semisweet chocolate chips
- ½ cup creme de menthe

Ice cream

1. In a large saucepan, combine the sugar, butter, water and corn syrup. Bring to a boil over medium heat, stirring constantly. Boil for 3 minutes. Remove from the heat. Add chocolate chips and creme de menthe; whisk until smooth.

2. Serve warm over ice cream or transfer to storage containers and refrigerate.

To serve: Scoop out desired quantity and reheat in microwave until warmed.

CHOCOLATE CHIP COOKIE MIX

SHELLEY FRIESEN
LEDUC, AB

PREP: 15 MIN. • **BAKE:** 10 MIN./BATCH
MAKES: 2½ DOZEN

- 1¼ cups all-purpose flour
- 1 teaspoon baking soda
- ½ teaspoon salt
- ½ teaspoon ground cinnamon
- ¾ cup packed brown sugar
- 1 cup (6 ounces) semisweet chocolate chips
- ½ cup dried cranberries
- ½ cup chopped walnuts
- ½ cup quick-cooking oats

ADDITIONAL INGREDIENTS:
- ⅔ cup butter, softened
- 1 egg
- ¾ teaspoon vanilla extract

In a small bowl, combine the flour, baking soda, salt and cinnamon. In a 1-qt. glass container, layer the flour mixture, brown sugar, ½ cup chocolate chips, cranberries, walnuts, oats and remaining chocolate chips. Cover and store in a cool dry place for up to 6 months.

YIELD: 1 BATCH (ABOUT 4 CUPS TOTAL).

To prepare cookies: In a large bowl, beat the butter, egg and vanilla until blended. Add cookie mix and mix well. Drop by rounded tablespoonfuls 2 in. apart onto ungreased baking sheets. Bake at 350° for 10-15 minutes or until golden brown. Remove to wire racks.

CHOCOLATE PEANUT BUTTER CANDY

HOLLY DEMERS
ABBOTSFORD, BC

PREP: 10 MIN. + CHILLING
MAKES: ABOUT 2½ POUNDS

- 1 pound white candy coating, coarsely chopped
- 1½ cups creamy peanut butter
- 2 cups (12 ounces) semisweet chocolate chips

1. In a large microwave-safe bowl, melt candy coating; stir until smooth. Stir in peanut butter; thinly spread onto a waxed paper-lined baking sheet.
2. In another microwave-safe bowl, melt chocolate chips; stir until smooth. Drizzle over candy coating mixture; cut through mixture with a knife to swirl the chocolate. Chill until firm.
3. Break into pieces. Store in an airtight container in the refrigerator.

ORANGE PEAR JAM

DELORES WARD • DECATUR, IN

PREP: 20 MIN. • **COOK:** 20 MIN. + STANDING • **MAKES:** ABOUT 7 CUPS

- 7 cups sugar
- 5 cups chopped peeled fresh pears
- 1 cup crushed pineapple, drained
- 2 tablespoons lemon juice
- 2 packages (3 ounces each) orange gelatin

1. In a Dutch oven, combine the sugar, pears, pineapple and juice. Bring to a full rolling boil over high heat, stirring constantly. Reduce heat; simmer for 15 minutes, stirring frequently. Remove from the heat; stir in gelatin until dissolved.
2. Pour into jars or containers; cool to room temperature, about 1 hour. Cover and let stand overnight or until set, but no longer than 24 hours. Refrigerate for up to 3 weeks.

PEACH RASPBERRY JAM

DONN WHITE • WOOSTER, OH

PREP: 10 MIN. **COOK:** 10 MIN. + STANDING • **YIELD:** ABOUT 5 CUPS

- 1¼ cups finely chopped peaches
- 2 cups fresh raspberries
- 2 tablespoons lemon juice
- 4 cups sugar
- ¾ cup water
- 1 package (1¾ ounces) powdered fruit pectin

1. Place peaches in a large bowl. In a small bowl, mash the raspberries; strain to remove seeds. Add raspberries and juice to peaches. Stir in sugar. Let stand for 10 minutes. In a small saucepan, bring water and pectin to a full rolling boil. Boil for 1 minute, stirring constantly. Add to fruit mixture; stir for 2-3 minutes or until sugar is dissolved.
2. Pour into jars or freezer containers; cool to room temperature, about 30 minutes. Cover and let stand overnight or until set, but no longer than 24 hours. Refrigerate for up to 3 weeks or freeze for up to 1 year.

FROZEN TREATS ARE
MELTED INTO MEMORY

It was the last day before Christmas vacation at St. Mary's Parochial School in Worthington, Minnesota, in 1952. Our class and several others had been practicing with Sister Dinah, our teacher and the music director, for the annual Christmas concert.

At about 2 p.m., Sister Dinah announced that she had a treat for all our hard work and took us downstairs to the cafeteria. We all sat around a few long tables as she brought out a frosty-looking box from the kitchen with vapors escaping from it. Inside were Fudgsicles for each of us!

We were to wait and not open them until everyone had one. We sat, hands folded in eager anticipation, until they were all passed out, then tore the wrappers off, almost as if we were in a race. Soon the Fudgsicles touched lips and tongues, but something was wrong. They quickly stuck.

No one knew that they had been packed in dry ice and were extremely cold. Imagine 23 fifth-graders sitting at tables with their tongues and lips frozen to their treats.

Panic set in. Some students pulled the sticks out but others among us sat there, Fudgsicles in hand, stuck to our mouths, not knowing what to do.

Luckily for us, previous dares about tongues and steel sled parts had taught us some hard lessons.

Almost on cue, my friend Tom and I got up, walked to the water fountain and helped each other use the water to thaw the treats until they separated from our mouths with minimal damage.

Others soon followed suit, although the damage had already been done to several students. Kids were crying, some with tongues bleeding, and Sister Dinah was in real distress, apologizing that she didn't know the frozen treats had been so cold.

Later, back in the classroom, parents arrived to take their children home early. Some still had swollen lips and tongues. There were even some absences the next evening at the concert.

Looking back, the whole thing seems almost hilarious, but those "treats" almost canceled our Christmas show.

STEPHEN NAVARA
WELLS, MN

THAT'S A MOUTHFUL! "Aunt Mary knew just what to buy for her eight nieces and nephews for Christmas in 1948," says Norman Middleton of Beech Grove, Indiana. "The faces of my sisters and brothers show their joy in every lick of their all-day caramel suckers. Pictured, from left, are Raymond, Walter, Boyd, Audrey, Doloris, James, me and John."

O HOLEY NIGHT

Although I was born at the start of the Great Depression, I never felt deprived. I had my best friends living right in my home in West Jordan, Utah—my five sisters and one brother. I had parents who cared, we never went hungry, and we all stuck together like glue.

As Christmas 1938 drew near, I counted the days, crossing each off with a great big black X.

When Dec. 24 arrived, we all looked for our best socks to hang up. I spotted one of my mother's nylon stockings. Wow, I thought, this will really hold a lot. I pulled it out with great excitement, then spotted a hole in the toe.

That was when my great plan formed. We always ran out of candy and nuts before the season was over, but if I put a big dishpan under the holey sock to catch more candy and nuts, we'd have enough to last all year!

I was so excited that I ran to tell my older sister, Jane. She smiled at me and said, "Oh, Wannie. He will hear them when they hit the bottom of the pan."

But I wouldn't be licked on this plan. I put a soft, fluffy towel in the pan, stood back and smiled. How very clever I was!

The sun had a hard time giving up the day as it streaked the sky and slowly rolled over the mountains. That night, we kids went to bed fully clothed so we could get up faster. Nothing was going to slow us down this Christmas morning.

We had our arms wrapped around each other like tangled fishing line. Low whispers and giggles could be heard until the wee hours of the morning, then silence.

Soon we were calling out to our parents, "Can we get up now?"

It seemed we asked a dozen or more times before the magic "yes" came back.

We sprang from our beds, flying feet hardly touching the floor.

SPUNKY TWOSOME. Lawana and her dog, Spunk, around the time of sock scheme. "We made our own fun," she recalls.

I ran to my sock as I pictured the heaping nuts and candy in the pan and then—what was this?—not one nut in the pan.

I clearly remembered putting a chubby finger on either side of the hole and pulling to make the hole a little larger so no big nuts would get stuck. Picking up my sock to investigate, I discovered a large orange wedged in the bottom, completely covering the hole.

Then I looked over at the excitement still going on under the shiny tinseled tree and wondered to myself:

Did Santa Claus do this on purpose, or was it an accident that he had clogged my holey sock?

LAWANA PETERSON • MIDVALE, UT

BRIGHT-EYED
BRUNCH

After the little ones have huddled around the tree and opened Santa's gifts on Christmas morning, continue the merry mood by gathering around the table for a bountiful breakfast. With the festive foods featured here, entertaining early in the day is a snap!

CHRISTMAS BREAKFAST CASSEROLE
DEBBIE CARTER
O'FALLON, IL

PREP: 20 MIN. • **BAKE:** 25 MIN.
MAKES: 10-12 SERVINGS

- 1 pound bulk Italian sausage
- 1 cup chopped onion
- 1 jar (7 ounces) roasted red peppers, drained and chopped, divided
- 1 package (10 ounces) frozen chopped spinach, thawed and well drained
- 1 cup all-purpose flour
- ¼ cup grated Parmesan cheese
- 1 teaspoon dried basil
- ½ teaspoon salt
- 8 eggs
- 2 cups milk
- 1 cup (4 ounces) shredded provolone cheese

Fresh rosemary sprigs, optional

1. Preheat oven to 425°. In a skillet, cook the sausage and onion over medium heat until the sausage is no longer pink; drain. Transfer to a greased 3-qt. baking dish. Sprinkle sausage with half of the red peppers and all of the spinach.

2. In a large bowl, combine flour, Parmesan cheese, basil and salt. Combine the eggs and milk; add to the dry ingredients and mix well. Pour mixture over spinach.

3. Bake 20-25 minutes or until a knife inserted near the center of casserole comes out clean. Sprinkle with provolone cheese and remaining red peppers. Bake 2 minutes longer or until cheese is melted. Let stand 5 minutes before cutting. Garnish with rosemary if desired.

ANY-SEASON FRUIT BOWL
FRANCES STEVENSON • MCRAE, GA

PREP: 5 MIN. + CHILLING • **COOK:** 25 MIN. + CHILLING
MAKES: 16-18 SERVINGS

- 2 cups water
- 1½ cups sugar
- ⅓ cup lime or lemon juice
- 1 teaspoon anise extract
- ½ teaspoon salt
- 3 oranges, peeled and sectioned
- 3 kiwifruit, peeled and sliced
- 2 grapefruit, peeled and sectioned
- 2 large apples, cubed
- 1 pint strawberries, sliced
- 1 pound green grapes
- 1 can (20 ounces) pineapple chunks, drained

1. In a medium saucepan, combine the water, sugar, lime juice, anise extract and salt. Bring to a boil over medium heat; cook for 20 minutes, stirring occasionally. Remove mixture from the heat; cover and refrigerate for 6 hours or overnight.

2. Combine fruit in a large bowl; add dressing and toss to coat. Cover and chill for at least 1 hour in the refrigerator.

PRONTO POTATO PANCAKES

DARLENE BRENDEN
SALEM, OR

START TO FINISH: 30 MIN.
MAKES: 8 PANCAKES

- 2 eggs
- 1 small onion, halved
- 2 medium potatoes, peeled and cut into 1-inch cubes
- 2 to 4 tablespoons all-purpose flour
- ½ teaspoon salt
- ⅛ teaspoon cayenne pepper
- 4 to 6 tablespoons canola oil

Applesauce, optional

1. Place eggs and onion in a blender; cover and process until blended. Add potatoes; cover and process until finely chopped. Transfer to a small bowl. Stir in the flour, salt and cayenne.
2. Heat 2 tablespoons oil in a large nonstick skillet over medium heat. Drop the batter by ¼ cupfuls into oil. Fry in batches until golden brown on both sides, using remaining oil as needed. Drain on paper towels. Serve with applesauce if desired.

SPICED APRICOT TEA

MARY HOUCHIN
LEBANON, IL

START TO FINISH: 25 MIN.
MAKES: 6 SERVINGS

- 2 cinnamon sticks (3 inches)
- 10 whole cloves
- 3 cups water
- 2 individual tea bags
- 3 cups apricot nectar
- ⅔ cup sugar
- ¼ cup lemon juice

1. Place cinnamon and cloves on a double thickness of cheesecloth. Gather the corners of the cloth to enclose spices; tie securely with string.
2. Place the water and spice bag in a large saucepan; bring to a boil. Remove from heat. Add the tea bags; steep, covered, for about 5 minutes according to taste. Discard tea and spice bags.
3. Add remaining ingredients to tea; heat through, stirring to dissolve sugar. Serve immediately.

TURKEY SWISS QUICHE

LOIS FOREHAND • LITTLE RIVER-ACADEMY, TX

PREP: 25 MIN. • **BAKE:** 30 MIN. + STANDING • **MAKES:** 6 SERVINGS

- 1 unbaked pastry shell (9 inches)
- 1½ cups finely chopped cooked turkey
- 4 eggs
- ¾ cup half-and-half cream
- 2 cups (8 ounces) shredded Swiss cheese
- 4 green onions, finely chopped
- 2 tablespoons diced pimientos
- 1 teaspoon dried oregano
- 1 teaspoon dried parsley flakes

Dash salt and pepper
- 3 slices (¾ ounce each) Swiss cheese, cut into thin strips

1. Line unpricked pastry shell with a double thickness of heavy-duty foil. Bake at 450° for 8 minutes. Remove foil; bake 5-7 minutes longer or until crust is golden brown. Reduce heat to 375°.
2. Sprinkle turkey into pastry shell. In a large bowl, whisk the eggs and cream. Stir in the shredded Swiss cheese, onions, pimientos, oregano, parsley, salt and pepper. Pour the mixture into crust.
3. Bake for 20 minutes. Arrange Swiss cheese strips in a lattice pattern over quiche. Bake 10-15 minutes longer or until a knife inserted near the center comes out clean. Let stand for 10 minutes before cutting.

EPIPHANY CAKE MADE LOTS OF CRUMBS AND MEMORIES

Mom celebrated the three kings' journey to Bethlehem with cake and symbolic gifts.

JOANN COOKE • RESEDA, CA

When my kids were growing up in Reseda, California, in the 1960s and '70s we didn't rush the holiday season.

Each Jan. 6, I baked a special cake to celebrate the Feast of the Epiphany, also called Twelfth Night. I decorated a yellow cake with white frosting, and on top were a crown and candy "jewels," since the cake commemorated the visit of the wise men to the town of Bethlehem to see Jesus, the newborn king.

Because the wise men brought gold, frankincense and myrrh to the Baby Jesus, I wrapped tiny gifts in aluminum foil and put them in the cake batter.

Each surprise meant something special. Whoever found a dried bean would be the king of the evening. A dried pea meant that one was the queen. A penny meant the child was destined to be poor, while finding a dime ensured great wealth.

A button meant the person would be a tailor or seamstress, and a raisin signified he or she was sweet. If there was nothing in that piece of cake, then certainly God loved you.

Since I had eight children, I usually put in extra raisins and pennies and, occasionally, extra dimes and buttons. But there could be only one king and queen.

The children couldn't wait to see what treasure would be found. They'd cut up their pieces of cake to find the surprises, then unwrap them with a groan or a joyous shriek and a lot of laughter. Finally, they'd eat the crumbled cake.

I don't know anyone else who ever made this cake. My children still talk about the Epiphany cake. Maybe it's time to renew the tradition and bake one for my grandchildren.

TASTE TESTERS. All eight of the Cooke family children—and their father, Jack—had to be wary when they were biting into the author's Epiphany cake. Pictured (from left) are Ted, 18; Kathy, 16; Connie, 15; Mary, 14; Pat, 11; Mike, 9; Debbie, 7; and Gina, 4.

BOUNTIFUL BASKET. "My father, Hadley Read, liked to take pictures on holidays," says Mary Beth Read of Urbana, Illinois. "That's me in the middle with my brothers Greg (left) and Phillip at our home in Champaign. We were waiting in sweet anticipation to try the fruit."

Sweet Indulgences

WORTH THE WEIGHT

The Christmas season was much anticipated in our small Ohio town when I was growing up in the 1930s. My favorite part of the holiday festivities was helping my grandma bake cookies.

Pfeffernusse, sand tarts, snickerdoodles, almond crescents, springerle, lebkuchen, gingerbread boys, spritz, mincemeat triangles and my very favorite, Christmas trees—the names roll off my tongue with pleasure, and I can almost smell the heavenly fresh-baked aroma.

Each cookie was special in itself, but a big plateful on the dinner table for dessert was a sight to behold!

Grandma didn't make just a few; she made hundreds and hundreds of cookies each year and sold them to the townspeople who had neither the time nor inclination to bake. The Depression was at its peak, and our family pitched in to do its share. What fun it was the first year I was old enough to help.
POLLY PIERCE DYER • COLUMBUS, OH

KEEPING AN EYE ON KOLACHE

Since my family's of Czechoslovakian descent, our favorite holiday treat was kolache, which is made with sweetened yeast dough and filled with cooked prunes or apples.

It was a test of patience to sit in the kitchen, warmed with the aroma of kolaches baking in the oven, waiting for the first bite!
JESSIE JEAN MOUCKA • APACHE JUNCTION, AZ

DREAMY CREAMY PIE

Christmas wasn't Christmas at our house without my mother's whipped cream pie.

After she baked the crust, my mom would whip the fresh cream to a thick consistency with sugar and added flavoring. She piled the filling high into the flaky pie crust, then dotted it with dollops of her clearest, tastiest homemade jelly.

We carry on her cream pie tradition every Christmas. These pies are wonderful, but they never taste quite like Mom's.
LILLIAN STEWART • MARSHALL, IL

SEASON'S EATING. "Dad, a busy minister, always made time for holiday meals with his family," says Rose Marie Hahn Higginbotham (in 1960, on right) of Parkville, Missouri.

LET'S EAT! There was time for one last photo before Dad carved the Christmas turkey in 1959. Nancy Castles of Coral Springs, Florida, shared this photo of her family.

LITTLE HELPERS. Got a sweet tooth? These sisters got involved in the fun of decorating classic Christmas cut-out cookies. "This picture of our two daughters, Sheri and Vicki, ages 6 and 2, was taken in 1960," says Fran Jones of Athens, Texas.

HOLIDAY HOSTESS. Ruth Larson of Batavia, Illinois, stands next to her mother-in-law while entertaining in 1960. "Mom and her friends polished off my treats quickly," she says.

FESTIVE TABLE. "The photo above calls to mind similar gatherings at my family's house during the holidays," says Jan Morton of Orlando, Florida. "After partaking of a meal fit for a king, we'd gather around several tables to play cards. An hour or so later, everyone would head for the kitchen to grab another bite of the delicious leftovers. Then it was back to the card games."

Kids in the Kitchen

By the time this 22-pound turkey was done roasting, we had all done our part to help our grandma, Lillian Stawarky, fix the feast. (I'm the hungry lad in back, third from the left.)

We grandkids had the "privilege" of polishing the pans, mashing the turnips and potatoes, and making sugar cookies out of the extra homemade pie crust.

You can see the pie on the counter to the left. I guarantee it was made from rhubarb out of Grandma's garden and had the flakiest from-scratch crust ever. She would never use a boxed crust mix or canned fruit.

A big believer in home cooking, Grandma often lamented, "You just can't get a good loaf of store-bought bread today."

After dinner, the whole family piled into the station wagon and drove to downtown Bridgeport, Connecticut, so we could enjoy the Christmas light displays.

My father, Vin, snapped this 1963 photo. It perfectly captures one of many fond memories of our family gathering in the kitchen and enjoying a bounty of blessings during the holidays.

MIKE SIMKO • BRIDGEPORT, CT